This perceptive book provides timeless insights into our business and personal visions and their relationship to creating the future. It is full of well-referenced examples and anecdotes which make its profound analysis of the subject easy to read and understand. *The 5th Dimension* is essential reading for anyone interested in directing their future.

Dr. Phillip Meddings, *Executive Chairman,*
TEC Australia and United Kingdom, an international
organization of Chief Executive Officers

The 5th Dimension provides a unique perspective into understanding what impacts the future, and what action we can take to influence it. It contains powerful tools and principles for corporate managers and individuals who want a say in their future.

Ronald J. Fitzgerald, *Division Chairman,*
American Society for Quality Control, and
Director, Total Quality, ABB Combustion Engineering,
Avon, Connecticut

Jim and Dave have reached the elusive goal of understanding, defining and, more importantly, accomplishing how to move mountains. *The 5th Dimension* needs to be in the library of anyone desiring to improve their course in life.

Craig M. Hagopian, *Director,*
Channel Strategy and Operations, Mtel Corporation,
Jackson, Mississippi

The 5th Dimension is a thought provoking, stimulating book asking the question every intelligent person has asked repeatedly, "What is the meaning of my life?" — if there is one. With courage and sensitivity, the authors address this question and provide life changing ideas and a course of action to help us gain greater awareness of our potential and power to become leaders in work and life. It is well written and has my wholehearted recommendation. Read it and find some answers.

Dr. Laura H. Ross, *Psychotherapist,*
Specializing in people,
Miami, Florida

This is a great book! I found it entertaining as well as informative and was immediately able to apply its message to both my personal life and my work groups. It illustrates the competitiveness of the arena of the future and clarifies what can be done today to help ensure more rewarding tomorrows.

Gene Kunde, *Business Consultant,*
Former Chief Operating Officer,
Epson America, Inc.,
Albuquerque, New Mexico

The Fifth Dimension

The Secret To Moving Mountains

James R. Puccino, M.S.

David M. Shoemaker, Ph.D.

The Fifth Dimension
The Secret To Moving Mountains

James R. Puccino
David M. Shoemaker

ProMotion Publishing
3368F Governor Drive, Suite 144
San Diego, California 92122

1 (800) 231-1776

ISBN 1-887314-00-8

Dedicated

To the person who is actually in the arena.

Whose face is marred by dust and sweat and blood; who strives valiantly; who errs, and comes short again and again, because there is no effort without error and shortcoming; but who does actually strive to do the deeds; who knows the great enthusiasms, the great devotions; who spends himself in a worthy cause; who at the best knows in the end the triumph of high achievement, and who at the worst, if he fails, at least fails daring greatly, so that his place shall never be with those cold and timid souls who know neither victory or defeat.

— Theodore Roosevelt

Contents

Preface

What does the Future hold for you? What will life be like for you ten years from now? With everything in the world changing so quickly, are questions like these ridiculous?

What you are holding in your hands is a book about the Future and the spirit which is the life force within each of us. For some, the Future merely will be, whatever it will be. For others, however, it is that which must be faced bravely. Anyone who has had to reach deep within their heart to find the courage to go just one more day understands the Future. It is where change is possible. It is the realm of hopes and dreams. It is the possibility of better. It may also be the worst that you can imagine, a source of deep despair and hopelessness.

We describe here what we have learned about the Future; it is a reflection of our own experiences and observations, those of others, and our intuitions. The themes we address are those about which most people wonder: What is the meaning of it all? What meaning has my life? and What can I do? These themes are timeless. They strike chords in everyone, chords which they themselves desire to have struck. Each of us has a desire and, indeed, a need for an awareness of the whole of which we are a part. But what part? What whole? What can we do?

Imagine this. A scientist approaches you one day, tells you his name and title, describes his background and training, shows you his credentials, and tells you that he has been closely studying you. Then he says:

"I have examined your life as no other person in history has been examined. I have studied your every move since birth, and I have interviewed every person with whom you have come into contact. In fact, I have a complete physiological and psychological profile on you. I know you as no one else does. I have used all of this information and my considerable expertise to devise a detailed day-by-day plan by which you should conduct the rest of your life. If you follow this plan, day-by-day, I guarantee that you will be happy for the rest of your life. It's all found in here. Yes, according to my plan, I know within a day or two the date of your death. Here is the plan; there will be no financial charge for my services."

The scientist hands you a beautifully-bound leather notebook with your name in bold, gold letters on the front. Would you accept it? Would you read it?

Only you know the answers to these questions. Your answers, however, reflect your orientation to the Future and to what you think you can do with your life.

To us, the vignette epitomizes the scientific attitude toward all that exists. We can picture in our minds a scholarly-looking professor wearing his colorful academic robe standing at his lectern asserting, "If anything exists, it exists in some quantity and, therefore, can be measured." and with each word thumping his fist upon his lectern. However, if you consider life to be a journey of the mind involving an increasing awareness and understanding of what *is* beyond what we see, science can only take you up to a certain point in your journey. It is as though you have begun a journey in an automobile or airplane; at a point in this journey you must leave that means of transportation and continue further with another. This will always be the case, regardless of what advancements are made in science and regardless of what advancements are made in logic.

You have to start using something else, something which is not created by science or the logic of your mind, and realize that there is at least one more dimension beyond *length*, *width*, *depth*, and *time*. There is at least *The Fifth Dimension*. We have no simple, one-word title for this dimension; perhaps there is no single word for it. It is the dimension, however, which contains the spiritual. It is timeless. The Fifth Dimension exists and is accessible to us only through our intuition; the result is an awareness on our part. This awareness may involve an increase in our knowledge, or a sensing of some relationship among the events which we see happening around us, or a sensing of what we should be doing, or a sensing of what is important. An awareness is knowing better what is. Everyone has experienced flashes of awareness at times in their life.

The goal of this book is increasing your awareness of life. But how is this done? For us, meditation is not the answer; reading is not the answer; being told by others is not the answer. You must act; you must act boldly; you must experience your own awareness. You've heard this before. It was true then and it's true now. What we offer you is very simple: ideas. A few powerful ideas. If you take these ideas, think about them for awhile, and then act on them in a way which is tailored to your life, you will be amazed with your own results.

Wait a minute! You're offering ideas when you know that what we want are specific steps, specific actions, which we can take to improve our lives, to make us happier! Just tell us what to do! Other books tell us steps to follow. Why don't you?

We present a specific set of ideas. We do not offer specific steps which we want you to follow. If we offered steps to be followed, and if you followed them, you would be living our lives, not your life. Nobody should lead your life but you.

While completing this manuscript we were fortunate in having some very talented people review preliminary drafts and offer suggestions. We have learned from them and we know that the material which you are about to read is better because of their contributions. All short-comings are solely our own doing.

J.R.P.
D.M.S.

Chapter I

Finding Life's Meaning

The universe is transformation; our life
is what our thoughts make it.[1]

Sir Christopher Wren (1632-1723), one of the greatest
of English architects, walked one day unrecognized
among the workmen who were building St. Paul's cathedral in London which he had designed. "What are
you doing?" he inquired of one man. The man replied,
"I am cutting a piece of stone." As he went on he put
the same question to another man. The man replied, "I
am earning five shillings two pence a day." To a third
man he asked the same question.

The third man's answer was powerful, classic,
and unforgettable. He hesitated, then with a deep conviction said, "I am helping Sir Christopher Wren build
a beautiful cathedral."[2] His answer, unlike that of the
other two men, reflected neither the drudgery of hard
work nor the fleeting gain of a few coins. He had a
purpose for being. He was doing more than cutting
stone and earning his daily wage. He was building a
great cathedral which would last forever. His expertise
and he himself would be a part of that beautiful cathedral as much as any stone, piece of wood, or pane of
colored glass. He knew the role which he would play
in this important project. He may not have been any
richer than his fellow workmen, but his life had a
degree of meaning and purpose which was priceless.

1

What would your life be like if you had a significant purpose for living? What if you had no purpose for what you were doing or planned to do? What effect would either of these two conditions have on you personally? How would you feel? Although these questions may not be ones which you ask yourself daily, you do think about them. You know in your heart that you want to lead a meaningful life, a life which is meaningful to you personally. But how is this done? Why should you even bother with trying to lead a meaningful life? Sooner or later, everyone asks himself these questions and wants answers. You may be doing this right now.

The Struggle For Meaning

Count Leo Tolstoy (1828-1910) was one of Russia's most celebrated writers of fiction. He wrote *War and Peace* (1869), perhaps the greatest work in Russian realistic fiction, and *Anna Karenina* (1877), one of the greatest love stories of the world. The former is the story of five families seen against the background of Napoléon's invasion of Russia in 1812; the latter, a powerful study of an unhappy woman. He wrote several other novels and a few plays. At the age of 46, seemingly happy, prosperous, and famous, Tolstoy began the most significant struggle of his life, his struggle to find meaning in life, a struggle which lasted for several years. The struggle, and what he learned from it, he described in his book *Confession* written in 1882.

2

This short work has been described as "...one of the noblest and most courageous utterances of man, the outpouring of a soul perplexed in the extreme by life's great problem."[3] Following the excerpt from *Confession* given below, you will be asked one simple question: What advice would you have given to Tolstoy? This is something which you should think about carefully. Now, Tolstoy tells us how it was:

"...five years ago something very strange began to happen to me. At first I began having moments of bewilderment, when my life would come to a halt, as if I did not know how to live or what to do; I would lose my presence of mind and fall into a state of depression. But this passed, and I continued to live as before. Then the moments of bewilderment recurred more frequently, and they always took the same form. Whenever my life came to a halt, the questions would arise: Why? And what next?"

"... The questions seemed to be such foolish, simple, childish questions. But as soon as I laid my hands on them and tried to resolve them, I was immediately convinced, first of all, that they were not childish and foolish questions but the most vital and profound questions in life, and, secondly, that no matter how much I pondered them there was no way I could resolve them. Before I could be occupied with my Samara estate, with the education of my son, or with the writing of books, I had to know why I was doing these things. As long as I do not know the reason why, I cannot do anything."

3

"...in the middle of thinking about the fame that my works were bringing me I would say to myself, 'Very well, you will be more famous than Gogol, Pushkin, Shakespeare, Moliere, more famous than all the writers in the world — so what?' And I could find absolutely no reply. ... If a fairy had come and offered to fulfill my every wish, I would not have known what to wish for. If in moments of intoxication I should have not desires but the habits of old desires, in moments of sobriety I knew that it was all a delusion, that I really desired nothing. I did not even want to discover truth anymore because I had guessed what it was. The truth was that life is meaningless. And this was happening to me at a time when, from all indications, I should have been considered a completely happy man; this was when I was not yet fifty years old. I had a good, loving, and beloved wife, fine children, and a large estate that was growing and expanding without any effort on my part. More than ever before I was respected by friends and acquaintances, praised by strangers, and I could claim a certain renown without really deluding myself."

"... And in such a state of affairs I came to a point where I could not live; and even though I feared death, I had to employ ruses against myself to keep from committing suicide. Several times I asked myself, 'Can it be that I have overlooked something, that there is something which I have failed to understand? Is it not possible that this state of despair is common to everyone?' And I searched for an answer to my ques-

4

tions in every area of knowledge acquired by man. For a long time I carried on my painstaking search; I did not search casually, out of mere curiosity, but painfully, persistently, day and night, like a dying man seeking salvation. I found nothing. I searched all areas of knowledge, and not only did I fail to find anything, but I was convinced that all those who had explored knowledge as I did had also come up with nothing. Not only had they found nothing, but they had clearly acknowledged the same thing that had brought me to despair: the only absolute knowledge attainable by man is that life is meaningless."

"... For a long time I could not bring myself to believe that knowledge had no reply to the question of life other than the one it had come up with. For a long time I thought I might have misunderstood something, as I closely observed the gravity and seriousness in the tone of science, convinced in its position, while having nothing to do with the question of human life. My question, the question that had brought me to the edge of suicide when I was fifty years old, was the simplest question lying in the soul of every human being, from a silly child to the wisest of the elders, the question without which life is impossible; such was the way I felt about the matter. The question is this: What will come of what I do today and tomorrow? What will come of my entire life? Expressed differently, the question may be: Why should I live? Why should I wish for anything or do anything? Or to put it still differently: Is there any meaning in my life that will

5

not be destroyed by my inevitably approaching death? Throughout human knowledge I sought an answer to this question, which is one and the same question in the various expressions of it. And I found that in regard to this question the sum of human knowledge is that (there is no answer to my question)."⁴

Now it is time for you to respond. What advice would you have given to Tolstoy? What would you have said to him? Think about this carefully. You may one day be engaged in the same struggle as Tolstoy, or you may have a friend who will be facing the same stone wall. Before you read Tolstoy's conclusion given in the Notes, have in mind your own conclusion.⁵ Tolstoy saved himself by realizing the incorrectness of his own thinking. Instead of depending entirely on his logic and power of reason, as he had been doing, he began to see that reason is only one part of his being.

There is more. At a deeper level there was a force he called his consciousness of life. According to him, intellectuals who relied solely on reason to sustain themselves were not representative of the average person. Tolstoy came to believe that most people avoided despair and found some kind of meaning in their life through a force which was beyond reason. It was as if ordinary people — the peasants, as he referred to them — had an irrational knowledge that he and his noble peers had throttled in themselves. Although these ordinary people had a harder life, suffered from physical deprivation, and were denied many of the pleasures which he had, they had access to a vital power which made it impossible for them to think that life has no meaning. Without much schooling and without a lot of deep thinking, they had learned how to live in a manner which puzzled him. They acted out of faith rather than reason, and he concluded that only a faith like theirs could make his life meaningful. Tolstoy began to live as the peasants lived, making, for example, his own shoes, all the while learning from them and trying to imitate their perspective on life.

Tolstoy's predicament is certainly not unique. Approximately 3,000 years earlier, the wise King Solomon (?-922 B.C.), son of King David and Bathsheba, and the third king of ancient Israel, was tormented by the same question.[6] King Solomon concluded that all of his notable accomplishments were mere vanity and grasping for the wind, soon to be forgotten upon his death.

Certainly the question about the meaning of life did not originate with Tolstoy, nor is it merely a Russian question. It is a universal question considered sooner or later by everyone. Before leaving Tolstoy, it is interesting to note that he thought people used four means to escape the terrible situation of a meaningless life.[7] They are:

Ignorance. Some people are simply incapable of understanding the problem which life presents. They are intellectually unable to realize that life is meaningless.

Epicureanism. The problem of life may be avoided by enjoying as much as possible the good which exists in the Present. Although people who do this are aware of the hopelessness of life, they avoid thinking about it by focusing on the pleasures of the Present. These people strive to forget the inevitability of sickness, old age, and death, which if not today then tomorrow will destroy all of their worldly pleasures. Tolstoy believed that most people of the upperclass used this means of escape. According to him, their moral stupidity enabled them to forget that all the advantages of their positions are accidental.

Suicide. The problem of a meaningless life can be eliminated by committing suicide. This escape requires, according to Tolstoy, both strength and courage, and only unusually strong and logically consistent people are able to commit suicide. These people realize that life is a joke and that the blessings of the dead are greater than those of the living. They put an end to the joke by putting an end to their life.

Weakness. This escape consists of continuing to drag out a life that is meaningless, knowing beforehand that nothing can come of it. These people know that death is better than life, but they do not have the courage to put an end to the delusion by killing themselves; instead, they seem to be waiting for something to happen.

Tolstoy decided that his method of escape was Weakness. Although he clearly favored suicide, he did not take his own life because he had "some vague notion that my ideas were all wrong."[8] This was a critical period in his life.

8

Viktor Frankl's Experience At Camp

The idea of a concentration camp, a place where a nation imprisons political enemies, is not new. They were first used by Great Britain during the First Boer War (1899-1902) in South Africa. Beginning in 1928 with the dictatorship of Joseph Stalin (1879-1953), the Russian secret police imprisoned millions of people in labor camps. And, the United States and Canada interned thousands of Japanese-Americans during World War II.

Although there have been other camps operated by other nations, the most infamous were those operated by the Germans before and during World War II, from 1933 to 1945. At the peak of their power, the Germans had 22 concentration camps which were used primarily to hold and execute Jews and, by 1945, approximately 6 million Jews had been executed. Although the primary means of execution was poison gas, many inmates died from starvation and disease. Suicide was not uncommon. Some camp inmates were allowed to live as long as they could work. Viktor Frankl, a doctor, was one such inmate, and one of the few survivors of the death camps. In the passage which follows, he describes a personal observation which was very important for him and for everyone:

"The death rate in the week between Christmas, 1944, and New Year's, 1945, increased in camp beyond all previous experience. In his (the chief doctor of the concentration camp) opinion, the explanation for

9

this increase did not lie in the harder working conditions or the deterioration of our food supplies or a change of weather or new epidemics. It was simply that the majority of the prisoners had lived in the naive hope that they would be home again by Christmas. As the time drew near and there was no encouraging news, the prisoners lost courage and disappointment overcame them. This had a dangerous influence on their powers of resistance and a great number of them died."

"... Any attempt to restore a man's inner strength in the camp had first to succeed in showing him some future goal. (The German philosopher, 1844-1900, Friedrich) Nietzsche's words, 'He who has a *why* to live for can bear almost any *how*,' could be the guiding motto for all psychotherapeutic and psycho-hygienic efforts regarding prisoners. Whenever there was an opportunity for it, one had to give them a *why* — an aim — for their lives, in order to strengthen them to bear the terrible *how* of their existence. Woe to him who saw no more sense in his life, no aim, no purpose, and therefore no point in carrying on. He was soon lost. The typical reply with which such a man rejected all encouraging arguments was, 'I have nothing to expect from life any more.' What sort of answer can one give to that?"

"What was really needed was a fundamental change in our attitude toward life. We had to learn ourselves and, furthermore, we had to teach the despairing men, that it did not really matter what we

10

expected from life, but rather what life expected from us. We needed to stop asking about the meaning of life, and instead to think of ourselves as those who were being questioned by life — daily and hourly. Our answer must consist, not in talk and meditation, but in right action and in right conduct. Life ultimately means taking the responsibility to find the right answer to its problems and to fulfill the tasks which it constantly sets for each individual."

"... A very strict camp ruling forbade any efforts to save a man who attempted suicide. It was forbidden, for example, to cut down a man who was trying to hang himself. Therefore, it was all important to prevent these attempts from occurring. I remember two cases of would-be suicides, which bore a striking similarity to each other. Both men had talked of their intentions to commit suicide. Both used the typical argument — they had nothing more to expect from life."

"In both cases it was a question of getting them to realize that life was still expecting something from them; something in the future was expected of them. We found, in fact, that for the one it was his child whom he adored and who was waiting for him in a foreign country. For the other it was a thing, not a person. This man was a scientist and had written a series of books which still needed to be finished. His work could not be done by anyone else, any more than another person could ever take the place of the father in his child's affections."[9]

Frankl saw in man's search for the meaning of his life a basic and fundamental need: the need for meaning. His discovery was that our need for meaning is so fundamental that its frustration *may* result in a neurosis, a mild mental illness accompanied by anxiety, insecurity, depression, unreasonable fears, and bodily aches and pains. To help people who have this kind of neurosis, Frankl created logotherapy, a form of therapy in which the therapist guides the patient to find a new sense of life, a new value, a new purpose, or a new responsibility in his life. Logotherapy is merely a replication of the process which he had successfully used in the concentration camp.

Lessons Learned From Tolstoy And Frankl

It is difficult to imagine two situations physically more different than those of Tolstoy and Frankl. The one, an estate basking in prosperity; the other, a death camp, drenched in the ash and odor of burning corpses. What they have in common is the mind of man asking, Why should I live one second more? Why should I continue the struggle? Why? Why! Had they been told a few years earlier that a day would come when they would welcome death with open arms, they probably would have laughed. But that day did come, and they weren't laughing. These two men saved themselves and others by finding a reason for not dying today. Perhaps tomorrow, but not today. And they lived that day. In each case, they found a meaning or a purpose for their particular lives; they found an answer to, Why should I not die today? Let's be clear on what happened, because we are easily led astray by the logic and orderliness of their prose which was written afterward.

What happened was not the result of logic or reasoning. It was their intuition which supplied their answers. To Tolstoy, it was a consciousness of life, an awareness that his life should continue. Period. He had not the slightest doubt that he must live and continue living; he merely had no logical reason for doing so. A logical reason was not necessary; he was aware of what he must do. To Frankl, it was an awareness that life demands something of everyone. You cannot die until you have done it. The *why* was unimportant and unnecessary. He knew in his heart that this was true. It was their intuition which saved them, not their logic, not their mind. They summoned the spiritual force within themselves and their answers were the result. Intuition. Why doesn't this happen to everyone in a similar situation? We don't know the answer to this question; we only know that it frequently happens. How often does this happen every day to people whose faces we shall never see, whose names we shall never know, and whose stories will never be told?

Do you need a sense of the purpose or meaning of your life when death seems like the only alternative? Yes. Do you need this sense of purpose or meaning at other times? Yes. We all have a fundamental need for meaning in our lives. We all desire to lead lives which are meaningful and not meaningless. This need of ours

13

is fundamental, so fundamental that we may not be consciously aware of it. We perhaps only become acutely aware of our need for meaning during crises in our lives. The need, however, is always with us and is in our very fiber. Clearly, "Man shall not live by bread alone."[10] To be sure, the struggle for bread is our first preoccupation, but as soon as we have food to eat and a shelter over our head, we ask ourselves *why* we struggle for it at all. This question is the first sign of man's search for meaning: *his* search for the meaning of *his* life. The answer is beyond logic. We will tell you right now that as you look deep within yourself during a moment of crisis and despair for the meaning of your life you will find a face, and the face will not be yours.

A Meaningless Life

According to Greek mythology, Sisyphus was the founder of the ancient Greek city of Corinth. He was also a notorious trickster who liked to deceive the gods. Sisyphus once outwitted the god Thanatos, the god of death. As the story goes, Zeus, ruler of the gods, had sent Thanatos to punish Sisyphus for revealing one of Zeus's love affairs. However, Sisyphus managed to capture Thanatos, bind him in chains, and no one died while he was chained. The god Ares freed Thanatos and gave him power over Sisyphus. Sensing his impending death at the hands of Thanatos, Sisyphus told his wife that when he died he should be buried without

14

the customary funeral rites. So he died and went to Hades, the land of the dead and ruled by a god of the same name.

Sisyphus then begged Hades to let him return to Earth so that he could punish his wife for not giving him a proper burial. His argument prevailed and Hades released him. However, once back on Earth, Sisyphus refused to return to Hades. He had tricked a god again. The god Hermes finally captured Sisyphus and returned him to Hades. As punishment for his trick, Sisyphus had to push a huge stone to the top of a hill. But, each time the stone reached the top, it would roll back down to the bottom, from where he had to start over again. And so it went, up and down, up and down, up and down, forever and ever and ever. Clearly the gods do not like being tricked, particularly by a mere man.

Let's think about Sisyphus for a moment. It is difficult not to chuckle at the way he tricked Hades. He seems to be the kind of person we would enjoy meeting. But who would want to take his place on the hillside? Would you? The answer, of course, is No. There isn't a person in the whole world who would willingly trade places with Sisyphus. Yet how many people are in fact pushing a stone just like Sisyphus because, and be clear on this point, they have chosen to do so? You may think that they have been forced into such a meaningless life but this is not the case. They have forced themselves into it, and they can, if they choose, force themselves out of it. As we shall

15

see, the arena in which this struggle will be waged is the mind. It is the mind which is the all-important tool.

Two Simple Questions About Life

There are two simple questions which have perplexed man for thousands of years, and they are as relevant today as they were for King Solomon. What is the meaning of life? What is the meaning of my life? These are not unusual questions, and they are not only considered by philosophers. Most people ask or wonder about life and their particular life. Asking about the why of what we observe around us is one of the distinctive characteristics of man. Certainly we long to know the secrets of the universe, that is, the secret of life itself. At the same time, however, we seek a meaningful way to live our own lives, whether or not we can find a separate meaning for the universe, that is, the larger whole.[11]

What Is The Meaning Of Life?

We are alive. We are aware of other people like us; we are also aware of many other forms of life as, for example, members of the plant and animal kingdoms. All are forms of life, and we wonder, What is the meaning of all this life? and What is its purpose? We assume that if anything exists, it has a purpose, a purpose which we can in some sense understand. We seek some kind of an explanation and, in light of this

16

explanation, to better understand the diverse and frequently bizarre-appearing events which occur on our planet and, indeed, occur to us in our daily lives. More fundamentally, perhaps, we seek to be reassured about the friendliness of the universe toward us, what we value, and what we are striving to do. We all need to feel secure and to live in a world which is understandable.

But what kind of answer would satisfy you? For us, the answer would center around knowing the relationships among a set of boxes, with each box inside a larger box. The smallest box is *You*. You are inside the box *All Humans*. This box is inside the box *All Life On Planet Earth*. This box is inside the box *All Life In The Universe*, which is inside the box *The Universe*, which is inside the box *All Universes*. This way of thinking is an application of a simple idea to the effect that everything is a component or a part of something which is larger. A corollary is that, for any one box, it is only possible to describe the events occurring within it; to understand the reason for the occurrence of these events (the why), the characteristics of the next larger box of which it is a part must be understood. It is here that the relationships *among* the boxes are very important.

As these relationships are progressively understood, our level of understanding progressively increases. If you understood the relationships among the boxes, you perhaps would say: Oh Yes, ...now I understand why it is that for the past 3,000 years only approximately 285 days on Earth have been without war. Now I understand the role played by the love between two people as, for example, mother and son. Now I understand why a person is inflicted with a serious infirmity and must endure the bodily pain and mental anguish for the rest of his life. Now I understand the role played by civilization. Now I understand the role played by humans. Now I understand what it is which I am to do with my life. Clearly, knowing the relationships suggested by our boxes would provide answers to many questions. The problems of living on Earth would be greatly simplified.

What if these relationships were known? Does not this imply that there is a purpose or goal toward which everything is directed? Doesn't this suggest that this goal is inescapable, predetermined, or already known by someone? Couldn't we conclude then that our decisions and actions follow some plan? Are we not automatons? Tools? Instruments? What about the concept of free will? Some might find this knowledge to be liberating; others might consider it damaging to their sense of personal freedom. However, everyone could feel that objective explanations had been discovered. Whatever the emotional response, the power of the human mind at least would have been established. Man would have proven the ability of his mind to solve the greatest of all puzzles. Ask yourself, Do I really want to know the answer?

This last question is rhetorical. Although the concept of relationships among our boxes is readily discussed, the specific relationships cannot be known by man, at least not for many centuries to come. That such is the case is easily demonstrated by the structure of the boxes itself. Taking *All Life On Planet Earth* as an example, we simply do not know the relationships between this component and the larger whole of which it is a part, the larger whole being *All Life In The Universe*. Therefore, the best which we can do is describe and analyze *All Life On Planet Earth*. There is no doubt that we are immersed in a universe and are a part of it. It is not clear, however, that we can stand back and look at the universe as a whole, as we might readily do with one or another of its parts as, for example, the planet Earth or its adjacent planets Venus and Mars. We have no awareness of a second universe with which to compare our own. We simply lack knowledge in these areas. In general, there are three categories of knowledge: what is known, what is unknown but able to be known, and what is unknowable. The relationships suggested by our boxes for the most part fall within the last two categories.

Thinking like this, the comments of G. Bernard Shaw (1856-1950), the famous British author, come as no surprise. Shaw was interviewed in 1901 and the interviewer asked for one word as to the meaning of the world comedy, referring to the meaning of life. Shaw replied with the following artillery salvo:

"It is this thoughtless demand for a meaning that produces the comedy. You ask for it in one word though we are not within a million years, as yet, of seeing the world as it really is. We are intellectually still babies: this is perhaps why a baby's facial expression so strongly suggests the professional philosopher."

"... Well, we are all still as much babies in the world of thought as we were in our second year in the world of sense. Men are not real men to us: they are heroes and villains, respectable persons and criminals. Their qualities are virtues and vices; the natural laws that govern them are gods and devils; their destinies are rewards and expiations; their reasoning a formula of cause and effect with the horse mostly behind the cart. They come to me with their heads full of these figments, which they call, if you please, 'the world,' and ask me what is the meaning of them, as if I or anyone else were God Omniscient and could tell them. Pretty funny this: eh? But when they ostracize, punish, murder, and make war to impose by force their grotesque religions and hideous criminal codes, then the comedy becomes a tragedy. The Army, the Navy, the Church, the (legal) Bar, the theatres, the picture-galleries, the libraries, and the trade unions are forced to bolster up their pet hallucinations. Enough. You expect me to prate about the Absolute, about Reality, and The First Cause, and to answer the universal Why. When I see these words in print the book goes into the basket. Good morning."[12]

Although we are very ignorant in most matters of life, we still have a fundamental need to understand and to feel secure. Given this, it is easy to see why so

20

many theories have been created over the years. Although each attempts to explain the larger picture (e.g., the relationships suggested among our boxes), each is nothing more than a perspective of one individual who, having a need to understand, created a set of relationships which made sense to him. We take these philosophies created by man over the millennia to be serious endeavors. Each is trying to share his understanding with us; each is trying to build upon and expand the understanding of his predecessors. Nevertheless, each is a theory, a perspective, and its value to us lies in its potential ability to challenge our own possibly narrow-minded way of thinking.

A relevant philosophy is one which creates a conflict within our mind which we seek to resolve by thinking about the issues. As we all know, what really counts is what we think, and we value most highly our own thoughts and opinions. Considering alternative philosophies is comparable to travelling to different countries. Through coming into contact with other cultures our understanding of our own culture is increased. We now understand how it is similar and different from the others. Without these potential differences, our understanding of our own culture is generally limited. The same is true for the values and ideals which we treasure so highly. It is important to recognize that modern philosophies are inherently neither superior or inferior to those developed by the ancients. The reason is that the nature of man has remained fundamentally unchanged over at least the

21

last 5,000 years and probably for the last 35,000 years. Man, as contemplated by the Roman Emperor Marcus Aurelius Antonius (121-180) as he described his thoughts while campaigning with the Roman army in what is now France, is the same man contemplated by modern philosophers. It is noteworthy that man has changed so little over the millennia while everything else has changed so much.

We conclude this section with comments made by the American philosopher Stern suggesting that the process of searching for meaning is never-ending: "... Man has been (placed) into the world, without his knowledge, will or consent, and is removed from it again without his will or consent. Between these two events man has to go through much suffering. Being not only conscious, like other animals, but conscious of his consciousness, i.e., self-conscious, man must ask himself earlier or later: Why am I here and for what purpose? What is the meaning of my sudden existence and my sudden disappearance?"

"Finding no answer in the nature which surrounds him, for nature is silent, man invents answers, first in the form of myths and religions, later in that of philosophic systems. ... But all these frames of orientation are children of their respective times and are worn out earlier or later, under the impact of growing empirical knowledge and increasing rational demands. A frame of orientation which appeared meaningful to a past age will no longer appear so to a later age, and will require its replacement by a more realistic and more rational framework. Thus the problem of meaning is a perpetual problem of mankind. It will remain with us as long as our species exists."[13]

We will ponder the meaning of life for as long as we exist. It is a part of our very fiber to do so. We agree with Stern that this questioning will continue forever. However, sooner or later, we must reach the understanding that the meaning of life is a riddle which will remain a riddle forever. There are no answers, only opinions, and in fact you may have an opinion. Fine. Now let's abandon this chase and focus our attention on the second question, a question which is far more relevant, and one which we can attack much more effectively.

What Is The Meaning Of *My* Life?

What is the meaning of *my* life? is the second of life's two simple questions and is probably the more commonly asked. It is here that you are examining yourself and what you are doing on Earth. What is the purpose of my life? Is my life worth living? What is it that I should be doing? Certainly, most people want to lead a meaningful life as opposed to one which is meaningless. Who wants to be an expert stone-roller like Sisyphus?

We must squarely face the fact that there is no obvious plan or grand design for what we should be doing during our life, day by day, and certainly the wide range of activities performed by man over the last

5,000 years is sufficient proof of this. As mentioned earlier, there are, however, a variety of orientations, each providing an answer to some degree. Historically, there are three major answers: the theological answer, the metaphysical answer, and the intellectual answer. The last is sometimes referred to as the critical, positive, or scientific answer.[14] These three answers were originally proposed by the French mathematician and philosopher Auguste Comte (1798-1857) and, according to him, constitute developmental stages in the thinking of man.[15]

Theological Answer. God, in creating man, did it for a certain purpose which we fulfill by merely existing, and fulfilling this purpose is the reason for our being. Our existence is meaningful because we merely are. It is not necessary for us to know the specific purpose. Here, the answer is based on the idea of a supernatural being.

Metaphysical Answer. The purpose of our existence is contained within or defined by an abstract force which produces all that exists and all that occurs. This abstract force controls everything. Two examples of this abstract force are Fate and Nature. Other titles are sometimes used. This answer is very similar to the theological answer; the concept of Fate has been substituted for that of God.

Intellectual Answer. Purpose or meaning is not found outside of us; it is found inside us. It is we who create our own meaning through reasoning and observation. There is no absolute meaning in and of itself.

Meaning is always a meaning to someone, whether it be to ourselves, to our ancestors, to our culture, or to our civilization. To determine the degree to which anything is meaningful, there must be a standard of measurement, and these standards are created by man and, therefore, are both changing and able to be changed over time.

Throughout history each answer has alternatively dominated the thinking of man. Even at a particular time each may be present, and even the thinking of a particular person may alternate among the three. In the average day, we frequently hear references in conversation to each. However steeped in history these answers may be, and regardless of the famous names with which they may be associated, and regardless of the number of brave and courageous men who have died in their defense, they are not very good answers. The first two answers are the same as saying, I don't know. The third answer, the answer which tells us to create our own meaning and then be satisfied with what we have created, is telling us to play a game with ourselves, all the while we know that it is a game which is being played, our little game. So, we find these three answers to be less than what we desire and, in fact, need. And, we are thankful that we have the liberty to make a statement such as this; it was only a few hundred years ago that a person would have been dealt with severely and often fatally for expressing such an opinion. Ask Galileo Galilei (1564-1642), the Italian astronomer and physicist. Under threat of torture by the Catholic Church, he recanted his theory of the solar system which is now accepted unquestionably. His theory challenged the dogmatic teachings of the Church. Church versus Galileo; Church wins.

There is an answer, better than the three just cited, which we call the Intuitional Answer. Our answer is distinctly different from those just listed. It is an answer focused on acquiring awareness, as opposed to facts and logical relationships, and is an answer applicable to everyone — Past, Present, and Future.

The Intuitional Answer

It is our intuition, and our intuition alone, which will provide the answer to the question, What is the meaning of my life? Everyone has the capability or power of intuition; indeed, it is one of the four basic psychological functions of man: thinking, feeling, sensing, and intuiting.[16] Intuiting and reasoning are entirely different processes and yield different kinds of awareness or understanding. We seek wisdom, and our intuition is the primary tool by which it may be acquired. The result of our intuition is an insight or a flash of awareness. It just happens. When it happens, we know and are certain that we know. It is the immediate apprehension of a truth. It is knowing without the use of prior knowledge or reason. Ralph Waldo Emerson (1803-1882), the great American poet, put his finger right on the mark when he wrote in 1841: "The primary wisdom is intuition. In that deep force, the last fact behind which analysis cannot go, all things find their common origin. ... We lie in the lap of immense intelligence, which makes us receivers of its truth and organs of its activity. When we discern justice, when we discern truth, we do nothing of ourselves, but allow a passage to its beams. If we ask whence this comes, if we seek to pry into the soul that causes, all philosophy is at fault. Its presence or absence is all we can affirm. Every man discriminates between the voluntary acts of his mind, and his involuntary perceptions, and knows that to this involuntary perception a perfect faith is due. He may err in the expression of them, but he knows that these things are so, like day and night, not to be disputed."[17] Indeed, the Buddhists believe that the essence of life itself may be understood through intuition.[18]

We all have the power of intuition, but frequently disregard what we intuit. Our culture generally defines what is real and acceptable. When the scientific method is the dominant theme in a culture, everything which is non-scientific is considered irrelevant and without value. Caught in the strong tide of science, we both question and discard our intuitions. The pressure brought to bear by our culture is very powerful.

How is wisdom acquired through intuition? Is not an intuition what happens spontaneously and unpredictably? The answer is Yes, but we can actively prepare the stage on which our intuition may choose to act. This preparation is essential. The first activity in seeking wisdom is acknowledging to yourself that you do desire such wisdom and to open yourself to receiving it. For us, this is done through what we call dancing. There is nothing magical about dancing. The first step in dancing is freely and without reservation admitting to yourself that you do not know very much. Then, in step 2, admit to yourself that what you think you know is probably only partially correct. In step 3, admit to yourself that knowing more begins by observing and asking questions, and all questions are valid. Then, in step 4, ask the first question and explore until you find a promising answer. Then ask the second question. Let the answer to the first question serve as the springboard for the second question. (If this is so, then why does...?) At this step, continue asking questions. Follow the path of your questions and answers, wherever it leads. What you gain from dancing is an enlarged perspective on what is knowledge, and the next question. There will always be one more question. What is important is to begin dancing. Dancing opens your mind.

The second activity in preparing your mental stage for intuition is performing to the best of your ability those activities which you believe will add meaning to yourself and to your life. This is a conscious, rational, and logical effort on your part. You select your meaningful goal. You strive to achieve it. You overcome the potential obstacles which stand in your way. All the while, you know exactly what you are doing and why. You know the game you are playing, and a game it is. Consider the building of St. Paul's cathedral described at the beginning of this chapter. For the third workman questioned, participating in the building of the cathedral provided meaning and importance to his life in that the greatness of the creation mentally accrued to him and to each of the workmen. He must have realized then, as we realize now, that the building will soon be gone, it is only a question of time and a few hundred years perhaps. But it will be gone! The important ingredient in this process is not what is created; it is the personal struggle and striving which the process entails. It is this struggle which is the essential prerequisite for our intuition. Indeed, the extent of intuition is directly related to the magnitude and duration of the struggle associated with the process.

Although Albert Einstein (1879-1955), the German-born American physicist, may have attributed his theory of relativity to a flash of insight, he also said that the insight occurred in the context of painstaking laboratory experiments and extensive efforts at analyzing data conducted over a period of years. The insight which occurred to Leo Tolstoy is of the same nature — occurring in the context of a serious personal struggle lasting for a period of years, a struggle described at the beginning of this chapter. The key is the struggle, supplemented by the desire to acquire wisdom and an openness to it when it becomes available.

The struggle begins when you decide to create meaning in your own life, and then strive to make it happen. This is a never-ending process. The book which you hold in your hand describes how you can create meaning in your life, or how to begin the journey. The by-product is the wisdom which you, like us, seek. For us the answer to, What is the meaning of my life? is the product solely of our intuition. This intuition is nurtured by, first, opening your mind to new understanding and awareness by admitting to yourself that you are not as smart as you think you are, and to start dancing. Second, consciously create meaning in your life by striving to the best of your ability to achieve a worthy goal. The primary tool for doing this is the project which we describe in the next section. This striving must involve a significant struggle on your part. It must challenge you as you have never been challenged before. It must arouse your emotions. These emotions are absolutely essential — an important relationship which we describe in a later chapter. It is on this mental stage that your intuition will make its appearance. We have no idea why this particular process is essential for increasing awareness; however, we are firmly convinced that it is necessary. Let's turn now to the important first step of this process, our consciously creating meaning in our own life.

How We Create Meaning

The majority of us desire to lead a meaningful life. But how is this done? What do we do to create a meaningful life for ourselves? Fortunately, the process is easily described, and has at its core the relationships among a project, a goal, and values and ideals.

The Tool For Meaning

The primary tool for creating meaning in our life is the *project*. A project is a set of activities focused on achieving a specific goal. At the start, this goal lies only in our mind and in the domain called the Future. But how does achieving a goal add meaning to our life? Certainly there are many goals which could be achieved. Would achieving just any goal add meaning to our life? The answer is No; the nature of the goal is important.

Consider the project of building the Panama Canal, a canal linking the Atlantic and Pacific oceans and completed in 1914. Imagine this. You are one of the 30,000 workers who made the canal possible. Because you worked on a project whose completion was highly desired and valued by everyone, your life during those years clearly had a meaning and a purpose. During those years you were able to justify your existence as a human being because you were the tool by which the goal was to be achieved. From this perspective, your life had two sources of meaning. The first is its meaningfulness from being linked to a highly desired goal; the second, meaningfulness from being the tool by which this goal was to be achieved. But what is a highly desired goal or purpose? It is here that we need to introduce the relationship between a goal and the values and ideals which you hold dear. A goal's degree of desirability is the degree to which it embodies the values and ideals which you consider important.

In this particular example, assume that you are one of the 5,000 Americans from the United States who worked on the Panama Canal. You may have taken the sea voyage to Panama because you wanted to be a part of the United States showing the world that Americans can solve any technological problem through hard work, creativity, persistence and determination. The first is an ideal, the latter are values. Other values and ideals could have been at play here. There are, of course, a large number of different projects and goals which could embody this particular ideal and these values. The important point is that values and ideals make a project and its goal desirable by placing them both in a larger context. For the person, there is almost no experience which will seem meaningful unless it can be related directly to values and ideals which he has chosen for himself. Ideals and values are the source of all consciously-created meaning, and the project with its goal is the tool by which you embody them.

We do not all build Panama Canals, and we may never be able to participate in a project of that magnitude. The following scenario shows how meaning in life may be acquired by a less complicated project. Imagine this. You are a combat veteran. You are a battlefield medic. You are the first person to apply immediate aid to the wounded, the majority of whom are soldiers, some are civilians. Because of you many soldiers and civilians, some whose names you can still recall right now, some whose faces you can still see, are alive today. You have been trained to do this, and you do it as well as any person could, given the circumstances. Your time is almost finished. You have already completed one tour of duty and will complete your second and last tour tomorrow. You will be flying home. Then, as if by magic, you find yourself sitting in the home of your parents. You have answered what seems like a million questions, but one lingers in your mind: Well, what do you plan to do now? What do I plan to do now? A few weeks pass. What do I plan to do now? You are getting dressed one morning when all of a sudden you remember a comment made several years ago: If you're looking for something to do, come see me. I guarantee that you'll sleep well at night. This was a comment made by your uncle 4 years ago. You think and think. He worked on an Indian Reservation in North Dakota. It all happened so quickly. You telephoned your uncle. You talked for awhile. Now you find yourself on an Indian Reservation digging a well with several other people. Everyone seems to be excited about digging this well. You hear them talking about the crops which will be planted. About the truck which brings fresh drinking water to this area once a week, weather permitting. Now the truck won't be needed here anymore. The well was finished after five weeks' work, pump installed, water flowing. What a celebration! You can't recall how many people thanked you for your hard work. It didn't seem to matter that you weren't an Indian. You think to yourself, All I did was help build a well! The thought must have been written across your forehead because one of your new friends comes up, stands beside you and staring at the well says, "To some people this is just a well, but, to my people, it's life." That was your first well; you're now finishing your third. The work is hard, but you're stronger now. I'm really needed here, you think. I can make a difference. I have made a difference. You find yourself smiling; in fact, you've been smiling a lot since you came to the Reservation. Your uncle is now standing by your side. With your medical training, he asks, do you think that you could...

Meaningfulness Versus Happiness

Happiness and meaningfulness are not necessarily one and the same. For happiness to occur, there must be a harmonious relationship between you and your surroundings. However, a person who finds himself out of harmony, his experience consisting largely in a struggle against a hostile environment, nevertheless, may have a meaningful life. The meaning in his life may even result from his refusal to adapt or adjust to his surroundings. Given the chance to have a happy life if only he conforms to something he doesn't like, he may renounce happiness and choose an uncomfortable resistance. This is the realm of heros. They may experience happiness, but they are prepared to sacrifice it for the sake of some value or ideal which has greater importance for them. Although their lives are not the only ones which are meaningful, they show that meaning and happiness are not identical. A life without much happiness, however, can be meaningful.

The relationship between happiness and meaningfulness is a dominant theme in the autobiography of the English economist and philosopher John Stuart Mill (1806-1873). Describing his life as a young man, he tells of his dedication to the principle of utilitarianism (the notion that the aim of society is striving to achieve the greatest happiness for the greatest number of people) which he inherited from his father and the noted English jurist and philosopher Jeremy Bentham (1748-1832): "I had what might truly be called an object in life; to be a reformer of the world. My conception of my own happiness was entirely identified with this object. The personal sympathies I wished for were those of fellow laborers in this enterprise. I endeavoured to pick up as many flowers as I could by the way; but as a serious and permanent personal satisfaction to rest upon, my whole reliance was placed on this; and I was accustomed to felicitate myself on the certainty of a happy life which I enjoyed, through placing my happiness in something durable and distant, in which some progress might be always making, while it could never be exhausted by complete attainment. This did very well for several years, during which the general improvement going on in the world and the idea of myself as engaged with others in struggling to promote it, seemed enough to fill up an interesting and animated existence. But the time came when I awakened from this as from a dream. It was in the autumn of 1826."[19]

At the age of 20 Mill suffered a severe mental depression. His suffering lasted for several years and taught him the difference between a meaningful life and a happy life. According to him, his difficulties began when he asked himself whether his strenuous attempts, to bring about the greatest happiness for the greatest number of human beings, would add to his own personal happiness if his efforts succeeded. Mill concluded that he was deceiving himself. Even if he did change society as he hoped, it would not make *him* any happier. Mill tells us what he learned from this episode in his life:

"The experiences of this period had two very marked effects on my opinions and character. In the first place, they led me to adopt a theory of life. ... I never, indeed, wavered in the conviction that happiness is the test of all rules of conduct, and the end of life. But I now thought that this end was only to be attained by not making it the direct end. Those only are happy, I thought, who have their minds fixed on some object other than their own happiness; on the happiness of others, on the improvement of mankind, even on some art or pursuit, followed not as a means, but as itself an ideal end. Aiming thus at something else, they find

36

happiness by the way. The enjoyments of life, such was now my theory, are sufficient to make it a pleasant thing, when they are taken *en passant*, without being made a principal object. ... Ask yourself whether you are happy, and you cease to be so. The only chance is to treat, not happiness, but some end external to it, as the purpose of life. Let your self-consciousness, your scrutiny, your self-interrogation, exhaust themselves on that; and if otherwise fortunately circumstanced you will inhale happiness with the air you breathe, without dwelling on it or thinking about it, without either forestalling it in imagination, or putting it to flight by fatal questioning. This theory now became the basis of my philosophy of life."[20] Mill is teaching us a valuable lesson here. Happiness is acquired indirectly.

Does Death Destroy Meaning?

Does our death erase the meaning which our lives may have acquired through our struggling to achieve goals which embody values and ideals which are important to us? Does our death make it all for nothing? The answer to both questions is No. Our life has the potential to acquire meaning both before we die and afterwards. If achieving your goals contributes to the achievement of goals considered important by larger groups as, for example, the family, the nation, or mankind, your life and you yourself continue to acquire meaning all the while you are alive. After death, your life continues to acquire meaning through the effect which your achievements continue to have on those who are still living. The meaning of your life does not necessarily end with your death.

A letter from a soldier to his wife reflects his awareness that the meaning of his life can extend beyond his death. The soldier is Major Sullivan Ballou of the Union army and the letter was written on July 14, 1861 — one week before the first Battle of Bull Run, the first major battle of the American Civil War between the Confederate States of America and the Union. Major Ballou wrote:

My Very Dear Sarah: The indications are very strong that we shall move in a few days, perhaps tomorrow. Lest I should not be able to write again, I feel impelled to write a few lines that may fall under your eyes when I shall be no more. ... I have no misgivings about or lack of confidence in the cause in which I am engaged, and my courage does not halt or falter. I know how strongly American civilization now leans on the triumph of the Government, and how great a debt we owe to those who went before us through the blood and suffering of the Revolution (Revolutionary War, 1775-1781). And I am willing, perfectly willing, to lay down all my joys in this life to help maintain this Government and to pay that debt. ... Sarah, my love for you is deathless: it seems to bind me with mighty cables that nothing but Omnipotence could break, and yet my love for country comes over me like a strong wind and bears me irresistibly on, with all these chains

*to the battlefield. The memories of all the blissful
moments I have spent with you come creeping over me,
and I feel most deeply grateful to God, and you, that
I have enjoyed them so long. And how hard it is for me
to give them up and burn to ashes the hopes of future
years, when, God willing, we might still have lived and
loved together and seen our sons grown up to honor-
able manhood around us. If I do not (return), my dear
Sarah, never forget how much I love you, and when my
last breath escapes me on the battlefield, it will
whisper your name. Forgive my many faults and the
many pains I have caused you. ... O Sarah, if the dead
can come back to this earth and flit unseen around
those they loved, I shall always be near you in the
gladdest day and in the darkest night, amidst your hap-
piest scenes and your gloomiest hours — always, always: and if there be a soft breeze upon your cheek, it
shall be my breath, or if the cool air cools your throb-
bing temple, it shall be my spirit passing by. Sarah, do
not mourn me dead: think I am gone, and wait for me,
for we shall meet again.*

Sullivan[21]

The first of two Battles of Bull Run took place
on July 21, 1861 near the town of Manassas, Virginia.
Some 35,000 Union troops commanded by General
Irvin McDowell were opposed by 29,000 Confederate
troops commanded by General Pierre Beauregard. During the 6-hour battle, the Confederates routed the
Union army, which retreated to Washington, D.C.

Union casualties were 481 killed, 1,011 wounded, and 1,210 missing or captured; for the Confederates, 387 killed, 1,582 wounded, and 13 missing.[22] One of the 868 killed was Major Ballou. Did he whisper Sarah's name with his last breath? He did most certainly in her imagination, and every time she thought of his death.

Each man, on each side of the confrontation, prays to his god for victory in battle and the triumph of the cause for which he fights. Undoubtedly, similar letters were written by soldiers of the Confederate army to their mothers, fathers, wives and sweethearts. Each wanted to live, but each would die if necessary for a cause or an ideal which extended beyond themselves and the relatively short span of their life. There is that which is more important than life itself. How often has this happened over the centuries?

The Potential Trivialness Of It All

Compared to the apparent magnitude of the universe, we, as physical beings, are insignificantly small. In fact, we are relative newcomers to the history of life (3,000,000,000 years old) on this Earth (4,500,000, 000 years old) in this universe (12,000,000,000,000 years old). If the history of the Earth were squeezed into one calendar year, man would be seen appearing on Earth only a few seconds before the very end of the last day of the year.[23] Extending this concept, it is relatively easy to think that any action and all actions taken by us are trivial and of no importance what-

40

soever. Compared to the universe, does anything which we do during our lives matter? Or, do all of the actions taken by all men in all times — Past, Present, and Future — matter? Although we have no answer to this question, we do offer one observation which we believe is worth considering: Man and the universe are distinctly different.

Imagine that you are standing in front of the 102-story Empire State Building in New York City, one of the tallest buildings in the world. As you stand there, do you think you would feel that any of your achievements were insignificant because of the physical presence of that building? We believe that your answer would be No. You realize that the building is not able to achieve anything; its size is irrelevant. And so it is with the universe. Its size is irrelevant to your achievements. Although you are a part of the universe, you are fundamentally different from the universe. You think. You imagine. You idealize. You evaluate. You intuit. You are able to conceptualize what you have never seen and, indeed, what may never exist in the world. These are capabilities which are lacking in the largest mountain, or any mountain. They are lacking in any universe; they are lacking in our universe. It is this concept which was worded so well by the French mathematician and philosopher Blaise Pascal (1623-1662) when he wrote:

"The greatness of man consists in thought. ... Not from space must I seek my dignity, but from the ruling of my thought. I should have no more if I possessed whole worlds. By space the universe encompasses and swallows me as an atom, by thought I encompass it. Man is but a reed, weakest in nature, but a reed which thinks. It needs not that the whole universe should arm to crush him. A vapour, a drop of water is enough to kill him. But were the universe to crush him, man would still be more noble than that which has slain him, because he knows that he dies, and that the universe has the better of him. The universe knows nothing of this."[24]

Our Strategy

Our first chapter has focused on our fundamental need for meaning. We all have a need for the meaning of our lives whether we care to admit it or not. It is there within us, perhaps encased currently in diversions, waiting to appear. Sooner or later the need will rise within us, become apparent, and we will recognize it as such. We will begin wondering to ourselves about our life.

In this chapter, we dealt with two questions: What is the meaning of life? and What is the meaning of my life? The first we discussed but discarded as being unknowable. The second, by contrast, cannot be discarded. It is embedded in our very fiber. We see ourselves everyday. We know of those who have gone before us; we know that others will follow us. What is the meaning of my life? is a question which we will all ask ourselves sooner or later.

The answer which we seek will not be a logical answer. It will not be derived from a series of equations. It will not be gleaned from algebra, calculus, or Venn diagrams. Instead, it will be an awareness, a sensing, a feeling. It will be the product of our intuition. What we intuit will be true, and we will immediately know it as such. What is particularly intriguing about awareness is that it cannot be sought directly; it must be sought *indirectly*. The concept is identical to that expressed so well by John Stuart Mill and included in this chapter. Mill was seeking happiness directly but found that it could only be obtained indirectly while striving for something else. And so it is with the awareness which we seek; we must seek it indirectly, as though it were incidental.

We believe that the something else toward which we must direct our efforts is creating a Future which is meaningful for us, a Future which embodies the values and ideals which we hold dear, and a Future which can only be achieved by a striving and struggling to the best of our ability. However, not just any desired Future will suffice; it must be a Future which benefits the lives of others. It must extend beyond ourselves. There is no doubt that we can do this, if we only chose to do so. But how does this lead indirectly to an increased awareness? We believe that the intensity of concentration and emotions evoked by the struggle are the impetus for our intuition, which is the source of all awareness. Awareness comes to a mind involved in an earnest and sincere struggle; conversely, no struggle, no increased awareness. Our strategy for increasing awareness is simply stated: Strive, strive again, and strive to the best of your ability to achieve a meaningful Future which is greater than yourself. The awareness which you seek will come indirectly.

In support of our strategy, the remaining chapters focus on achieving a desired Future which, because it resides solely in our mind, we refer to as a vision of a desired Future or, more simply, as a vision. Each chapter focuses on a different facet of achieving a desired Future, your desired Future, your vision.

We all have a vision of a desired Future and this vision is very important to us and our lives. In Chapter II *Moving Mountains* we look at some visions of other people. How are visions acquired? What is an effective vision? We also look at the differences between achievement visions and avoidance visions.

We do not merely react to what occurs in our environment. We act. We initiate. We seek to tailor the environment to us. Power is essential and it lies within us, able to be tapped by us. How this is done is described in Chapter III *The Force Is With You*. It is here that we address the spirit which is in each of us.

In Chapters II and III, the discussion focuses generally on the vision of one person. However, for that one person to achieve his vision, the cooperation of a group is required. We need others. This is the realm of the leader, and his use of his vision to muster the cooperation of a group which he needs to achieve his vision. How this is done is discussed in Chapter IV

Casting Your Net Upon The Waters. To succeed, we all must be leaders to some degree. This is essential.

Chapter V *The Future Is In Your Mind* looks carefully at what is meant by "the Future." What is the Future? Does tomorrow already exist? We think that the Future is not predetermined but created. There are 6 strategies by which we may create our Future, and each is described. The path of our life will involve one or more of these strategies.

But, given the rate of change in the world and the potential unpredictability of it all, is it realistic to think that a desired Future may be achieved? Is this belief on our part merely a psychological opiate which we use to sooth our anxiety about the Future? This fundamental question is addressed and answered in Chapter VI *The Alternative Is Unthinkable.* It is here that we look carefully at the principles of warfare.

The environment in which we live is competitive, and principles play an important role in our survival. In Chapter VII *Choose Your Principles* the purpose of a principle is explored. From where do principles come? It is here that the relationships among principles, values, ideals and desired Futures are considered. We also explore the ideal of striving to achieve that which extends beyond ourself.

Any vision operates in a competitive environment, and in striving and struggling to achieve our vision we must be aware of alternative outcomes, outcomes other than our vision. We need to be aware of what we want to happen as well as what we do not want to happen. We must face both the desirable and the undesirable. Scenarios force us to do just this. How scenarios are developed and how they are used are described in Chapter VIII *All Roads Don't Lead To Rome*.

Our closing comments are given in the *Epilogue: Leave Some Footprints*. We talk about heroes and what it means to be one. We exhort you and ourselves to be heroes, and to leave some footprints for those coming after us.

Chapter II

Moving Mountains

If you have built castles in the air, your
work need not be lost; that is where they
should be. Now put the foundations
under them.[1]

Although we may not be able to physically move
mountains, we frequently aspire to do what for us,
with our physical and mental capabilities, is comparable to just that — moving mountains. Let's consider for a moment the two largest pyramids in the
world ever constructed by man. The first is the Pyramid of the Sun at Teotihuacán approximately 25 miles
north of Mexico City, Mexico. It is approximately 215
feet high and the length of its side at the base is
roughly 1,200 feet. The Toltecs are thought to have
built it sometime between 300 A.D. and 600 A.D. The
second is the Great Pyramid at Giza, Egypt located
about 10 miles west of Cairo. In its current condition,
it is about 450 feet high and the length of its side at the
base is approximately 745 feet. The Great Pyramid
was built around the year 2,500 B.C. In the presence
of these two pyramids, you certainly feel as though
you are in the presence of man-made mountains.

The Great Pyramid and the Pyramid of the Sun
are well-known and have been visited by numerous
travelers over the centuries. Although each traveler
admires what was built and is understandably amazed,

we want to consider what to us is even more amazing: what was there *before* these two pyramids were built. The answer, of course, is nothing. Nothing, that is, except two visions in the minds of two men. For us, it is thrilling to imagine these two men standing one afternoon on their respective plateaus and *seeing* their pyramids. Each can almost reach out and touch it. As each stands there admiring it, each thinks of what it will look like at different times during the day. Each thinks of the wonderment of others as they stand just where they are right now and see it for the first time. There is a big smile on both their faces. Nothing in the world has ever been built as grand and magnificent as that which they can see right now. They think of the rock and earth which must be moved, the countless number of stones which must be put in place, the many laborers and builders, the challenges to be overcome, and the years of hard work ahead. Can this be done? Year after year after year? Each is quite reasonably concerned. The smiles have left their faces. For both, failure is clearly possible. After awhile, both turn around and begin walking down the path to their homes. And, as they walk, they begin to grin again. Both know that they will do it! They will build great pyramids the likes of which have never been seen in the world before.

Although these two men wore different clothes, practiced different customs, prayed to different gods, and spoke different languages, there is no doubt in our minds that at one moment in their lives each had the same magnificent thought. The same vision. The same doubt. The same determination. Each said to himself, I will do it! Is it not possible that each thought to himself that on what they were to embark was like moving a mountain?

You have much in common with these two pyramid builders as they stood looking at their pyramid on the plateau where it would be built. You have a desired Future. You have a vision. You know what it is. You know the obstacles. You know how you will feel after you have done it.

Behind every great achievement and every great failure lies the vision of a single person. In the striving to achieve this vision, to achieve a desired Future, there is pain, suffering, agony, joy, happiness, the potential for meaning, wisdom and increased awareness. It is this vision, this picture of a desired Future, which provides the goal toward which you strive, guides your actions in the Present, and is a source of meaning in your life.

Creating in our mind mental images of a desired Future is a process as ancient as man himself. Undoubtedly, the last person on Earth will have in his mind images of a desired Future.

Power Of Your Vision

What do you envision? What propels you into the Future? Let's look at a few examples of a vision. The six which we have selected are those of the great and famous. Although to us they are merely examples, the visions given here have each affected many people.

Walter E. Disney

In the United States and the world, Walter (Walt) E. Disney (1901-1966), the creator of the famous Disneyland amusement parks, is a legend. Almost everyone has heard of Walt Disney. His parks are in several foreign countries. This was his vision: "The idea of Disneyland is a simple one. It will be a place for people to find happiness and knowledge. It will be a place for parents and children to spend pleasant times in one another's company: a place for teachers and pupils to discover greater ways of understanding and education. Here the older generation can recapture the nostalgia of days gone by, and the younger generation can savor the challenge of the future. Here will be the wonders of Nature and Man for all to see and understand. Disneyland will be based upon and dedicated to the ideals and dreams that have created America. And it will be uniquely equipped to dramatize these dreams and send them forth as a source of courage and inspiration to all the world. Disneyland will be something of a fair, an exhibition, a playground, a community center, a museum of living facts, and a showplace of beauty and magic. It will be filled with the accomplishments, the joys and hopes of the world we live in. And it will remind us and show us how to make those wonders part of our own lives."[2]

President Ho Chi Minh

Ho Chi Minh (1890-1969), whose real name was Nguyen That Thanh, was the President of North Vietnam from 1945 to 1969. He successfully led the communists of Vietnam in their efforts to drive all foreign armies from Vietnam. Ho's directives to the peasants, the soldiers, the political groups, and to the people of Vietnam generally, were unremitting. He never ceased to stimulate everyone to greater effort, to hope, and to victory. This was his *Appeal For Patriotic Emulation* issued to the people of Vietnam on June 11, 1948:

"Patriotic zeal has a triple end. To conquer famine. To conquer ignorance. To conquer the enemy. And the way to do it is this: Rely on the people's army plus the people's morale in order to obtain the welfare of the people. This is why every citizen, whatever his calling, whether he be intellectual, peasant, worker, businessman or soldier, has a duty to work fast, work well, work hard. Every Vietnamese, irrespective of age, sex or status must become a fighter on one of these fronts: military, economic, political or cultural. Each one should make real the password: Resistance of the whole people, *total* resistance. As to the results of this dedication, here they are: Everyone will eat his fill and be adequately clothed. Everyone will know how to read and write. All our soldiers will have proper subsistence and enough arms. The nation will become entirely independent and unified. In order to achieve these ends, I ask everyone to dedicate himself: The old

51

(should) encourage youth to help us vigorously in our work. The children (should) outdo each other both in schoolwork and helping their elders. Merchants and manufacturers (should) increase their businesses. Peasants and workers (should) increase their output. Intellectuals (should) create. Technicians (should) invent. Officials (should) serve the people more devotedly. Regular army and guerilla units (should) strike even heavier blows against the enemy and particularly to seize weapons."[3]

Martin Luther King, Jr.

Martin Luther King (1929-1968) was a Civil Rights activist in the United States and for his accomplishments was awarded the Nobel Peace Prize in 1964. In 1968, he was assassinated in Memphis, Tennessee. His most well-known and quoted speech is his *I Have A Dream* keynote address presented on August 28, 1963 in Washington, D.C. before the Lincoln Memorial to approximately 250,000 participants in a March for Civil Rights. Given here is the second half of his speech, the part in which he described his dream.

"... So I say to you, my friends, that even though we must face the difficulties of today and tomorrow, I still have a dream. It is a dream deeply rooted in the American dream that one day this nation will rise up and live out the true meaning of its creed, we hold these truths to be self-evident, that all men are created equal. I have a dream that one day on the red hills of Georgia, sons of former slaves and sons of former slave-owners will be able to sit down together at the table of brotherhood."

"I have a dream that one day, even the state of Mississippi, a state sweltering with the heat of injustice, sweltering with the heat of oppression, will be transformed into an oasis of freedom and justice. I have a dream that my four children will one day live in a nation where they will not be judged by the color of their skin but by content of their character. I have a dream today!"

"I have a dream that one day, down in Alabama, with its vicious racists, with its governor having his lips dripping with the words of interposition and nullification, that one day, right there in Alabama, little black boys and black girls will be able to join hands with little white boys and white girls as sisters and brothers. I have a dream today!"

"I have a dream that one day every valley shall be exalted, every hill and mountain shall be made low, the rough places shall be made plain, and the crooked places shall be made straight and the glory of the Lord will be revealed and all flesh shall see it together. This is our hope. This is the faith that I go back to the South with. With this faith we will be able to tear out of the mountain of despair a stone of hope. With this faith we will be able to transform the jangling discords of our nation into a beautiful symphony of brotherhood. With this faith we will be able to work together, to pray together, to struggle together, to go to jail together, to stand up for freedom together, knowing that we will be free one day."

"This will be the day when all of God's children will be able to sing with new meaning — 'my country 'tis of thee; sweet land of liberty; of thee I sing; land where my fathers died, land of the pilgrim's pride; from every mountain side, let freedom ring' — and if America is to be a great nation, this must become true."

"So let freedom ring from the prodigious hilltops of New Hampshire. Let freedom ring from the mighty mountains of New York. Let freedom ring from the heightening Alleghenies of Pennsylvania. Let freedom ring from the snowcapped Rockies of Colorado. Let freedom ring from the curvaceous slopes of California. But not only that. Let freedom ring from Stone Mountain of Georgia. Let freedom ring from Lookout Mountain of Tennessee. Let freedom ring from every hill and molehill of Mississippi, from every mountainside, let freedom ring."

"And when we allow freedom to ring, when we let it ring from every village and hamlet, from every state and city, we will be able to speed up that day when all of God's children — black men and white men, Jews and Gentiles, Catholics and Protestants — will be able to join hands and to sing the words of the old Negro spiritual, 'Free at last, free at last; thank God Almighty, we are free at last.'"[4] This was the vision which was the theme of King's many speaches across the country.

Henry Ford

Henry Ford (1863-1947) was a leading manufacturer of automobiles in the United States during the first half of the twentieth century. The Ford Motor Company exists to this day. This is the early vision of Ford: "I will build a motor car for the great multitude. It will be so low in price that no man making a good salary will be unable to own one, and enjoy with his family the blessing of hours of pleasure in God's great open spaces. The horse will have disappeared from our highways, the automobile will be taken for granted."[5]

Sir Winston L. Churchill

During World War II, Sir Winston Churchill (1874-1965) was the Prime Minister of England and at the same time the Minister of Defense. These are excerpts from two of his speeches made to the House of Commons within the first month of his administration. We begin with the conclusion of his first speech as Prime Minister to the House of Commons on May 13, 1940:

"... In this crisis (the beginning of World War II) I hope that I may be pardoned if I do not address the House at any length today. ... I would say to the House, as I said to those who have joined this Government: I have nothing to offer but blood, toil, tears and sweat. We have before us an ordeal of the most grievous kind. We have before us many, many long months of struggle and of suffering. You ask what is our policy? I will say: It is to wage war, by sea, by land and air, with all our might and with all the strength that God can give us: to wage war against a monstrous tyranny, never surpassed in the dark, lamentable catalogue of human crime. That is our policy."

"You ask, What is our aim? I can answer in one word: Victory — victory at all costs, victory in spite of all terror, victory, however long and hard the road may be; for without victory, there is no survival. Let that be realized; no survival for the British Empire; no survival for all that the British Empire has stood for, no survival for the urge and impulse of the ages, that mankind will move forward towards its goal."

"But I take up my task with buoyancy and hope. I feel sure that our cause will not be suffered to fail among men. At this time I feel entitled to claim the aid of all, and I say, Come, then, let us go forward together with our united strength."[6]

Now, the conclusion of a subsequent speech given to the House of Commons on June 4, 1940:

"... I have, myself, full confidence that if all do their duty, if nothing is neglected, and if the best arrangements are made, as they are being made, we shall prove ourselves once again able to defend our island home, to ride out the storm of war, and to outlive the menace of tyranny, if necessary for years, if necessary alone. At any rate, that is what we are going to try to do. That is the resolve of His Majesty's Government — every man of them. ..."

"The British Empire and the French Republic, linked together in their cause and in their need, will defend to the death their native soil, aiding each other like good comrades to the utmost of their strength. Even though large tracts of Europe and many old and famous States have fallen or may fall into the grip of the Gestapo and all the odious apparatus of Nazi rule, we shall not flag or fail."

"We shall go on to the end, we shall fight in France, we shall fight on the seas and oceans, we shall fight with growing confidence and growing strength in the air, we shall defend our island whatever the cost may be, we shall fight on the beaches, we shall fight on the landing grounds, we shall fight in the fields and in the streets, we shall fight in the hills; we shall never surrender, and even if, which I do not for a moment believe, this island or a large part of it were subjugated and starving, then our Empire beyond the seas, armed and guarded by the British Fleet, would carry on the struggle, until in God's good time, the new world, with all its power and might, steps forth to the rescue and the liberation of the old."[7]

President John F. Kennedy

Ever since the presidential campaign of 1960, the American President John F. Kennedy (1917-1963) had become convinced that the United States must be the world leader in space exploration, regardless of the cost. He believed that in the 1960s the United States desperately needed a spectacular space achievement to regain its leadership role in the world. President Kennedy decided that the United States must place a man on the moon before the Russians. His decision to land a man on the Earth's moon before the Russians was communicated to the U.S. Congress, the American people, and the world in his Message To Congress on May 25, 1961 entitled *Urgent National Needs*. Here President Kennedy publically set forth the goal of placing a man on the moon by the end of the decade.

"... Finally, if we are to win the battle that is now going on around the world between freedom and tyranny, the dramatic achievements in space which occurred in recent weeks should have made clear to us all, as did Sputnik in 1957, the impact of this adventure on the minds of men everywhere, who are attempting to make a determination of which road they should take... I believe that this nation should commit itself to achieving the goal, before this decade is out, of landing a man on the moon and returning him safely to earth. No single space project in this period will be more impressive to mankind, or more important for the long-range exploration of space; and none will be so difficult or expensive to accomplish... But in a very real sense, it will not be one man going to the moon... it will be an entire nation. For all of us must work to put him there."[8]

The Congress of the United States and the American public were inspired on hearing their President publically challenge the Russians. With very

58

little debate, the Congress subsequently approved and funded President Kennedy's space program which, as the then Senator Robert S. Kerr explained, "will enable Americans to meet their destiny."[9]

Land Of Utopia

There is generally no limit to what may be envisioned. It may be a particular event, a set of events, or it may be society as a whole — all people, all events. The grand vision. We turn now to these grand visions and step into the world of utopia. Over the centuries scholars have described what would be either a desirable or undesirable Future for mankind. The word commonly used to describe a desirable world is *utopia*, a Greek word meaning *no place*. A utopia is generally an imaginary society perfectly organized in all ways, particularly with regard to laws, government, and social conditions. A description of a utopia tends to contrast a more desirable Future with a less desirable Present.

The adoption of the label *Utopia* relates directly to a novel by that name published in 1516 by the English statesman Sir (Saint) Thomas More (1478-1535). The novel is a report of the Portuguese sailor Raphael Hythlodaye who made three voyages to America with the explorer Amerigo Vespucci. Hythlodaye tells of his travels through wild and unexplored places; the greatest wonder, however, was the island of Utopia, where all men are equal, prosperous, educated, happy, wise, and work together harmoniously. Hythlodaye lived among the Utopians for five years and described in detail how these conditions were brought about and maintained.

Sir Thomas More was not the first to envision a better organization for society. The Greek philosopher Plato (427-347 B.C.) described his ideal society, referred to as *The Republic*, in 375 B.C. St. Augustine described his *City Of God* (as opposed to his City Of Man) in 426. More recently, the English philosopher Sir Francis Bacon (1561-1626) presented his *New Atlantis* in 1622; the Italian monk Tommaso Campanella (1568-1639), his *City Of The Sun* in 1623; the Frenchman Count Claude Henri de Saint-Simon (1760-1825), his plan appearing in *The Organizer* in 1819; the American writer Edward Bellamy (1850-1898), his *Looking Backward, 2000-1887* in 1888; the Austrian economist Theodor Hertzka (1845-1924), his *Freeland: A Social Anticipation* in 1890; and, finally, the English novelist and historian Herbert G. Wells (1866-1946), *A Modern Utopia* written in 1905.

In addition to the few mentioned here, a variety of other authors over the years have described their notions of a social utopia. All were describing what to them would be an ideal organization for society, an ideal way for mankind to live. Certainly they believed or hoped that society could be changed for the better, and that the forces at play could be manipulated, if so desired, to ultimately produce the desired outcome. They had hope and an idea.

But, who reads such material? It is interesting to note the success of the American writer Edward Bellamy: "The story of Bellamy's success in his own lifetime is astonishing. Within a year of its publication in 1888, *Looking Backward 2000-1887* sold a quarter of a million copies in the United States alone; by the time of the publication of its sequel *Equality* in 1897, it had sold half a million copies in America and hundreds of thousands more throughout the rest of the world. It was the best-selling novel in nineteenth-century America after *Uncle Tom's Cabin*, and the second novel in American literature to sell a million copies."[10]

As utopian authors envisioned societies characterized by orderliness, happiness and contentment, others envisioned potential societies which are depressingly wretched. Such a society is referred to as a *dystopia*, meaning in Greek not surprisingly *bad place*. The premier dystopian author was the Russian Evgenii I. Zamyatin writing in 1920 the novel *My (We)*, a story of the Single State, an authoritarian state which suppresses individual freedom to provide for personal happiness.[11] In the Single State, complete conformity in behavior and thinking has been achieved and individuality almost eradicated. All citizens wear uniforms and are known by number, e.g., D-503, E-330, instead of by name. They live in a city constructed completely of glass, so that there can be very little individual privacy, and their lives are regulated by a centrally-controlled device, called the Hour Schedule, at whose command the citizens in unison conduct their daily activities. Control is maintained by a single dictator, the Benefactor, who has a small but powerful police force, the Guardians, to aid him.

A dystopian, such as Zamyatin, frequently is opposed to the utopias proposed by others. For example, consider *orderliness*. At first, it would seem that orderliness, as opposed to disorderliness, is desirable. However, producing orderliness to an extreme degree could result in a society described by Zamyatin. Similarly, it may be argued that, to increase the level of individual happiness, the degree of individual freedom must be reduced. As the degree of freedom increases, so also increases the likelihood of pain and suffering. Two other dystopian writers, both strongly influenced by the writing of Zamyatin, are the English authors Aldous Huxley (1894-1963) and George Orwell (the pseudonym of Eric Blair, 1903-1950). The first wrote *Brave New World* in 1932 and, the second, *Nineteen Eighty-Four* in 1949.

Origins Of Visions

How is it that a vision of a desired Future comes to be in our mind? There is not one way, but several ways. All of these ways, however, may be divided into two broad categories. With the first, we create our own vision; with the second, we acquire it from another person or group. In either case, for us to accept a vision, we *must be predisposed* to accepting it or *have a compelling need* to accept it. Some examples of a compelling need are a strong desire for a change, fear of potential Future events, and a need to acquire something not currently possessed. Most of our visions, however, we create ourselves. Let's consider the ways in which we might acquire a vision.

Intuition

Intuition is the ability to perceive knowledge or understanding without reasoning. When a vision is the product of our intuition, it just appears, whole, one day in our mind. When this happens, the vision is understood immediately, although the rationale as to why this is an appropriate vision may not be understood. A vision appearing in this manner is frequently preceded by an intense desire on our part to acquire a vision which is appropriate for us.

Management theorist Burt Nanus, in developing the concept of visionary leadership, asks the question, Where does vision come from? Although the dangling preposition certainly puts a frown on the face of his English teacher, it, nevertheless, is an interesting question. His answer centers around the notion of intuition or, as he calls it, insight as being the source of vision: "Every remarkable artistic achievement starts as nothing more than a dream, usually of one individual, and not infrequently contested and ridiculed by friends and colleagues. Such a dream is a vision not much different from one a leader develops for an organization, for leadership itself is also an art form. Visionary leaders, like artists, are astute and perhaps idiosyncratic observers and interpreters of the real world. Leaders, like artists, try to rearrange the materials at their disposal — that is, the people, processes, and structures of an organization — to create a new and more powerful order that will succeed and endure over time. And the best visionary leaders, like the best artists, are always seeking to communicate directly and viscerally a vision of the world that will resonate with the deepest meanings of people and cause them to embrace it as worthwhile and elevating."

"... So where does a leader's vision come from? Vision is composed of one part foresight, one part insight, plenty of imagination and judgment, and often, a healthy dose of chutzpah.[12] It occurs to a well-informed open mind, a mind prepared by a lifetime of learning and experience, one sharply attuned to emerging trends and developments in the world outside of the organization. Creativity certainly plays an important part, but it is a creativity deeply rooted in the reality of the organization and its possibilities."[13]

Nanus' comment suggests that a vision, like art, is an intuition of the individual. A major ingredient, however, of this intuition or insight is, in the opinion of Nanus, a large dose of knowledge acquired through study and experience, or hard work. It is as though the concepts of the Future were building blocks, able to be configured in a variety of ways by the creativity of the mind of the individual, with the one configuration then intuitively selected by the individual as being more appropriate or more desirable than all others. For Nanus, intuition is all-important.

An example which illustrates the insight and creativity suggested by Nanus is found in the process by which the Gillette safety razor came to be. This particular shaving tool was invented by King C. Gillette (1855-1932) who in 1895 was a traveling salesman and a frustrated inventor. Employed by the Crown Cork & Seal Company, Gillette was envious of its president, William Painter, who had invented the company's best-selling product — a bottle stopper consisting of a tin cap with a cork lining. Painter encouraged Gillette, who had patented several minor inventions, to cultivate his inventive talents.

One day Painter gave Gillette some advice. "King, you are always thinking and inventing something. Why don't you try to think of something like the Crown Cork which, when once used, is thrown away, and the customer keeps coming back for more? And with every additional customer you get, you are building a foundation of profit."

Gillette never forgot these words. For years he tried unsuccessfully to think of a product to fit Painter's criteria for success. Sometimes he mentally stepped through the alphabet, A to Z, trying to think of a new product starting with each letter, a product which would be useful, saleable, and disposable. Then, one day in the spring of 1895, the idea for which he had been waiting finally fell into his mind. The following is Gillette's personal account of his initial vision of the safety razor with disposable shaving blades:

"It was born as naturally as though its embryonic form had matured in thought and only waited its appropriate time of birth. One morning when I started to shave, I found my razor dull, and it was not only dull but it was beyond the point of successful stropping. It needed honing, which meant it would have to be taken to a barber or cutler. A razor is only a sharp edge, I said to myself, and the back of it is just support. Why do they go to all the expense and trouble of fashioning a backing that has nothing to do with shaving? And why do they forge a great piece of steel and then spend so much labor in hollow grinding it when they could get the same result by putting an edge on a piece of steel only thick enough to hold an edge? As I stood there with the razor in my hand, my eyes resting on it as lightly as a bird settling down on its nest, the Gillette razor was born — more with the rapidity of a dream than by a process of reasoning. In that moment I saw it all: the way the blade could be held in a holder; the idea of sharpening the two opposite edges on the thin piece of steel; the clamping plates for the blade, with a handle halfway between the two edges of the blade. All this came more in pictures than in conscious thought, as though the razor were already a finished thing and held before my eyes. I stood there before that mirror in a trance of joy. My wife was visiting in Ohio, and I hurriedly wrote to her: I've got it! Our fortune is made! Fool that I was, I knew little about razors and nothing about steel, and I could not foresee the trials and tribulations I was to pass through before the razor was a success. But I believed in it with my whole heart."[14]

Critical Incident

A vision may be the result of a critical incident, and examples of such incidents are numerous. Although only three are described here, you will be able to think of several from your own life. A critical incident is an event, observed and experienced by you, which produces a sudden and abrupt change in your thinking, level of understanding, or level of awareness. The distinguishing characteristic of a critical incident is that, before the incident, you were not aware of the level of understanding which was clearly present after the incident.

Although any learning experience is the result generally of some incident, the incidents referred to here are those where the new level of understanding is spectacular. A particular incident may be critical only for one person; others present at the same time may be completely unaffected. This suggests that the affected person was in some manner predisposed for the level of understanding which occurred, a predisposition possibly the result of previous work, experience, or a strong desire to understand. What is interesting is that the incident itself need not be grand or spectacular; most frequently, it seems, it is relatively small.

Our first example of a critical incident is the death of a close friend. You are attending the funeral service and hear the many kind words spoken about your friend. All of a sudden, you can see yourself lying in the casket just as your friend is now, and you wonder what people will be saying about you at your funeral. You can not imagine them making the same positive comments about you as they are now making about your friend. In your heart, you know that you must treat people, your friends, your colleagues, differently than you have in the Past. You know that this is true. You decide then and there to change your behavior.

For our second example, imagine yourself as a teenager suffering from an illness which has confined you to a hospital bed for several months. You have been treated by several doctors and over the weeks you and they have become friends. You see daily how they treat you and you know that your steady improvement is in large measure due to their expertise. When in the hospital you talk to the nurses and occasionally to other patients, all of whom share your opinion of these doctors. You can imagine yourself being one of these doctors. You can imagine yourself helping people in a hospital. You can feel even now the pride and sense of joy which this would bring to you. You can imagine being thanked afterward by your patients for what you have done. When you are released from the hospital, you will start down the path of study and hard work which leads to a medical degree, your medical degree.

Our third example of a critical incident is that reported by Nikola Tesla (1856-1943), the Yugoslavian-American scientist, whose invention of the alternating current transmission system revolutionized the use of electricity. Disturbed by the many shortcomings of the direct-current system, Tesla was convinced that he could devise an entirely new electrical system based on alternating current. But first he would have to invent an alternating current motor, a device which many scientists had tried unsuccessfully to build. However, Tesla was determined to solve this problem and was confident that the answer lay somewhere deep in his mind.

The design for the alternating current motor came to him in February 1882 as he was walking with a friend in a park. The sunset with its panorama of brilliant colors filled the sky, moving Tesla to recite a passage from Goethe's *Faust... The glow retreats, done is the day of toil; it yonder hastes, new fields of life exploring; ah, that no wing can lift me from the soil, upon its track to follow, follow soaring...* As he spoke, his body swayed from side to side, his arms waved about in the air. Suddenly he became immobile and fell into a trance-like state. This is how he described his experience: "As I uttered these inspiring words the idea came like a flash of lightning, and in an instant the truth was revealed... The images I saw were wonderfully sharp and clear and had the solidity of metal and stone, so much so that I told (my friend), 'See my motor here; watch me reverse it.' I cannot begin to describe my emotions. Pygmalion see-ing his statue come to life could not have been more deeply moved. A thousand secrets of nature which I might have stumbled upon accidentally I would have given for that one which I had wrested from her against all odds."[15]

A year later Tesla constructed a working model of his alternating current motor. He built it without any blueprints or rough sketches, with nothing except his memory to guide him. Gifted with amazing mental powers, Tesla was able to see a machine in his mind, take a mental photograph of it, store the information in his mind, and recall it at will. The parts for his motor were exactly built from mathematical calculations worked out in his mind and fit together exactly as he had pictured them. When the motor was ready to be tested, he confidently threw a switch, and the machine responded as planned. Tesla knew he had a motor which would revolutionize technology around the world.

Logical Analysis

A vision may be the result of logical analysis or reasoning on your part. Logical analysis is the antithesis of intuition. Imagine this. One day you decide to find a quiet, secluded place where you can be alone. You want to think. You want to think about your life, what you want to do with your life, and what you have done up to this point in time with your life. You have paper and pen at hand and, as you draw various boxes denoting key decisions and events in your life, you begin to realize what the goals of your life really are. You see that the pattern of events and decisions, if continued into the Future, will not allow you to achieve the goals of your life. On a separate sheet of paper, you begin to roughly sketch what could happen so that these goals, or most of them, could be achieved. As you think about this, you find that there are several scenarios possible. Next, for each scenario, you list what you would have to do to make each scenario occur for you. Each scenario would require a considerable amount of work on your part. There is one scenario, however, which seems within your grasp. As you start to think more about this scenario, the initial activities required, the work involved, the changes which you would have to make in your life, and what you would feel like as you are living the scenario, you sense the excitement within you swell. You can finally visualize the scenario which you want to be a part of your life.

The vision of a corporation may be the result of logical analysis and the process described here may be followed by one individual or a group of employees. The process begins by focusing on a point in time in the Future as, for example, 6 to 8 years from the Present. For this time period and for the relevant industry in which the corporation is a part, consider what the competition will be doing and what will be the needs and desires of the clients. In this particular arena, identify several areas where there will be a client demand associated with a relatively weak response from the competition. For two or three of these areas, determine what would be the general nature of the product or service which would be most appropriate for the client and possibly not able to be serviced sufficiently well by the competition. These are the potential weak points in the marketplace. Then, for each potential product or service, conjure alternative scenarios by which the desired product or service could be made available to the client. What resources would be required to implement each scenario? Of the required resources, what are currently available to the corporation? What additional resources would have to be acquired by the corporation?

Considering all of the scenarios and products as a set, there will be one or two in the set which sound interesting, involve a certain amount of risk, and would certainly pose a significant challenge for the corporation. But, if one of these risky scenarios could be carried out, what would the Future be like for the corporation. What would happen in 6 or 8 years? How would the employees feel? What would they be thinking at that time? It is the description of events such as these which constitute a potential desired Future for the corporation, a vision of a desired Future.

Clearly, the process involves an unusual amount of what-if thinking, a determination to think anew, an appraisal of the potential of the competition, and an appraisal of the client's needs. Determining a corporate vision by group consensus, of course, is not a novel idea. Some examples of the questions which a group might consider when starting down the path to a corporate vision are: What do we as a company really want to do? What have we done as a company that gives us the most pride? Looking back on our company's history, of what ought we to be ashamed? What could we as a company do in the future that would make us all proud? What do we as a company do effectively? What could we as a company do effectively? Ten years from now, looking back, what will we as a company have done to make us the most proud?[16] Although these are interesting questions and undoubtedly of value, their value might be increased were they to address more directly the potential competition and the potential needs and desires of the client. Perhaps the group should consider initially the question, What will cause our corporation to be in business 10 years from now?

Vision Acquired From Others

If you are predisposed to accepting a vision, a vision may be acquired from another person or a group. The degree to which you maintain this vision is related to the creditability of the vision, the benefit to you from striving to achieve it, and the cost to you if the vision is not achieved. There are four methods by which you may acquire a vision from another: persuasion, imitation, group consensus, and formal indoctrination.

Through daily or frequent contact with another person, you may be persuaded or influenced by that person to believe that their vision is important to you and that it is in your best interests to share in this vision. Their vision becomes your vision. Here, you have been persuaded.

After learning of a vision held by a person whom you admire greatly, you decide that his vision is equally appropriate for you. You adopt the vision, equating the quality of the vision with the degree of admiration which you have for him. Here, you imitate what has been done by another.

You may be a part of a group. With all members participating, a group may collectively derive over time a vision which is judged appropriate for it. Striving to achieve the vision is a requirement for group membership. Here, you are acting in accordance with the group consensus.

Through the training process, you are instructed as to what is the appropriate vision for you to hold in your mind, and exactly how you are expected to act and think in keeping with this vision. The degree to which you are rewarded for your actions is a function of the degree to which you strive to achieve this vision. Here, you have been formally indoctrinated.

More Than A Dream

If a mental image or series of images does not in any way influence your behavior and actions, it is merely a dream, idea, or concept. But not a vision. A dream, however, may lead to a vision when you decide to act to achieve it.

Your vision must have at least three character-istics. First, it must address a Future situation or con-dition. Second, it must be specific and imagined suffi-ciently clearly so that, when it has occurred, you know that it has occurred. And, third, when it is visualized, it must evoke emotions within you, and inspire or stim-ulate you to act to achieve that envisioned. Your vision may address a situation or condition which has never been experienced by you or by anyone. Also, a vision may address a situation or condition which may or may not occur during your lifetime. Lastly, your vision may involve individuals other than yourself. At any time, you may have more than one vision.

A vision may address what you desire to achieve, or a vision may address what you desire to avoid or not have happen. The examples given below address both categories of visions. *Achievement* vi-sions, as a category, address accomplishments or striv-ing for excellence; *Avoidance* visions, what is to be avoided or assumed to be detrimental to you. General-ly, all visions are achievement visions in that you are trying to cause specific Future events to occur.

Achievement Visions

Imagine this. You are a college student and you can see yourself being an engineer upon graduation. Each

75

day you study persistently. The course of study is difficult but you can see yourself one day being an engineer and building large and magnificent bridges. You can see yourself one day standing beside a new, large bridge where, off to one side of the bridge, there is a plaque bearing the inscription: THIS BRIDGE WAS BUILT BY (your name). You sense even now the pride and feeling of accomplishment of that Future moment.

Imagine this. You have been employed by a large corporation for the past 25 years. You will retire next February and look forward to this time. You envision yourself fishing for trout in a mountain pool fed by a small river. As you think about this, you can almost feel the cool mountain breezes across your face. You can almost see the ripples in the water from the fish occasionally swimming close to the surface. You can sense the feeling of peace and tranquility of the moment. These moments you know you will enjoy very much. You even enjoy thinking about them and planning for them.

Imagine this. You are a parent. You can envision your son or daughter graduating from college. It is this thought which causes you to save the necessary monies, each month deposited in the bank, so that the funds will be available when your son or daughter is ready to attend college. You know the sense of joy that you will experience as you watch your son or daughter accept their diploma on graduation day. You will be there. You know that you will.

76

Imagine this. You work for a company. You can envision what this company will be like 10 years from now. In your mind, everyone will admire the products and services produced by the company. Everyone will think that the company is the greatest. The products will be known throughout the entire world as the best, the absolute best, of their kind. Each day as you work, you know that each and every task which you perform must be performed to the best of your ability. Because this is the way the best products in the world are made.

Avoidance Visions

Imagine this. You are sitting in your company office one day, working as always. Your immediate supervisor enters unexpectedly saying, due to economic factors, management has determined that your services may no longer be required. In fact, your last day on the job may be three months from now. You can sense the feeling of surprise and disappointment and, indeed, anger. You have worked at this company for sixteen years, yes, sixteen long years. What will you tell your family, your friends. How difficult will it be for me to find another job? you wonder to yourself. You begin to work harder on the job, taking on difficult assignments, working longer hours.

Imagine this. It is the final day of your life. During your last hours, someone at your side asks, What did you accomplish with your life? The answer is difficult, and, in fact, there is no answer. Because you know that there is really nothing of what you wanted to do that you really did. You feel the sadness as you say, "Well, if I had it all to do over again..." You can see the not-totally-hidden look of disappointment on the inquirer's face as he or she realizes that this was a question which should not have been asked. This answer will not be my answer, you think. Each day is a new opportunity to begin doing or to do what I have always wanted to do. You will not let this happen to you! Yes! You reach for the telephone to contact a very dear friend with whom over the years you have lost contact. This person had been very helpful to you. Now, perhaps, you can begin being helpful to them.

Imagine this. You are a parent who, over the years, has read newspaper accounts of children accidentally drowning in swimming pools. You can feel the anguish, horror, and disbelief which the parent of a drowned child must feel as they watch paramedics attempting unsuccessfully to revive their child. You can imagine your own child lying on the ground with a paramedic bending over him or her. You can see the paramedic rhythmically pressing hard on your child's chest, then blowing air into their lungs, pressing on the chest, blowing air into the lungs, pressing and blowing, pressing and blowing. This will never happen to you. This will never happen to your child. Never. It is for this reason that you carefully watch your child every time they go swimming. Every time you do this.

Inspiring Others

You may have a vision which is yours and yours alone. There is no need to communicate it to anyone else. Whether or not anyone else knows about it, understands, or agrees with it is unimportant. You can travel the path to your desired Future alone. However, if the nature of your vision is such that the cooperation of others is essential for its achievement, then it must be communicated to them. The tool for doing this is the vision statement, which is an expression of the vision in a form so that it may be understood by others. A vision statement is effective to the degree that, when communicated, it creates in the mind of another person a series of specific mental images associated with the desired Future, and causes the person to act with determination in performing those activities necessary for the vision to be achieved. For your audience, the Future described and communicated must be perceived as desirable, creditable, relevant, understandable, and simple.

A Few Lessons From Napoléon

Because the vision statement is chiefly a communication tool, it follows that it will differ among groups of people to reflect the differing and potentially unique characteristics and interests of each group. This is true whether the vision statement is expressed in writing, by word of mouth, or by observed behavior and actions. Some practices of Napoléon Bonaparte I (1769-1821), Emperor of the French from 1804 to 1815, are both interesting and instructive. The majority of the correspondence and writing of Napoléon was published in French in 32 volumes from 1858 to 1879, and this literature has been extensively studied for years. Napoléon fully realized the power of words.

"All his life Napoleon was conscious of the power of words to influence events. He knew that armies march, treaties are made, policies formed, nations moved to action only as a result of words, and that the way these are chosen and used profoundly influences their effectiveness. ... He would carefully revise the drafts of public documents, often showing in marginal notes or covering letters why one phrase was to be preferred to another. His subordinates received constant admonition and advice about their own style and sometimes stern but wise criticism of what they wrote; often enough their papers were returned to them for redrafting. Words must be weighed, he said to Eugène (Eugène de Beauharnais, Napoléon's stepson).[17] To Eugène he also wrote: The circular is too long-winded; authority reasons less and explains itself more briefly. You would have done better to write six lines.[18] To Murat (Joachim Murat, General): Your Order of the Day is wretched. Good God! Where should we be if I had to write four pages to tell the soldiers not to let themselves be disarmed? You never learnt that from me.[19] Such comments abound; they show both the value he placed on the right use of words and his faith in his own ability to achieve it. The brevity that he urges he almost always practiced. To waste words was to waste time, and that seemed to him a calamity; in politics as in war, he said, the lost moment never returns.[20] But he also knew that the fewer the words, provided they are the right ones, the more influence they will wield. I have read the proclamation, he wrote to Lucien (Lucien Bonaparte, Napoléon's brother, French Ambassador to Spain), it is worthless. There are too many words and not enough ideas. That is not the way to speak to the people."[21]

Napoléon was adept at what he called tact. He was very concerned that the style and content of his writing be appropriate for the audience to which it was directed. He believed "there is an appropriate mode for each subject, each person, each community, and that if the ruler is to achieve his aims he must be able to call them up at will. His own writing has an adaptability resembling the suppleness of his military manoeuvering ...and from the style alone it is often possible to tell whom he is addressing."[22] The notion of tact dominated the writing style of Napoléon. If writing to a priest the language must be sought in the spirit of religion, not in that of philosophy.[23] In Egypt it was easy, from some of his papers, to think him a Moslem. Letters about finance are mostly columns of figures. His staff and soldiers received precise, detailed orders leaving no room for misunderstanding or for the 'ifs' and 'buts' that infuriated him. ... For the common man he would often refer to 'his star,' or Destiny or the will of God; the educated got reasoned, forceful argument. Each letter is exactly adjusted to the personality of the recipient and carefully designed to produce the intended effect; it is unlikely that any of those addressed realized how far they were being managed."[24]

The lessons to be learned from Napoléon are very simple. The wording of the vision statement is very important, whether communicated in writing or by word of mouth. The presentation of the vision statement must be tailored to each audience. Clearly, the concept of a single vision statement is not appropriate.

An Effective Vision Statement

To be effective, a vision statement should (1) focus on a positive achievement, large in scope, (2) outline the strategy for achieving success, major areas of emphasis, and challenges to be overcome, (3) identify the behavior required of each person for success, (4) state when success is expected and how it will be determined, (5) cite the benefits to each person from achieving the vision, and (6) state the attitudes, feelings, and emotions which should be had by each person as they contribute to achieving the vision.

At the beginning of this chapter we gave several examples of vision statements. Let's take a look at how Ho Chi Minh did it according to the six criteria given above.

What was the positive achievement, large in scope? Patriotic zeal has a triple end: To conquer famine. To conquer ignorance. To conquer the enemy…to obtain the welfare of the people and…for the nation to become entirely independent and unified.

What was the strategy by which success was to be achieved and what were the challenges to be overcome? Every Vietnamese, irrespective of age, sex or status must become a fighter on one of these fronts: military, economic, political or cultural. Each one should make real the password: Resistance of the whole people, *total* resistance. Rely on the people's army plus the people's morale in order to obtain: the welfare of the people.

What must each person do to contribute to success? Every citizen…has a duty to work fast, work well, work hard. The old are to encourage youth to help us vigorously in our work. Children are to outdo each other both in schoolwork and helping their elders. Merchants and manufacturers are to increase their businesses. Peasants and workers are to increase their output. Intellectuals are to create. Technicians are to invent. Officials are to serve the people more devotedly. Regular army and guerilla units are to strike even heavier blows against the enemy and particularly to seize weapons.

When is success expected and how it will be determined? Ho Chi Minh implies that success will be achieved when the nation is entirely independent and unified.

How does each person benefit from achieving the vision? Everyone will eat his fill and be adequately clothed. Everyone will know how to read and write. All our soldiers will have proper subsistence and enough arms. The nation will become entirely independent and unified.

What are the attitudes, feelings, and emotions which should be had by each person as they contribute to achieving the vision? Ho Chi Minh does not describe this.

Each of the visions given in this chapter could have been analyzed in this manner. In fact, you could analyze your vision in the same way.

The Vision Tapestry

What happens when a vision is achieved? For example, assume that you have for years envisioned graduating from college. What happens when you graduate from college? The answer is that you still remember this previous vision, but that it no longer inspires you to act. It is replaced by another vision, a new opportunity to create meaning for yourself and your life. This new vision may be a vision of similar magnitude or it may be one of larger magnitude. Here, the development may be vertical (expanding to a larger, more comprehensive vision) or horizontal (replacing one vision with another of similar magnitude). The magnitude of a vision refers to the number of your life's activities which are influenced by it.

Every vision is potentially a component of a larger vision. Consider the famous Bayeux Tapestry located not surprisingly in Bayeux, France. This particular tapestry is approximately 231 feet long and 20 inches high, and was completed in the years 1073 to 1083. The tapestry presents the events from 1064 to 1066 and the story of the final conflict between Harold II of England and William of Normandy, rival claimants to the English throne. Included in the tapestry are scenes of oath-taking, banquets, ship-building, the Norman invasion, soldiers fighting on foot, armored knights with swords in hand riding on horses, arrows flying through the air, somersaults of falling horses, dead and wounded soldiers lying on the ground, and finally the Battle of Hastings (1066) during which Harold II was slain and William the Conqueror seized the English crown. The tapestry contains more than 600 human figures and over 200 animals, as well as ships, trees, and buildings.

Imagine this. You are standing in front of the Bayeux tapestry. At first, you are standing very close to it and you see only a small part of it. The part which you are seeing is like a vision. If you move parallel to the tapestry, you will see different parts of the tapestry, that is, different scenes, but each scene will be of the same magnitude as that seen previously. These different scenes are like different visions, all of the same magnitude. However, as you step back, you will see more of the tapestry and the relationships among the smaller scenes which you previously observed, but you will not see all of the tapestry. You will just see more of it. What previously had been your vision will now be a part of a larger vision. You can seen both your old vision and the new vision of which it is a part.

Think For A Moment

The vision statements given at the start of this chapter are known to us because of the significance to our lives and the publicity of the events associated with them. What of the countless number of visions in the mind of man today of which we know nothing? How are they affecting our lives and our world at this very moment? For the vision statements given at the start of the chapter, consider what is it about them which motivated men to act. As you read them, what images were conjured in your mind?

It is interesting to speculate what the world would be like if visioning was not done, or not able to be done, by anyone. Would this constitute the framework for a dystopian novel? What would be the effect on your life if you either could not or did not care to envision desirable Future events?

Everyone with the capability of imagination envisions the Future to some degree. Do you have a vision which is worthy of you?

Chapter III

The Force Is With You

> I never work better than when I am in-
> spired by anger: for when I am angry, I
> can write, pray, and preach well, for
> then my whole temperament is quicken-
> ed, my understanding sharpened, and all
> mundane vexations and temptations de-
> part.[1]

How it starts we all know very well. We, of our own
free will, select desired Future events, and then strive
to cause them to happen. In our mind, there is some
potential series of events which is thought to bring
about or produce this desired Future. Actions taken in
the Present are the product of decisions made in the
Present, and are evaluated by us according to the degree to which they bring about our desired Future.
From this perspective, the Future as envisioned in our
mind clearly influences what we do in the Present. We
create a Future in our mind and then this Future shapes
our behavior and attitudes. The concept is similar to
that suggested by Sir Winston Churchill when he said,
"We shape our buildings: thereafter they shape us."[2]
It is how our desired Future shapes our behavior and
attitudes which is considered here. We also consider
what it is within us which allows us to frequently act
with such power and determination. As we shall see,
our emotions play an important role.

87

Before beginning, let's turn for a moment to a more general question. Why do we find ourselves doing this at all? Why do we find ourselves creating images of Future events and then striving to achieve them? Why has this been done by every man, and will be done by every man? The answer is very simple. Change. The environment in which we find ourselves is continually changing, as we ourselves are changing. Specifically, we are ill-suited for the changing environment on the planet Earth. We must act to survive; taking no action will result in our death. If the Present is acceptable, we must strive to maintain that condition. If the Present is unacceptable, we create in our mind an idea of what is more acceptable. The desirable exists only in the Future, in our mind. It is for this reason that we look to the Future, to what could be, to what provides the only basis for all hope. If there were no change, concepts of goal, value, and, indeed the Future would be meaningless. It is only in the context of change that these terms acquire any meaning at all.

We do not merely react to what occurs in our environment. We act. We initiate. We seek to tailor the environment to our best interests. One way in which we attempt to manipulate our environment is envisioning a desired Future and then striving to achieve it. We are a presence in the universe, and a presence clearly different from anything else living on the planet Earth. There is, however, a conflict between our will and our environment. A changing environment forces us to act in our best interests. It is the very possibility of change which allows us the possibility of changing the Present to what is more desirable. Although we may struggle with change, it is this very change which allows us the possibility of altering the environment according to our desires. Clearly, change affords us the opportunity of creating meaning in our life. However, with change there is what cannot be changed, is undesirable, and which is judged significant to his life. This must be endured. Courage comes in many forms.

The Spirit Connection

The ultimate source of power resides in our human spirit. It is our spirit through our mind which empowers our seemingly frail body to act. The mind alone is incapable of generating such a force. The fundamental connection is the connection between our emotions and our spirit. It is our *emotions* which call our human spirit into action. An emotional response is the critical factor for the quickening of our spirit. Our vision is a source of power to the degree to which it evokes our emotions. Our vision must arouse our emotions to be effective. The quotation given at the beginning of this chapter was taken from Martin Luther (1483-1546), the German leader of the Reformation Movement and the founder of Protestantism. For Luther at that time of his life, the driving emotion was anger. Is anger the only emotion? Of course not. Other emotions are fear, joy, sadness, acceptance, disgust, surprise and curiosity — with fear being the most powerful of all. These basic emotions combine to form others, just as the basic colors combine to produce all colors.

We are able to generate an energy or force from within ourselves. This force we call the *psychological force*. We could have called it the spiritual force. Regardless of the label, it is this force, this energy, which will allow us to persist or persevere for an extended period of time or in difficult circumstances. When we reach deep within ourselves, this is the force we seek and often find.

What is meant by the human *spirit*? We consider every person to be composed of three closely interrelated parts: body, mind, and spirit. The spirit is the life force which has been extended to and resides in our body. The body without the spirit is dead. The life force in the body is an extension of the life force which exists in the universe. The source of the life force is God. It is because the spirit in our body is an extension of the universal life force that the potential in each of us is so great.

Examples Of The Psychological Force In Action

Why do some people act as they do, with persistence and determination, in the face of seemingly dominating events? What enables them to do what others consider either impossible or too difficult? The answer is the psychological force within them. Although this force is easily recognized when it occurs, and its absence equally conspicuous, it is a force difficult to describe. Nonetheless, it is real and potentially very powerful. When it is the product of a group, it has the potential to compensate for a variety of inadequacies in any plan, tactic, or strategy. It is a significant force multiplier. What is constant throughout history is the potential for the psychological force to exert a dominant influence on events.

Although the psychological force of a person or group is intangible, we should not underrate or ignore it because it is difficult to describe, and certainly more difficult to analyze. The force may be intangible; its effects are not. The history of man is ennobled by innumerable instances in which a person or group seemingly through sheer determination and will power performed the impossible.

Four examples of the psychological force in action are presented here. Many could have been presented. For the first two, we travel to ancient Italy and the city of Rome; the year is 505-504 B.C. For the third example, we travel to ancient Greece; the year is 480 B.C. For the last example, we travel to what is now the United States of America and state of Texas; the year is 1836. By delving into the Past we show that the psychological force is nothing new to man; it is not a modern factor. In every case — Past, Present and Future — it is man struggling to force his will upon the environment to bring about a change which he considers desirable.

Horatius At The Bridge. The year is 505 B.C. and the city of Rome is just 246 years old. To the North lies the country of Etruria in central Italy (in what is currently Tuscany and part of Umbria). The king of the Etrurians, Porsena, has marched his army to Rome with the intent of capturing the city. Some parts of the city are defended by walls; other parts are secured by the Tiber River (currently the Tevere River which runs through the center of modern Rome). On this day, Roman soldiers are guarding the one bridge across the Tiber and, from that vantage point, see the Etrurian army suddenly assault and capture the Janiculum Hill on the West bank. The Etrurians then proceed at full speed for the bridge leading to Rome. The Roman soldiers on the bridge, seeing the enemy army rapidly approaching, flee in terror, abandoning their weapons as they run to Rome. Only one soldier remains behind on the bridge: Horatius Cocles. Unable to persuade his comrades to stand and fight, and seeing that the enemy would soon be across the bridge and on to Rome, Cocles tells the fleeing soldiers to demolish the bridge by any means possible. Remaining on the bridge, he will hold off the enemy as long as possible.

"(Cocles) then advances to the first entrance of the bridge, and being easily distinguished among those who showed their backs in retreating from the fight, facing about to engage the foe hand to hand, by his surprising bravery he terrified the enemy. ...he for a short time stood the first storm of the danger, and the severest brunt of the battle. But as they who demolished the bridge called upon (him) to retire…(he cast) his stern eyes round all the officers of the Etrurians in a threatening manner (and) challenged them singly… They hesitated for a considerable time, looking round one at the other, to commence the fight; shame then put the army in motion, and a shout being raised, they hurled their weapons from all sides on their single adversary; and when (the spears and javelins) all stuck in the shield held before him, and he with no less obstinacy kept possession of the bridge with firm step, they now endeavored to thrust him down from it by one push, when at once the (bridge begins to collapse. Cocles)…armed as he was, he leaped into the Tiber, and amid showers of darts hurled on him, swam across safely to his party, having dared an act which is likely to obtain more fame than credit with posterity."[3]

Scaevola, The Man With One Hand. After his ordeal, Rome expressed its gratitude to Cocles by erecting a statue in his honor and giving him as much land as he could plough around in one day. Meanwhile, Porsena, failing in his first attempt to capture Rome, decided to lay siege to the city. Inside the besieged city was a young nobleman named Caius Mucius. It was a disgrace, he thought, that the Roman people were confined within their walls by the very Etrurian army they had often beaten in the Past. To him, such an indignity should be avenged by a great and daring deed. Mucius decided to sneak into the camp of Porsena and assassinate him. However, when he eventually found himself in the vicinity of the king, he was unable to identify Porsena because the men standing around him were dressed similarly. Mucius knew that any inquiries by him would betray his true identity. So, he stabbed the person he thought was the king, only to have killed the wrong man. His capture is sudden, and he is brought immediately before the king.

"...(Mucius) standing alone before the king's tribunal; even then, amid such menaces of fortune, more capable of inspiring dread than of feeling it, 'I am,' says he, 'a Roman citizen, my name is Caius Mucius; an enemy, I wished to slay an enemy, nor have I less of resolution to suffer death than I had to inflict it. Both to act and to suffer with fortitude is a Roman's part. Nor have I alone harbored such feelings towards you; there is after me a long train of persons aspiring to the same honor. Therefore, if you choose, prepare yourself for this peril, to contend for your life every hour; to have the sword and the enemy in the very entrance of your pavilion; this is the war which we the Roman youth declare against you; dread not an army in array, nor a battle; the affair will be to yourself alone and with each of us singly.' When the king, highly incensed, and at the same time terrified at the danger, in a menacing manner, commanded fires to be kindled about him (Mucius), if he did not speedily explain the plots, which, by his threats, he had darkly insinuated against him; Mucius said, 'Behold me, that you may be sensible of how little account the body is to those who have great glory in view;' and immediately he thrust his right hand into the fire that was lighted... When he continued to broil it as if he had been quite insensible, the king, astonished at this surprising sight, after he had leaped from his throne and commanded the young man to be removed... says, 'Be gone, having acted more like an enemy towards thyself than me. I would encourage thee to persevere in thy valor, if that valor stood on the side of my country. I now dismiss you untouched and unhurt, exempted from the right of war.' Then Mucius, as if making a return for the kindness, says, 'Since bravery is honored by you, so that you have obtained by kindness that which you could not by threats, three hundred of us, the chief of the Roman youth, have conspired to attack you in this manner. It was my lot first. The rest will follow, each in his turn, according as the lot shall set him forward.'"[4]

Coming so close to being killed by Mucius and sensing the risk to his life from those determined to follow in his footsteps, the king decided that it was in his best interests to make peace with the Romans. A peace was concluded, and Porsena withdrew his troops from the Janiculum Hill and marched out of the Roman territories. The fathers (of Rome) gave Mucius, as a reward for this valor, lands on the other side of the Tiber river, which were afterwards called the Mucian meadows in his honor. His bravery was to be remembered for all times. From the loss of his right hand, Caius Mucius was given the nick-name of *Scaevola*.

The 300 Spartans. In 480 B.C. the Persian king, Xerxes, was invading Greece from the north with a large army, numbering approximately 210,000 men.[5] At that time, a narrow mountain pass, about 50 feet wide, lay between Mount Kallidromos and the Gulf of Malia, and provided the only way for a large army to conveniently march from northern to southern Greece. Leonidas I, the Spartan king, led a Greek army of 6,000 men to hold the Pass at Thermopylae. For two days the Greeks stopped the Persians but, on the evening of the second day, a large Persian force threatened them from the rear. The Persians had discovered an old mountain trail which they used to come up behind the Greeks, having been shown the way by a shepherd. Knowing that the Persians would soon be attacking and not wanting all of his Greek soldiers to die in the Pass, Leonidas ordered most of the Greeks to leave. He would hold off the Persians with a small force of 300 Spartans and 1000 or so other Greeks. Their fortress was an old stone wall which had been built many years earlier to block the Pass. The Persians overran the Spartans, killing Leonidas and the three hundred Spartans who stood with him. Herodotus (490-425 B.C.), the Greek historian, describes the final moments of the battle:

"As the Persian army advanced to the assault, the Greeks under Leonidas, knowing that they were going to their deaths, went out into the wider part of the Pass much further than they had done before; in the previous days' fighting they had been holding the wall and making sorties from behind it into the narrow neck, but now they fought outside the narrows. Many of the invaders fell; behind them the company commanders plied their whips indiscriminately, driving the men on. Many fell into the sea and were drowned, and still more were trampled to death by their friends. No one could count the number of the dead. The Greeks, who knew that the enemy were on their way around by the mountain track and that death was inevitable, put forth all their strength and fought with fury and desperation. By this time most of their spears were broken, and they were killing Persians with their swords. In the course of that fight Leonidas fell, having fought most gallantly, and many distinguished Spartans with him. Their names I have learned, as those of men who deserve to be remembered; indeed, I have learned the names of all the three hundred."

"There was a bitter struggle over the body of Leonidas; four times the Greeks drove the enemy off, and at last by their valor rescued it. So it went on, until (the Persians coming from behind) were close at hand; and then, when the Greeks knew that they had come, the character of the fighting changed. They withdrew again into the narrow neck of the Pass, behind the wall, and took up a position in a single compact body, all except the Thebans, on the little hill at the entrance to the Pass, where the stone lion in memory of Leonidas stands today. Here they resisted to the last, with their swords, if they had them, and, if not, with their hands and teeth, until the Persians, coming on from the front over the ruins of the wall and closing in from behind, finally overwhelmed them with missile weapons (arrows and javelins)."

"Of all the Spartans and Thebans who fought so valiantly, the most signal proof of courage was given by the Spartan Dieneces. It is said that before the battle he was told by a native of Trachis that, when the Persians shot their arrows, there were so many of them that they hid the sun. Dieneces, however, quite unmoved by the thought of the strength of the Persian army, merely remarked: 'This is pleasant news that the stranger from Trachis brings us: if the Persians hide the sun, we shall have our battle in the shade.'"[6]

In our mind's eye, we can see the final moments of the Spartans at Thermopylae. There are about 25 Spartans remaining, in phalanx formation, with their large circular bronze shields held to the outside, standing shield pressed on shield, holding long iron swords. They are completely surrounded by the Persians who, for the moment, have stopped fighting. King Xerxes approaches on his golden chariot to watch for himself the end of these Spartans who, for two days, have stopped the advance of the mightiest army in the world. He studies the Spartans briefly, then, with a wave of his arm, signals his archers to kill them with arrows. He will waste no more of his men killing these Spartans. Arrows rain down on the Spartan phalanx. After several volleys, all that remain are three or four Spartans protecting with their shields the fallen body of Leonidas. One final volley, and they too are dead.

After the battle, King Xerxes ordered that all dead Persian soldiers be buried so that his troops following up from behind would not become demoralized from seeing what a relative handful of Greeks could do. He also had the head of Leonidas displayed on the top of a stake for all to see as they marched south.

The Battle Of The Alamo. Dated February 24, 1836, the following is a letter written by Lieutenant Colonel William B. Travis, commander of the Alamo,[7] to General Sam Houston, Commander-in-Chief of the Armed Forces of Texas:

To the people of Texas and all Americans in the world. Fellow citizens and compatriots.

I am besieged, by a thousand or more of the Mexicans under (General) Santa Anna. I have sustained a continual bombardment and cannonade for 24 hours and have not lost a man. The enemy has demanded a surrender at discretion, otherwise, the garrison are to be put to the sword, if the fort is taken. I have answered the demand with a cannon shot, and our flag still waves proudly from the walls. I shall never surrender or retreat. Then, I call on you in the name of Liberty, of patriotism and everything dear to the American character to come to our aid with all dispatch. The enemy is receiving reinforcements daily and will no doubt increase to three or four thousand in four or five days. If this call is neglected, I am determined to sustain myself as long as possible and die like a

99

soldier who never forgets what is due to his own honor and that of his country. VICTORY OR DEATH.

William Barret Travis, Lt. Col., Comdt.

P.S. The Lord is on our side. When the enemy appeared in sight, we had not three bushels of corn; we have since found, in deserted houses, eighty or ninety bushels, and got into the walls twenty or thirty head of beeves. T.[8]

On March 6 at 4 A.M. the first assault on the fortress was launched by the Mexican army, numbering approximately 6,000 men, and commanded by General Antonio López de Santa Anna, the President of Mexico. The rifle and cannon fire from the Alamo was deadly. Hundreds of Mexicans fell and the first assault broke off in confusion, with no Mexicans getting within ten yards of the walls of the fortress. The second assault was also beaten back with cannon and rifle fire. Texan sharpshooters on the walls had a half-dozen loaded rifles each. Mexican officers said after the battle that most of their men killed outside the walls were shot through the top of the head. A number of Texans were shot off the walls of the Alamo during the second assault. Many Mexican troops had made it to the walls during the second assault, where it was impossible for the Texans to fire at them without standing on the walls and exposing themselves to enemy rifle fire. With the outcome of the battle still in doubt, General Santa Anna ordered his entire reserve into the third assault, the final assault. The Alamo was completely overrun. No prisoners were taken; any Texan found alive was bayonetted to death. General Santa Anna ordered the bodies of the 189 defenders of the Alamo piled in a stack in front of the main entrance to the church compound and burned. According to witnesses, the huge funeral pyre burned with a sickening smell well into the night. Today, a large stone memorial marks this spot.

Regarding the final moments of Colonel Travis: "He was shot in the forehead during the third and last charge. He fell back, then picked up his sword. A Mexican colonel entered a breach in the wall, saw Travis holding his ground and started to plunge his sword into him. Travis drove his sword home first. Together, the two men fell dead by the ramparts."[9] At the Alamo, approximately 1,500 Mexican soldiers were killed.

The Battle of the Alamo was the first of 8 battles which the Mexican army would wage against the Texans. The Battle of San Jacinto would be the final battle for their independence from Mexico. The delay forced upon the advance of the Mexican army by the defenders of the Alamo allowed General Sam Houston (1793-1863) time to gather the forces he needed to ultimately save Texas. After the fall of the Alamo, General Houston's army continually retreated to the east, with the Mexican army pursuing and destroying Texan settlements along the way. Approximately 7 weeks after the Battle of the Alamo, both armies were in the vicinity of the western bank of the San Jacinto River, near its mouth. It was here that the Texans stopped retreating and attacked the pursuing Mexican army. The Mexican army consisted of approximately 1,600 infantry, one cannon, 50 cavalry, and were commanded by General Santa Anna; the Texan army numbered approximately 800 infantry, with 2 cannon, and were commanded by General Houston. At about 4 P.M. in the afternoon of April 21, 1836, the Texan army attacked. General Houston, mounted on his white stallion, drew his sword and, pointing it toward the Mexican lines, cried to his troops, "Remember The Alamo." The Texans then advanced, taking up the cries "Remember the Alamo" and "Remember Goliad," without stopping until they were almost on top of the enemy line.

The Mexican army was taken by surprise. For reasons unknown, they had posted no sentries or scouts around their camp. At the time of the attack, most of the Mexican soldiers were resting or sleeping, including General Santa Anna. When the two armies came into contact, there was a brief flurry of fighting, and the Mexican army was completely routed. By General Houston's own calculation, from the first shot to the capture of the Mexican camp, the battle lasted only 18 minutes. Even though the Mexican soldiers threw down their arms and attempted to surrender, the Texans shot, clubbed, and stabbed them to death — including the wounded. For several hours after the battle, they pursued the fleeing Mexicans and killed as many of them as they could. Officers of the Texan army, including General Houston, were unable to stop the slaughter. All in all, 9 Texan and 630 Mexican soldiers were killed. Surprisingly, several hundred Mexican soldiers were taken prisoner. General Santa Anna, who had escaped during the battle, was captured the following day and later forced to sign a treaty granting Texas its independence from Mexico. The treaty was subsequently repudiated by the Mexican Congress and General Santa Anna was removed from power, again.[10]

Importance Of The Psychological Force

The potential magnitude of the psychological force within us is large, with generally unknown limits. The words *perseverance, determination, esprit de corps, will*, and *drive* are used commonly to describe a high degree of this force; *indifference* and *apathy*, to describe a low degree. By extension, the psychological force of a group is an interactive combination of the psychological forces of each of its members. This situation has the potential for synergy in which the effect of the whole is greater than the sum of the effects of its individual parts. It is important to remember that the psychological force within a person is an energy without value. Only its effects have potential value, as evaluated by an observer. It is merely a force. We assign a value to it.

The psychological force is a characteristic of man and, because man has changed little during the past 45,000 years, it has been a relevant and important force throughout history. There is nothing to suggest that this will change in the Future. The military historian Sir Basil Liddell-Hart has made this same point, referring to the importance of the moral factor and moral considerations, the equivalent of what we are calling the psychological force: "...(there is a) predominance of moral factors in all military decisions. On them constantly turns the issue of war and battle. And in the history of war they form the only constant factors, changing only in degree, whereas the physical factors are fundamentally different in almost every war and every situation."[11]

Napoléon Bonaparte knew well the importance of the psychological force. In a letter dated August 27, 1808, he said, "In war, moral considerations account for three-quarters, the balance of actual forces only for the other quarter."[12] Approximately 30 years earlier, Captain John Paul Jones (1747-1792), a Scottish-born American naval officer in the American Revolutionary War (1775-1781), is reputed to have said: "Men mean more than guns in the rating of a ship." Similarly, John Stuart Mill (1806-1873), the English philosopher and political economist, wrote that "One person with a belief is a social power equal to ninety-nine who only have interests."[13] By moral considerations or the moral factor, Napoléon and other writers then and since are referring generally to the fighting spirit of individuals.

Clausewitz describes well the potential contribution of the military spirit (a gradation of the psychological force) to victory or success: "Military spirit...is one of the most important moral elements in war. Where this element is absent, it must be either replaced by one of the others, such as the commander's superior ability or popular enthusiasm, or else the results will fall short of the efforts expended. How much has been accomplished by this spirit, this sterling quality, this refinement of base ore into precious metal, is demonstrated by the Macedonians under Alexander, the Roman legions under Caesar, the Spanish infantry under Alexander Farnese, the Swedes under Gustavus Adolphus and Charles XII, the Prussians under Frederick the Great, and the French under Bonaparte. One would have to be blind to all the evidence of history if one refused to admit that the outstanding successes of these commanders and their greatness in adversity were feasible only with the aid of an army possessing these virtues."[14]

The high regard for the psychological force was not limited to Europeans. As one of his ten principles of war, Mao Tse-tung (1893-1976), leader of the People's Republic of China from 1949 to 1976, described his *Principle Of The Military Spirit* as follows: "In war, the quality and quantity of arms are important; without them, one cannot win. Even with them, one can lose. The most important attribute of a victorious army is the military spirit. In every conceivable way, thought of possible defeat must be eliminated from the army and replaced with an iron will to win."[15] What we are calmly referring to as the psychological force is more enthusiastically called the fighting spirit of man.

The Psychological Force And You

Horatius Cocles. Caius Mucius. Leonidas. William Travis. How many more names could be added to the list! Their stories are inspiring; they are heroes and the stuff of which legends are made. They have struggled on the battlefield of life. But what of the people who are not as famous? Each and every day there are innumerable people, people whose faces and names we shall never see or know, who summon the courage and conviction to act resolutely on their own particular battlefield of life. They struggle for their family; they struggle for their friends; or they struggle for a cause which only they know. They have reached within themselves to find the courage and determination to persist, and they have persisted. We must never forget that the force which our legendary heroes were able to tap within themselves is the same force which we are able to tap within ourselves. Our fighting spirit.

Vision And Vitality

We experience vitality in the process of striving to achieve, to force our will upon the environment in which we find ourself. It is struggling which spawns vitality. Vitality is not the same as happiness; it is a sense of being alive, of realizing the potential which is in ourselves. It is excitement. Because of the positive nature of vitality, experiencing it serves as a stimulant for continued action. The sensation of vitality while striving to achieve is equivalent to the pleasure of sexual intercourse in propagating the human race. Vitality is a reinforcement for striving to achieve in the face of competition. Vitality comes only from the struggle and the possibility of overcoming perceived obstacles.

Description Of The Process

An existing or anticipated change produces an opposition of forces, one force of which is man. In our mind there is a conflict because of the presence of a desired goal. Competition is produced when we act to eliminate the perceived conflict. This action may require an exertion of our will, our determination, and produce an emotional response. It is striving to achieve in the face of competition which produces vitality in us. This striving is also the impetus for increased understanding and awareness.

A continually changing environment forces us to continually define more desired and less desired Future events. These are relative distinctions. We strive to achieve the more desirable and to avoid the less desirable. Conflict is a mental perception; events in and of themselves have no meaning or value. They just occur. Conflict is directly related to what is desirable and what is undesirable. The nature of the struggle in which we choose to engage determines what we value and the principles we consider relevant. If there is no struggle, values and principles are adopted and discarded randomly.

Leaders generate conflict between a group and some other clearly-defined entity. As long as this state of conflict exists, leaders know that there is within each person the potential for vitality, emotion, and the evocation of the power of the spirit to achieve.

Levels Of Competition

All competition involves *the struggle* and the potential for vitality. There are, however, different levels of competition. These levels are described below and form a hierarchy. For each person, the most important question to ask is, What is the nature of the struggle in which you are engaged? Everyone is engaged in some struggle, and it is only with death that the struggle as we know it ceases to exist. With each level of competition, it is the resultant vitality which is the reinforcement for the continued striving to achieve.

Level 1: Person Versus Environment. The environment consists of everything external to the person. The intent is initially survival and subsequently adaptation. The focus is on the Present.

Level 2: Person Versus Person. The person has adapted successfully to his environment and now seeks to dominate both the environment and those people who directly affect his well-being. The focus is on the Present and the Future. The influence of the will and degree of determination is paramount.

Level 3: Person Versus Concept. The struggle for dominance takes place in the person's mind. The person is seeking to understand. Concepts generated by his mind are challenged by those generated by others. Reason is the primary tool and the product is increased knowledge and understanding.

Level 4: Person Versus Universe. The person seeks understanding and awareness beyond that related to content. There is the realization that any particular content learned is relatively unimportant. There is something more important. What the person seeks is an increased awareness of the relation between the self and the universe. Within this arena, most, if not all, topics which had previously seemed important are now judged to be relatively trivial.

Your Future Or Theirs

The most important vision to anyone is his own vision, a vision which he has generated, fully supports, and is striving to achieve. The visions of others are of interest only when they are in direct competition with his vision, or achieving the vision of another facilitates to some degree his achieving his own vision. The arena of life is a competitive arena. To think otherwise is simply incorrect.

Complementary Versus Contradictory Visions

We all have a Future. As soon as we create the desirable in our mind and, necessarily, the undesirable, and strive to achieve the desirable we becomes a force with a direction. The magnitude of this force is a function of the resources supporting it. Opposition of forces is to be expected and, concomitantly, conflict among forces. Indeed, it is difficult to honestly envision an environment containing man in which conflict does not exist. Within this context, there will be visions which are complimentary and those which are contradictory. Two visions are complimentary when one facilitates the achievement of the other. Two visions are contradictory when the achievement of one excludes the achievement of the other. There is nothing new in this concept; it is merely a thumb nail sketch of all history and the Future.

Effect Of A Group Vision

An effective group vision inspires each member to act, while at the same time provides each member with a sense of personal pride, self-worth, and a sense of achievement. To be maximally effective, the incentive to the member for striving to achieve the group vision is that doing so contributes to or supports the vision which he has for his own life. From this perspective, participating in the group is a supporting activity for the life vision of the person. An effective group vision links the successful performance of the person's activities within the group with his own life vision.

Consider the work done by an employee of a corporation. This work is an unnatural, contrived activity. Performing such activities runs counter to our basic nature. We would not of our own free will assemble, for example, electronic appliances. We are forced to perform such activities. In our search for meaning, we see an occupation for what it is: what we do to occupy our time as the seasons of life unfold, beginning with birth, then adolescence, then maturity, and finally death. At best, an occupation is a stepping stone to something else. From our perspective, the primary opposing forces are the employee, wanting to do only those activities which add meaning to his life, and the corporation, wanting the employee to perform contrived activities for reasons which may not be well understood. An effective corporation links the achievement of the corporate vision with the achievement of the personal vision of the employee.

After You've Done It

It can come about; the vision can be achieved. The desired Future toward which you have been striving can happen. At this moment in time there is the feeling of exuberance, joy, and happiness, a sense of fulfillment. Man has successfully exerted his will over a cruel and unforgiving environment; man, the triumphant. These feelings are easily understood, and are

111

those which have been experienced by most people at one time or another. However, there are other potential feelings which may follow on the heels of these. What do we do now? What's next? While striving toward the desired Future, there was no question as to what was to be done and why it was to be done. But what happens when this reason for being no longer exists? The answer is malaise and complacency, and a feeling that something is missing.

Jan Carlson, Chief Executive Officer of Scandinavian Airlines, described the result of his corporation's achieving its desired Future as follows: "We had a dream, and we reached it, and we reached it very quickly. But we didn't have another long-term objective. So people started to produce their own new objectives. You see, it had all been a little too easy. And we created frustration, because this is a psychological game. ... I learned that before you reach an objective you must be ready with a new one, and you must start to communicate it to the organization. It's not the goal itself that's important. It's the fight to get there."[16] The founder of a successful computer products corporation described the effects on his employees when the corporation finally reached financial stability. For the first seven years, employees and managers worked 12-hour days in tiny cubicles. At that time, "It was us against the world. We were a great team them." Because of its success, the corporation moved into a prestigious office complex with modern sculptures, perfectly manicured green lawns, thick carpets on the floors, fine furniture, and its own parking lot. It was then that the corporation began to flounder, being eventually placed on the market for sale. As described by one of its founders: "What was once a great *esprit de corps* degenerated into intense factions and we lost all sense of team spirit. People began working 9 to 5 and, worse, they acquired a 9 to 5 attitude! We looked around and found that success had brought malaise. We just didn't have that same fighting spirit. From there it was all downhill."[17]

The pattern of behavior illustrated by these two examples has been labeled by management consultants Collins and Lazier as the *We've Arrived* syndrome.[18] This syndrome involves five developmental phases. In Phase 1, the group has a compelling drive to achieve a particular desired Future. There is a challenge to be met by the group. The activities of the group are focused on achieving the desired Future. In Phase 2, there is group cohesion, team work, high performance, and enthusiasm. In Phase 3, the desired Future is achieved. The group has successfully met the challenge. They have arrived. In Phase 4, a new desired Future has not been envisioned. There is no new challenge to motivate the group. And, in Phase 5, the group experiences the feelings of malaise, complacency, and that something is missing. Members form factions, with each going off in its own direction, setting its own goals. There is internal strife.

The completion of the Panama Canal provides an interesting insight into the effect of achieving a vision. Beginning in 1904, the United States built the Panama Canal in 10 years by taming a jungle, dividing a continent, and uniting two oceans. It was the greatest engineering achievement of the twentieth century. The Canal opened to commercial ships of all nations on August 15, 1914 and by doing so fulfilled a centuries-old dream of connecting the two oceans and reducing the long voyage around Cape Horn by about 7,000 miles. But what were the feelings of the workers as the first ship passed through the Canal?

"Dredging had continued on the Cucuracha (land)slide from the time it had closed the Canal. When the date of formal opening approached, there was a channel 150 feet wide and 35 feet deep — large enough to pass the Panama Railroad ship *Ancon*, which had been selected for the inaugural transit from the Atlantic to the Pacific. Although Canal diggers had looked forward for years to the opening of the Canal, they hated to see the end. Some hoped an earthquake would ruin the Canal so it would have to be built all over again. They looked back to the days of the great urge to get the Canal dug; but those days were gone forever. ... All along the Canal, thousands waited and watched from vantage points as the *Ancon* passed. They thought of the years of work it took to build the Canal. They visualized the years of routine operation ahead. They knew the passage of the *Ancon* marked the end of an epoch in their lives. They knew that they had witnessed the realization of the dream of four centuries."[19]

The lesson to be learned from these examples is that there must always be a sense of competition, a challenge to be met and overcome. As one desired Future is achieved, it must be replaced by another. This is the nature of man.

Stress And Vitality

We have identified vitality as one potential effect of striving to achieve a desired Future. For us, vitality, the sensation of being alive, the zest of life, lies primarily in the self-initiated struggling to achieve. We all have the potential to experience the sensation of vitality. Now we briefly consider both *vitality* and its opposite *stress*. If you have the potential to experience vitality, you also have the potential to experience stress. In so doing we will also show what is meant by *courage* and its opposite *cowardice*. Our explanation of these terms requires a broader perspective than what has been presented so far. One such perspective is our Sphere Of Relevant Events, and it is within this Sphere that the discussion of vitality, stress, courage and cowardice will be placed.

Experience The Shaolin Monastery Examination

Our discussion of vitality and stress, two topics which collectively constitute the fabric of each and every person's life, begins with a famous examination, and you will be there. This examination is one which many

years ago, approximately 600 to 800 A.D., students of
karate at the Chinese Shaolin Temple and Monastery
were required to pass before leaving the monastery and
becoming masters.[20] Leaving the monastery denoted
the completion of their formal training. If you are
unfamiliar with karate, karate is a martial art in which
the primary weapons used by the person in defending
himself are the parts of the body, particularly the
hands and feet. This was the examination:

"The test would begin early in the morning at
sunrise. The air is filled with excitement, for the most
difficult of all tests is to *leave* the monastery. To do
this, the student must walk through a hallway, leading
to the outside, lined with 103 wooden dummies, each
of which is armed with a weapon. Each dummy is trig-
gered to strike out at the passing student as he walks
down the hallway. The triggering mechanism is contained within the wooden floor planks, so that the
student himself activates the dummy, his opponent, as
he walks down the hallway. Each dummy is constructed differently; some have spears, others have maces
(heavy wooden clubs with metal spikes at one end), but
each is capable of delivering a lethal blow. Selected
dummies act individually; others strike two or three at
a time. Except for his hands and feet, the student has
no weapons. If he does not make his way through the
hallway, he is taken back to recover, if still alive, to
try another day. But if he is successful in walking
down the corridor, the test is not yet over, for then he
must enter a room in the center of which is a five-

hundred pound caldron filled with burning embers. This caldron must be lifted to activate a mechanism which opens the door leading to the outside of the monastery. On the right side of the caldron is a relief of a tiger; on the left, a dragon. Each relief is positioned such that, when the student lifts the caldron, imprints of the animals are burned into his forearms. This imprint was the sign of the master and would be carried with him for life."[21]

There can be no doubt that each student took their examination very seriously, because it was a matter of life or death. Similarly, striving to achieve a desired Future is a very serious matter. It is your life. It is your desired Future. This is an important point, and the example of the Shaolin examination was selected solely to bring this to your attention. The path that you will take in striving to achieve your desired Future will have many "hallways" in it. The primary difference between these hallways and the hallway in the Shaolin examination is that, in your life, the "dummies" are not always wooden.

Imagine this. You are standing inside the Shaolin Monastery. You are standing before the door which opens into *the* hallway. Your teacher, the master, is standing off to one side and, when he nods his head, you will open the door, step inside, and begin the examination. Other students, friends you have known for many years, are also there, standing as a group off to one side. As you stand there, alone, you think of the fifteen years that you have been studying at the monastery. You think of the early years when everything you did seemed so clumsy. You think of the improvements in physical stamina, dexterity, speed of hand and foot, concentration and perception which gradually came with time and practice. You think of the many times when you have imagined yourself standing exactly where you are now standing. These thoughts, and all thoughts, you now cast from your mind; your eyes are on the master. You hope that he does not notice the ever so slight grin on your face; but you have learned that the master notices everything. The master nods his head, you quickly step forward, open the door, and step inside.

Now imagine this. You are again standing inside the Shaolin Monastery. A student is ready to take his final examination and you have come to watch, to give moral support. You are one of the students in the group standing to one side. You know that the day will come when you will be taking the examination, but that day is a long way off. You see the master, you see the student who will be tested, and you wonder what must be going through the student's mind as he stands there waiting for the master's nod of the head. All of a sudden the master turns and points his finger at you. He indicates that you should stand in front of the hallway door. You will be tested today. You step forward and position yourself before the door, feet together, arms at your sides, head up, because the master has requested it. Why am I here, you wonder, when I have only been studying for *eight* years. Your legs begin to have a strange sensation in them, as though they are not part of your body. You feel your heart pounding in your chest. Your mouth is dry. Your breathing is shallow and rapid. You feel the perspiration accumulating on your body; the sweat drips down your forehead and burns your eyes. You find it very difficult to stand still. Your mind seems to be going blank. You turn your eyes toward the master, and wonder why your eyelids seem to be blinking so rapidly. The master nods his head, you cautiously step forward, with sweating hand open the door, and step inside.

What were your feelings in each of these two situations? In which situation do you think that you would have been more successful? What is the role played by training? What is the role played by the mind? Where was the sense of vitality? Of stress?

Sphere Of Relevant Events

The Sphere Of Relevant Events consists of all events of which you are aware and which you judge to be significant to you. An event is a unit of analysis created by your mind into which everything of which you are aware is divided. Each event is a "mental chunk" of your environment. Events may be of different magnitudes, ranging from the "small" to the "large." A few examples of possible events are: (1) a comment made by a friend, (2) a professional career spanning 10 years, (3) the birth of a child, and (4) graduating from college six years from the Present. It is important to remember that it is you who create the events; what is real or factual is nothing more than a consensus among people. Events in and of themselves have no inherent value. They merely exist in your mind. Events are important to you because they constitute the building blocks by which you attempt to establish relationships among what occurs in your mental environment — Past, Present, and Future. One example of such relationships is a causal relationship: Event A leads to event B which, in turn, leads to event C, and so on. These relationships are typically referred to as problem-solving.

Your mind creates many events. Those events in the Sphere Of Relevant Events are a subset of this total, a subset which you consider to be important, functional, significant or relevant. Using this criterion, you are continually revising the population of relevant events in this Sphere, with those judged to be relatively unimportant pushed to the recess of your mind, not lost but merely stored. One interesting facet of the Sphere Of Relevant Events is the relative numbers of events which you have placed in the categories of Past, Present, and Future. Remembering that an event is in this Sphere only if it is important to you, the relative numbers of events in each category indicate your general orientation. A predominance of events in the Future category suggests that you are being "pulled by the Future;" a predominance in the Present, being "pulled by the Present;" and, a predominance in the Past, being "pulled by the Past."

Evaluating Events

Many events reside within your mind, a subset of which we have labeled the Sphere Of Relevant Events. Events in and of themselves have no value; they merely exist. It is you who both create and evaluate each event of which you are aware. Each event is evaluated according to its association with a relevant value or the achievement of a desired Future. From this perspective, events may be categorized as desirable, undesirable, or neutral — that is, neither desirable nor undesirable. The value of an event is your assessment of it. The same event may have different values depending on who performs the evaluation. Striving to bring about a desired event is vitality-producing. An undesirable event is stress-producing. The degree of desirability (or undesirability) of the event determines its potential degree of vitality or stress. It is your perception which determines whether a particular event is vitality-producing or stress-producing. An event in and of itself is valueless.

Given the existence of one or more values or a desired Future which you are striving to achieve, the potential for both desirable and undesirable events exists. In fact, each category of events cannot exist without the other; the meaning of one is derived from the existence of the other. Similarly, the potential exists for both vitality-producing and stress-producing events. And, one cannot exist without the possibility of the other.

121

Courage And Cowardice

In the Sphere Of Relevant Events, there are events which will be vitality-producing and those which will be stress-producing. If one exists, the other must also exist. Courage is participating in or initiating one or more stress-producing events knowing or believing that doing so will contribute to the realization of an accepted value or the achievement of a desired Future. Courage involves having faith. Cowardice, by contrast, is the refusal to be involved with stress-producing events, knowing full well that participating in such events may lead to a desired outcome. Despair stems from a belief that the effects of possible actions will result neither in the realization of a desired value nor the achievement of a desired Future. Despair may result from the inability to act, or from a perceived absence of any desired Future. If the possibility of courage exists, the possibility of cowardice also exists. Either both exist or neither exists.

A General Perspective

When striving to achieve your desired Future there will always be the potential for both vitality- and stress-producing events, as well as courage and cowardice on your part. The preferred strategy, of course, is one which increases the number of vitality-producing events and decreases the number of stress-producing events. An alternative strategy is attempting to minimize the numbers of events in both categories by, for example, abandoning the notion of striving for any desired Future and decreasing the number of values clutched to one's chest. In this latter strategy, the minimum desired Future consists primarily in continuing to live.

You Be The Judge

How do you know if a vision which you hold is appropriate for you? Ask yourself these questions:

1. What is the effect of this vision on my life?

2. What should be the effect of this vision on my life?

3. What is my compelling reason for holding this vision?

4. What price do I have to pay for striving to achieve this vision?

5. Am I willing to pay this price?

6. What will be the effect on my life when this vision is achieved?

7. What is the effect of this vision on other people?

123

8. What is the relationship between this particular vision and others which I may hold?

9. What is the relationship between this vision and the visions which are held by other people important to me?

10. To what degree am I able to act to achieve this vision?

11. How does the achievement of this vision add meaning to me and my life?

Chapter IV

Casting Your Net
Upon The Waters

You see things; and you ask "Why?" But
I dream things that never were; and I ask
"Why not?"[1]

On July 20, 1969, U.S. astronaut Neil A. Armstrong
stepped from the *Apollo 11* spaceship *Eagle* and put his
left foot down on the rocky surface of our Earth's
moon saying, "That's one small step for a man, one
giant leap for mankind." After he walked around for
18 minutes, astronaut Edwin E. Aldrin, Jr. joined him
and for about two hours the two astronauts explored
the moon's surface and conducted scientific experiments. *Eagle* was on the moon for almost 22 hours before Armstrong and Aldrin rejoined the spaceship
Columbia, piloted by astronaut Michael Collins, which
had been circling the moon. All three astronauts returned to Earth safely.

This story is well-known. Now, let's look at it
from another perspective. On May 25, 1961 President
John F. Kennedy described one of his visions to the
American people: "I believe that this nation should
commit itself to achieving the goal, before this decade
is out, of landing a man on the moon and returning
him safely to earth." As these words were spoken,
everyone hearing them could clearly picture in their

mind a man dressed in a spacesuit stepping out of a spaceship and planting the American flag on the surface of the moon. It was a thrilling thought. Simple and powerful. However, there was no doubt that this was the vision of *one man*: President Kennedy. He not only envisioned what many considered the impossible, he also stated clearly when it was to be achieved. But could President Kennedy achieve his vision alone, by himself? Of course the answer is No. He needed the help of others, many others. He needed a group of dedicated people to help him achieve his vision. His group was everyone associated with the multi-million dollar U.S. space program administered by the National Aeronautics and Space Administration. The space program was the tool by which his vision was achieved. Others may have adopted his vision, may have embraced it, may have worked courageously to achieve it, but it nevertheless was President Kennedy's vision which was achieved. And his vision was achieved by effectively marshalling the efforts of a group.

We all have visions, and it is seldom that what we desire to achieve can be achieved solely by ourselves. We need the cooperation of others. We need our own "space program." We can join an existing group or we can form a new group, or both. But one or more groups we need. As soon as the assistance of another person is required for us to achieve our vision, we come face to face with the topics of effective communication and seeking cooperation. These are the skills of the leader, and it is a leader which you must become. These skills are always important, but even more so when what is to be achieved lies in the distant Future and the necessary intermediate activities are challenging and difficult. We must always remember that no one is just standing around patiently waiting for us to announce the moment when they should begin striving diligently and persistently, perhaps courageously, to help us achieve our vision. They must be convinced, and they must have a reason for helping you. Others are also competing for their attention, time and expertise. To them, you are just another person with a vision, just another dreamer.

To achieve your vision, you must communicate it, and you must seek the cooperation of others. The how and why of this process are important. How should a vision be communicated? Why should a vision be communicated? These and other questions are addressed here in the context of becoming an effective leader.

The British Lion That Roared

History bursts at the seams with instances where a group is faced with a significant environmental challenge requiring what will be a fateful response. But, What is the most appropriate response? and What can be done to cause the group to respond as one, with all its energy and resources at its disposal? Failure is clearly possible, but so is success. This is the milieu of

127

the leader, whether it be the leader of a family, a team, an organization, a corporation, an army, or a nation. You can be a leader, most certainly that of yourself, and perhaps that of others. For all, the situation is conceptually identical; what differs is the time, the place, and the specific circumstances.

An excellent example of a speech by a leader which created an inspiring vision of the Future is that given by Sir Winston Churchill (1874-1965) at the start of World War II. At that time, Churchill was the Prime Minister of England and also the Minister of Defense. On June 18, 1940, he addressed the House of Commons and discussed candidly the threat of a military invasion of England by Germany. Before presenting the conclusion of his speech, however, remember what had happened in Europe just a few weeks before he made his momentous speech. The German army had completely overrun Europe. The British army in Europe had been forced to evacuate at Dunkirk, suffering great losses of men and materiél. The French army had been trounced and forced to surrender. There was every indication that the German army would invade England in the very near future.[2] Now, the conclusion of the speech given by Sir Winston Churchill:

"... What General Weygand (the commander-in-chief of the French army) called the Battle of France is over. The Battle of Britain is about to begin. On this battle depends the survival of Christian civilization. Upon it depends our own British life and the long continuity of our institutions and our empire. The whole fury and might of the enemy must very soon be turned upon us. Hitler (of Germany) knows he will have to break us in this island or lose the war. If we can stand up to him all Europe may be freed and the life of the world may move forward into broad sunlit uplands; but if we fail, the whole world, including the United States and all that we have known and cared for, will sink into the abyss of a new dark age made more sinister and perhaps more prolonged by the lights of a perverted science. Let us therefore brace ourselves to do our duty and so bear ourselves that if the British Commonwealth and Empire last for a thousand years, men will still say 'This was their finest hour.'"[3]

The situation faced by many groups is similar to that faced by Sir Winston and England. The environment is competitive and failure of the group is a possibility. Concentration of energies, both physical and psychological, is essential. It is the leader who must inspire the group and focus its efforts on meeting the challenge. This has been done throughout history, and will be done in the Future. Leaders have always understood that their power or degree of influence was built upon their vision of the Future, and the degree to which it was shared by others.

Desired Effect Of A Group Vision

The responsibility for identifying and communicating the vision for the group falls squarely on the shoulders of its leader and no one else. An effective group vision should produce a significantly higher concentration of the psychological force of its members than what would normally be present. In any group, the psychological force will be present to some degree and may be associated with a variety of mental images. A group vision must provide a common or single mental image to which the psychological force may be directed. The desired effect is that, through identifying and communicating a relevant and clearly understood vision of a desired Future, everyone will be inspired and motivated to act with persistence and determination over the long-term to achieve it.

Once again, we turn to the master, Napoléon Bonaparte, for an example. In 1798, Napoléon was the Commander-in-Chief of the French Army of the East as it headed toward Egypt. Imagine what thoughts would be racing through your head as you heard this proclamation. This is the Order of the Day issued by Napoléon on board the ship *Orient*. "Soldiers! You are going to undertake a conquest whose effects on civilization and the commerce of the world will be incalculable. You will strike the surest and most painful stroke possible against England until you can deal her final death-blow. We shall undergo tiring marches; we shall fight several battles; we shall succeed in all our enterprises; Destiny is with us. The Mameluke beys, who favour English trade exclusively, who have covered our merchants with insults and tyrannize over the unfortunate inhabitants of the Nile, will have ceased to exist a few days after our arrival. The people amongst whom we are going to live are Mohammedans; the first article of their faith is: 'There is no other God but God, and Mahomet is his prophet.' Do not argue with them; behave towards them as we behaved towards the Jews and the Italians; show respect to their muftis and imams as you have to rabbis and bishops. Have for the mosques and the ceremonies prescribed by the Koran the same tolerance that you showed for convents and synagogues, for the religion of Moses and of Jesus Christ. The Roman legions protected all religions. You will find here customs different from those of Europe; you must get used to them. The people amongst whom we are going treat women differently from us; but, in every country, he who commits rape is a monster. Pillage enriches but a few; it dishonors us, it destroys our resources, it makes enemies of the people it is to our interest to have as friends. The first city we are going to meet was built by Alexander. At each step we shall find memories worthy to excite emulation."[4]

From Your Mind To Their Mind

Your vision resides in your mind. It is known only to you. Observing your behavior, others might infer a rationale for your actions and all the while not know if their inferences were correct or incorrect. They would only be guessing. Clearly, if your vision is to become the tool for concentrating the psychological force of a group, it must be communicated to others and translated so that it can be understood by them.

131

Bringing The Vision To Light

The all-important tool for communicating the vision is the *vision statement*, which is a translation of the vision in the leader's mind into a form which may be understood by the group. A vision may be communicated by word of mouth, expressed in writing, or illustrated by pictures. A vision which is not communicated, not communicated clearly, or communicated but not understood is at best harmless and at worse counter-productive in concentrating the psychological force. A poorly communicated vision is counter-productive because it creates in the minds of each member a sense of lack of direction, purpose, and, most importantly, lack of leadership. The conclusion here is simple. Both the vision statement and the manner in which it is communicated are critical. It is the vision statement which must be carefully created. It is the all-important link between the mind of the leader and the mind of the follower.

Another Fundamental Connection

Why would a person strive to the best of their ability to bring about your desired Future? Why is it that your vision is of interest to them at all? The answer is very simple. There is no inherent reason why a person should care one wit about your success or failure and, particularly, your vision of a desired Future. However, what the person does care about is his own needs, aspirations, and achieving his own desired Future. It is these which are foremost in his mind, not your desired Future. Cutting to the heart of the matter, the leader is nothing more than a tool used by a group to achieve what it is unable to achieve by itself. Conversely, the group is a tool used by the leader to achieve what he is unable to achieve by himself.

As the leader has a vision of a desired Future, so too does the individual have visions of a desired Future. These personal visions may be achievement visions or avoidance visions, but they are visions nevertheless. The incentive to the person for striving to achieve your vision must be that doing so contributes to or supports the visions which the person has for his own Future. It is important to remember that what a person desires for the Future may relate to a personal benefit or a benefit associated with others. Your vision, then, will be increasingly effective in generating and concentrating the psychological force inherent in a group to the degree to which it is related to achieving, bringing about, or facilitating the personal visions of the members of the group. Any vision statement from the leader which does not address the personal visions of the membership will generally be ineffective in mustering anything more than a token level of support.

This is the concept behind tailoring the vision statement to an audience. Participating in the group must be a supporting activity for the person's life visions. An effective vision statement links the successful performance of group activities with these life visions. Leaders must be aware of the potential visions of individuals when communicating their vision of a desired Future.

Sell It To The Monks

The leader must communicate his vision, both formally and informally, to all members of the group. When the vision is communicated formally, it must be communicated by the leader himself, and not by anyone else. He must clearly define the desired Future, and assert his conviction that everyone is expected to contribute to achieving it. This message must be communicated consistently, frequently, and in a variety of situations. It must be communicated with conviction and in a language appropriate for each audience.

As this is done over time, the leader also must communicate the progress made toward achieving the vision, including successes as well as failures. Informally, but no less importantly, the leader must communicate the vision by he himself acting the way he expects others to act. He must communicate by example. In light of the inevitable successes and failures of the group, he must consistently reward those members whose performance is consistent with achieving the vision. Clearly, everyone must be trained to successfully perform those activities which support the vision.

Peters, a management consultant, offers similar advice for disseminating the vision of a corporation. According to him, the first and most important step is for the leaders of the corporation to act day-by-day in keeping with the vision, that is, "living it." It is only after the vision has been shown to be workable should cards, banners, slogans and the like be printed.

In fact, says Peters, if a corporation begins with a formal declaration, the effort is probably doomed to failure. When this happens, the leadership of the corporation does not know what the vision really means, let alone any employee. The leaders should focus primarily on living the vision, and secondarily on generating slogans and the like.

Another important component, according to Peters, is preaching the vision. He suggests a three- to five-minute speech with many variations which should be used several times a day, regardless of the setting. No opportunity is, in fact, inappropriate for reiterating the vision, using a pertinent detail that happens to be at hand. If possible, the speech should include examples of employees following the vision in their daily work activities.

An even better example, says Peters, is one showing how an employee took a small risk to support the vision. The final ingredient for Peters is the intensity of the emotions linked to the vision. The vision lives through the intensity of the emotions of the leaders, an intensity which draws others to it.[5]

To better appreciate the notion of tailoring the presentation of the vision to the audience of the moment, consider how the vision statement of, for example, a corporation would have to be modified in explaining its desired Future to different groups of people. Consider how the presentation of the vision would have to be tailored to each of the following groups:

1. First-line supervisors
2. Custodians
3. Representatives from a major supplier of the corporation
4. A heterogeneous group of employees of the corporation, where heterogeneous refers to different occupations
5. A small group of employees who have been temporarily laid-off from the corporation
6. Second-line supervisors
7. Visitors from another country
8. Persons having highly desired skills who currently are employed by other corporations
9. Monks from a religious monastery
10. Students ranging in age from 13 to 14 years at an eighth-grade elementary school class

The intent of the presentation is inspiring confidence in the leadership of the corporation, and instilling a desire for personal accomplishment and corporate achievement above and beyond the ordinary. For the monks — group 9 above, they should be firmly convinced that, should they choose a worldly occupation, it would be with this particular corporation. These are the demands placed on the leader of any group.

Some Possible Problems

There are potential problems associated with identifying and disseminating a vision to all members of a
group. For example, once a vision of a desired Future
is identified for a group, all members are expected to
abide by it. Some may not like the constraints on their
behavior dictated by the vision. Also, a vision requires
group members to have a degree of faith in the course
set by the leader. Some may be uncomfortable in doing
this, particularly if the early efforts of the group are
not successful. Not to be ignored is that the reputation
and creditability of the leader are associated with the
quality of the vision. If the vision is frequently
changed or modified, the impression is created that the
leader is uncertain and faltering, and that the success
of the group is in doubt. Lastly, the vision, once
known, may be challenged by the members of the
group as inappropriate. Some may believe that a different Future is more appropriate.

The Hopi Solution

An interesting technique by which a leader may communicate to a group is that used by the Hopi Indians of
the southwestern United States. The process begins
with the tribal elders, in the presence of other members
of the tribe, conducting an open discussion among
themselves and then making a preliminary decision.
This group of elders is surrounded by several rings of

tribal members who listen to the discussion. The ring adjacent to the tribal elders consists of people who have status just below that of the inner ring. This pattern continues to the last ring on the outside, a ring composed of adolescents. After the opening discussion and preliminary decision, the tribal elders move to the outer most ring, and then all groups move one ring closer toward the center. The group now in the center discusses what its members *think they heard*, with all others listening. The process repeats until the tribal elders are again in the center ring. The tribal elders, now back in the center of the ring and aided by their reflections on the opinions of others, reconsider their original decision and make the final decision.[6] Clearly, this is an unusual process and one which could only be implemented in certain situations. Still, it is intriguing. For what types of decisions is this particular process most appropriate? What basic principles does the process incorporate? In what other cultures and situations might this process be used effectively?

How Moving Is Your Vision?

There are two criteria to be considered when evaluating your vision: its likelihood of occurring in the Future, and how effectively it inspires others to act. Determining the degree to which an existing vision is right for the group is the responsibility of the leader. Evaluating the vision according to the first criterion, its likelihood of occurring in the Future, involves a careful consideration of the likelihood of alternative and competing Futures. Does the desired Future have a reasonable chance of occurring? Clearly a vision of a desired Future which has a low estimated probability of occurrence, as compared to alternative Futures, may be a beacon of failure. An assessment of the vision according to the second criterion, how well it inspires all members to act, is a sensing over time of the degree of determination in the actions performed by its members. This is clearly intangible, and the obtained result is a function of the experience of the leader.

The Vision Pyramid

The vision of the leader is a vision for the group as a whole, and it is applicable to all activities performed by the group. In a large group, however, the relationship between the vision and the activities performed by a particular subgroup as, for example, a team or a department, within the group may be ambiguous. To remove this ambiguity, what is required is a *sub-vision* tailored to the duties and responsibilities of the members within each subgroup. The sub-vision is a version of the group vision tailored specifically to the activities performed daily by the members of the sub-group. Although each person may understand the group vision, it is the sub-vision which is directly related to what they do every day. A sub-vision is an important concept. In a large group there may be a variety of subvisions.

139

Assume that, for example, a particular corporation is composed of five divisions. The sub-vision appropriate for each division is constructed by the leadership of the division, working closely with the leadership of the corporation. Although a division could develop a sub-vision on its own, it may not appropriately support the corporate vision. To avoid this potential problem, the subgroup must develop their sub-vision in cooperation with the leadership of the corporation. A similar process is followed when developing a sub-vision appropriate for each team within a division. When this process is followed throughout the corporation, the sub-visions of each organizational unit conceptually sum to the corporate vision. The final product resembles a pyramid, with the vision of the whole group at its apex. The blocks under the apex are the sub-visions of the subgroups.

Let's consider the vision pyramid for a moment. The largest vision, the vision of the leader, will be larger in scope than any sub-vision under it. The magnitude of each sub-vision is constrained by the vision of which it is a part or a component. If we assume that the motivational effect of a vision is a function of its magnitude, we would expect that, the lower a person is in an organization, the less effective is the sub-vision in motivating a person to act. The smaller the vision, the smaller is its potential motivating effect. Following this way of thinking, we could easily conclude that a vision is only effective for the top leaders of any large group; for all others, their sub-visions may be interesting but certainly not effective in inspiring people to act. This conclusion is unavoidable if we assume that each person only has knowledge of the sub-vision for the group of which he is a part. To change this conclusion, we must change what is in the person's head. Each person must know two visions. The first is the sub-vision of the group of which he is a part. The second, and a very important second it is, is the vision of the entire group, the vision of the leader. When a person knows both of these visions, and the link between the two, he will be as motivated to act as is the leader.[7]

The Vision Pyramid is an important concept. Consider the sub-vision held by a person working in a particular team within the larger group. It is this sub-vision which provides the foundation for his daily decisions and actions. If this sub-vision is directly linked to the group vision, and all activities are guided by the sub-vision, then *all* activities are logically integrated within the group as a whole. The immediate impact of this is that one person, acting within a team and potentially unaware of what the group as a whole is doing, is able to act in a manner which benefits the whole. This concept is valid for all large groups.

Take The Lead

What has pulled each group, be it a family, team, organization, corporation, or nation, from the Past to the Present is the ability of its leader. What will pull it from the Present to its desired Future is the ability of its leader. Leadership is essential for achieving any group vision. In fact, the primary tool of the leader is his vision of the Future.

The attention received by the topic of leadership reflects the historical evaluation of mankind that it is a fundamental ingredient of success, regardless of the nature of the endeavor. But leadership is a heavy burden to bear. Many desire the title but not the hard work required to lead successfully. Regarding the leadership of a corporation, consider the candid comments made by Michael H. Walsh, President and Chief Executive Officer of Tenneco Incorporated: "I believe there is a shortage of people who realize that a (Chief Executive Officer's) job is to lead. This is one of the things that I've learned: We have to get people in positions of leadership in companies to understand what their job is. It is fundamentally leadership. It is not doing somebody else's job. If you look at people in leadership positions and do a time analysis of what they do, I submit you'll find a great deal of the time they're doing somebody else's job rather than shaping the concept and structure by which the concept will be implemented across the board in a large, complex organization. That's a very time-consuming task — and frankly, what I've found is, it's sufficiently exhausting that a lot of people don't want to take it on."[8] Walsh is suggesting that effective leadership requires energy, determination, and the will to lead. Walsh is telling us why there are so few good leaders.

142

Your Responsibilities As Leader

It is important to distinguish between the responsibilities of *the leader* of the entire group and the responsibilities of all others in the group who may be performing leadership activities. Understanding this distinction is equivalent to recognizing the hierarchy of leadership which must exist in any group, particularly a large group. *The leader,* as a position, is quite different from that of all others. The person occupying the position of *the leader* has two, and only two, responsibilities: (1) to maintain the continued existence of the group, and (2) to increase the vitality of the group, that is, its capability to function successfully in a competitive environment. No other person in the group has these two responsibilities, and the combined activities of all members of the group assist the leader in fulfilling them. This distinction is also important because it conceptually separates *what* is to be achieved by the leader from the *means* by which he is to achieve it. In short, all activities of the group are the tools by which the leader meets these two responsibilities. Clearly, the degrees to which a leader fulfills these two responsibilities constitute the primary criteria by which his performance should be evaluated. All else is secondary.

The relationship between *the leader* and the group is of some interest. *The leader* is a position which exists for the life of the group, a position sequentially occupied by particular people. The leader knows that he will be replaced and, in fact, is eventually replaced. Certainly one perspective is that the group is a tool used by the leader to realize his personal intentions. Alternatively, and from the perspective of the group, the leader is a tool used by the group to maintain its continued existence in a competitive environment.

Leading Versus Managing

In the many discussions of leadership, the difference between leadership and managership has been described in a number of ways. Certainly, the concept is not new, and some examples of how others have struck the difference between the two are given below. We now present a few differences drawn by others.

"Keeping one's hand on the tiller is different from sighting the distant horizon. Maintaining one's course in the present is different from envisioning the new lands of the future. ... Managers make the most of the current situation, often seeing that goals are accomplished when it would appear that resources are inadequate for the purpose. ... Leaders take people toward a future destination, encouraging others to leave the familiar situation for unknown shores. Management requires the effective supervision of a work unit, no matter what the size. Leadership requires the ability to envision, make strategies, and plan what the work unit will do years later, and establish present goals in that context."[9]

144

"You can manage what you do not understand, but you cannot lead it."[10]

"A peacetime army can usually survive with good administration and management up and down the hierarchy, coupled with good leadership concentrated at the very top. A wartime army, however, needs competent leadership at all levels. No one yet has figured out how to manage people effectively into battle; they must be led. ... The manager plans and budgets; the leader sets the direction. The manager organizes people; the leader aligns people. The manager controls people; the leader motivates people."[11]

"I tend to think of the differences between leaders and managers as the difference between those who master the context and those who surrender to it. There are other differences...managers learn through training...(and) leaders opt for education. ...the manager administers; the leader innovates. ... The manager focuses on systems and structure; the leader focuses on people. ... The manager relies on control; the leader inspires trust. ... The manager asks how and when; the leader asks what and how."[12]

"The words manager and leader are metaphors representing two opposite ends of a continuum. Manager tends to signify the more analytical, structured, controlled, deliberate, and orderly end of the continuum, while leader tends to occupy the more experimental, visionary, flexible, uncontrolled, and creative end. Given these fairly universal metaphors of contrasting organizational behavior, I like to think of the prototypical manager as the person who brings the thoughts of the mind to bear on daily organizational problems. In contrast, the leader brings the feelings of the soul to bear on those same problems. Certainly, managers and leaders both have minds and souls, but they each tend to emphasize one over the other as they function in organizations. The mind represents the analytical, calculating, structuring, and ordering side of tasks and organizations. The soul, on the other hand, represents the visionary, passionate, creative, and flexible side. ... Both managers and leaders have attained success in the Past, and they will go on doing so."[13]

"We shall define management as the process of working with and through individuals and groups and other resources to accomplish organizational goals. ... The achievement of organizational goals through leadership is management. ... In essence, leadership is a broader concept than management. Management is... a special kind of leadership in which the achievement of organizational goals is paramount. The key difference between the two concepts, therefore, lies in the word organization. Leadership occurs any time one attempts to influence the behavior of an individual or group, regardless of the reason. It may be for one's own goals or for those of others, and they may or may not be congruent with organizational goals."[14]

Although activities associated with leadership are different from those of managership, both categories of activities are essential for any group attempting to achieve its desired Future. What is particularly criti-

146

cal in any group is avoiding the condition in which managership consistently dominates leadership.

It's Up To You

The conclusion is unavoidable. For you to achieve your desired Future, you must be a leader of others. You must solicit their cooperation. You must inspire people to act on your behalf. You must lead. There is no other way.

We all have visions and it is seldom, if ever, the case that what we desire to achieve can be achieved solely by ourselves. We need the cooperation and expertise of others. Period. You must ask yourself and answer for yourself a very simple question, "Why should someone else help me?" There must be an answer, a very convincing answer, which is easily understood by others. This answer must be very simple. They must understand why they want to help you, and they must maintain this awareness and understanding until your vision has been achieved.

You must face the reality that others care very little about you, you as a person. What people care about is their being able to achieve their own desired Future, their own vision. Never forget that they will help you achieve your vision if doing so allows them the promise or possibility of achieving their own vision, their own desired Future. As they are a tool by which you will achieve your desired Future, you are a tool by which they will attempt to achieve their own desired

147

Future, their own vision. Never forget this fundamental relationship between your vision and their vision.

Chapter V

The Future Is In Your Mind

If you do not think about the future, you
cannot have one.[1]

"I want to do away with everything behind man, so
that there is nothing to see when he looks back. I want
to take him by the scruff of his neck and turn his face
toward the future!" These are the words of Savva
Tropinin, a young inventor who wants to build a new
world replacing the old one which, in his opinion, is
hopelessly constrained by the prejudices, misconcep-
tions, and the illusions of society. He is the hero in the
play *Savva* written in 1906 by the Russian author and
playwright Leonid Andreyev (1871-1919).[2] Not unexpectedly, Tropinin is murdered in the end by the very
people whom he is trying to help.

In our mind's eye, it is easy to imagine Savva,
grabbing some poor bystander by the neck, turning his
face in some direction and saying, "Look! Look there!
That is the Future. Keep facing it and go forward.
Don't look behind you for even one moment. Forget
the Past! The Future is there, and there is where you
must go! Now!" Stepping back from the commotion,
it is of interest to the impartial observer to see just
where the bystander's face is being directed by Savva.
Is it this way? Or that way? Of course, the orientation
of the face is unimportant. The turning of the face is a
metaphor for what is to be done by the mind of man.

THE FIFTH DIMENSION

The Future resides only in your mind and is created by your imagination. It is not "out there," waiting to be discovered as was the tomb of the pharaoh Tutankhamen on November 4, 1922 by the Englishman Howard Carter (1873-1939). The tomb was there long before Carter; he merely discovered it. Similarly, the continent called America was there long before the 41-year-old Italian explorer Christopher Columbus (1451-1506), one of its many discoverers, landed at Watling Island in the Bahamas on October 12, 1492. Quite the contrary, with the Future, the explorer does not discover but instead creates. The Future resides *inside*, in your mind and is nothing more than a collection of mental images and relationships among these images. The Future is not a direction but a mental domain, the domain of what *could be*.

We live, think, and act in the Present. The Future and the Past reside only in our mind and are solely the products of our mind. The first is continually created by imagining; the second, by remembering. It is through the power of the mind and its functions of memory and imagination that we traverse the Past, Present, and the Future. It is our mind's memory which creates the apparent continuity.

That the Past and the Future do not exist apart from our mind is not a recent conclusion. For example, St. Augustine (354-430), the monumental writer and Christian theologian, ponders the topic at great length in Book XI *Time And Eternity* of his 13-volume

Confessions written during 397 to 400 A.D. He reaches this conclusion and describes well the relationship between the mind of man and these three concepts of time, that is, Past, Present and Future: "What is by now evident and clear is that neither future nor past exists, and it is inexact language to speak of three times — past, present, and future. Perhaps it would be exact to say: there are three times, a present of things past, a present of things present, a present of things to come."

"In the soul there are these three aspects of time, and I do not see them anywhere else. The present considering the past is the memory, the present considering the present is immediate awareness, the present considering the future is expectation. If we are allowed to use such language, I see three times, and I admit they are three. Moreover, we may say, There are three times, past, present, and future. This customary way of speaking is incorrect, but it is common usage. Let us accept the usage. I do not object and offer no opposition or criticism, as long as what is said is being understood, namely that neither the future nor the past is now present. There are few usages of everyday speech which are exact, and most of our language is inexact. Yet what we mean is communicated."[3]

Although frequently overlooked in discussions of memory is the ability of our mind to remember feelings, emotions, colors, odors, sounds, sensations and tastes. Truly, the maximum capacity of our mind is incomprehensible. St. Augustine frequently expresses his amazement and wonder regarding the mind of man, particularly its function of memory. For example, he writes: "Great is the power of memory, an awe-inspiring mystery, my God, a power of profound and infinite multiplicity. And this is mind, this is I myself. What then am I, my God? What is my nature? It is characterized by diversity, by life of many forms, utterly immeasurable. See the broad plains and caves and caverns of my memory. The varieties there cannot be counted, and are, beyond any reckoning, full of innumerable things. Some are there through images, as in the case of all physical objects, some by immediate presence like intellectual skills, some by indefinable notions or recorded impressions, as in the case of the mind's emotions, which the memory retains even when the mind is not experiencing them, although whatever is in the memory is in the mind. I run through all these things, I fly here and there, and penetrate their working as far as I can. But I never reach the end. So great is the power of memory, so great is the force of life in a human being whose life is mortal."[4]

The process of our life on this planet Earth is irreversible. Literally, each step is a step toward, and hopefully beyond, the grave. We may look back, indeed, may desire to go back, but there is no stopping. The Past is completed and done; what *could be* resides in the Future. The Future is the only realm which may be created by us. Bernard de Jouvenal, the French economist and philosopher, expresses this point very well: "For man in his role as an active agent the future is a field of liberty and power, but for man in his role as a cognizant being the future is a field of uncertainty. It is a field of liberty because I am free to conceive that something which does not now exist will exist in the future; it is a field of power because I have some power to validate my conception though, naturally, not all conceptions indiscriminately! And indeed the future is our only field of power, for we can act only on the future. Our awareness of this capacity to act supports the notion of 'a domain in which one can act.'"[5]

While the Future may be created by us, it is realizing this which gives rise to the notion of alternative Futures. More than one Future is clearly possible, and the question of importance is, Which Future is it to be? Yours or someone else's? A future must occur. Certainly the notion of alternative Futures, paired with the notion that we have some influence over which alternative Future actually occurs, suggests that the Future is most appropriately thought of as a competitive arena.

The Past is past and, as remembered in the Present, gives rise to the feelings of regret, remorse, joy and happiness. It is the Future, however, which gives rise to the feelings of anxiety, fear, and hope.

While it is certainly true that only the Future may be changed by us, the inherent difficulty is that the Future *must* be changed by us. There really is no choice in the matter. The universe and everything in it is continually changing; no two seconds of time are alike. If our Present is considered acceptable, merely maintaining that status requires changing or creating the Future. Similarly, and perhaps more obviously, replacing what is undesirable in the Present with what is more desirable requires us to create the Future. To do nothing in this regard is either to die, or to comply with a Future created by another, or possibly both.

It is the relative complexity of man as an organism which demands foresight as the absolute minimum requirement for survival. An organism of lesser complexity would find this discussion meaningless were its meaning able to be understood. Although we may agree with the old adage *All is flux, nothing is stationary* attributed to the famous Greek philosopher Heraclitus (544-483 B.C.), the implications of his fragmentary remark require careful consideration.

Several topics and questions are addressed in this chapter, and all have to do with the Future. While this chapter was being prepared, a 16-year-old teenager, happening to notice the section *The Future Influences Your Present* at the end of this chapter, asked "How can the future influence us if it hasn't happened yet?" A good question. Hopefully, the answer to this particular question and a few others will be given here. More specifically, in this chapter we address the nature of the Future, considered both as a concept or idea and as a product. We also consider what it means to create a Future, and we present six fundamental strategies for doing just this. We all use one or more of these strategies. And lastly, we show how the Future does, in fact, influence the Present, and discuss some implications of this for each of us. As a whole, this chapter provides the conceptual scaffolding for the lofty notion of a *desired Future*.

What Is *The Future*

What task could be simpler than defining *the Future*? Although it is a word included in every language and one spoken everyday by everyone, what does it mean? As defined by the dictionary, the Future is the indefinite period of time yet to be; time that is to come. The dictionary definition seems to be correct in that the meaning of the Future found there corresponds with its conversational use. There was no surprise. A difficulty arises, however, when the definitions of the Past and Present are also considered. The Present is found to be a moment or period of time perceptible as intermediate between Past and Future; now. And, the Past, is defined as the time before the Present. Although the Past, Present, and Future are each defined, each is defined in terms of each other, and all relate to what is called *time*. What is happening here is that time is considered to be divisible and, when divided, produces the three distinct categories of Past, Present, and Future. Not surprisingly, time is defined as a nonspatial continuum in which events occur in apparently irreversible succession from the Past through the Present to the Future.

Now to the point. Considering time as divisible produces a paradox: the Present tends to not exist. To

155

demonstrate quickly this outcome, consider any period of time as, for example, the 24-hour today. It is easy to divide today into the Past (those hours which have already passed), the Present (the current hour), and the Future (those hours still to come.) What has been done for the day could be done equally well for the present hour, producing those minutes having passed, the present minute, and those minutes still to come. And, continuing to the present second, the three parts also logically follow. Dividing the second, and subsequently any part of it into Past, Present, and Future takes us to the point of having what is absolutely the smallest unit but still reducible into three parts. So, the Present logically tends toward nothingness, providing our paradox. In short, any consideration of time as divisible will produce a paradox. This paradox also shows the shortcoming of our power of reason. To the question What is time? the answer historically is that it is not able to be understood by man.

St. Augustine's conclusion comes as no surprise: "What is time? Who can explain this easily and briefly? Who can comprehend this even in thought so as to articulate the answer in words? Yet what do we speak of, in our familiar everyday conversation, more than of time? We surely know what we mean when we speak of it. We also know what is meant when we hear someone else talking about it. What then is time? Provided that no one asks me, I know. If I want to explain it to an inquirer, I do not know."[6] Augustine generally concludes that the mind of man is not capa-

156

ble of truly understanding time. He does, however, identify memory as the critical component for the human comprehension of time. Certainly, everyone knows what is meant by the Future. But do they?

One approach for understanding time is to consider it a characteristic of a particular subsystem which is part of a larger system. Through attempting to identify and understand the characteristics of the *system*, the characteristics of the subsystem will acquire additional meaning. The key is not analysis, but synthesis. The difficulty, however, with such an easy answer is that contemplating such a system may be beyond our mental capability. The question to be answered is, What is the system of which the universe is a part? In defining such a system, one result will be defining the absence of time.

The concept of the Future can have a profound psychological influence on a person. George Steiner, the linguist, recalls the shock he experienced when, as a young boy, he first realized that statements could be made about the distant Future.

"I remember a moment by an open window when the thought that I was standing in an ordinary place and 'now' and could say sentences about the weather and those trees fifty years on, filled me with a sense of physical awe. Future tenses, future subjunctives in particular, seemed to me possessed of a literal magic force."[7] He then compares this feeling with the mental vertigo often produced by contemplating extremely large numbers, and draws attention to the suggestion made by some scholars of Sanskrit, the oldest known Indo-European language, that "the development of a grammatical system of futurity may have coincided with an interest in recursive series of very large numbers."[8]

From Steiner's perspective, the ability to think about the Future is what sets man apart from the lower animals: "...the proper start (when contemplating the future) is wonder, a tensed delight at the bare fact, that there are future forms of verbs, that human beings have developed rules of grammar which allow coherent utterances about tomorrow, about the last midnight of the century, about the position and luminosity of the star Vega half a billion years hence. Such supple immensity of linguistic projection, and the discriminations it allows between nuances of anticipation, doubt, provisionality, probabilistic induction, fear, conditionality, hope, may well be the major achievement of the neocortex, which is that part of the brain that distinguishes man from more primitive mammals."[9]

The Future As A Product

Although the idea of the Future is painfully challenging, more easily embraced is the Future as a product. The product consists generally of mental images created by the imagination and cast forward in time. As considered here, imagination is one of the four primary capabilities of the mind; the other three being perception, thought, and memory.[10] Indeed, if it were not for our continual imagining and remembering, there would not exist the apparent continuity among the Past, Present, and Future. Fortunately for us, for the majority of the time, this process is performed unconsciously. Although the mind is truly an amazing engine, its capability of imagining is of primary interest now and, in particular, what may be referred to as *controlled imagining*, as opposed to *spontaneous imagining*. With controlled imagining, we use our will to guide or channel what we imagine; spontaneous imaging, by contrast, happens suddenly and effortlessly, and is a constant source of surprise to us.

It was to controlled imagining that Aristotle was referring when he wrote, "For imagining lies within our own power whenever we wish, e.g., we can call up a picture, as in the practice of mnemonics by the use of mental images."[11]

Now, we wish.

Imagine this. The warm, dry air is blowing steadily in your face and the sun is high in the cloudless blue sky. Looking to the West, there is nothing but desert extending to the horizon. Rolling hills of sand and rock as far as the eye can see. To the East, the largest city in Africa — Cairo, looking grayish on the whole with the tops of several buildings reaching higher than the rest. Scanning the immediate vicinity, there is the 448-foot-tall pyramid built for the Pharaoh Khafre, sides resembling large brown stairways, but still having at its pointed apex the covering of polished white limestone placed there by the original builders.

The rest of the white limestone casing stones were removed long ago by the mosque-builders in Cairo. Such is man.

There is also the smaller 203-foot-tall pyramid built for the Pharaoh Menkaure, of the same brownish color, with its casing stones also removed. Noteworthy is the large hole in its North face, a scar left long ago by those seeking treasure within. You can also see the large Moslem cemetery adjacent to the Christian cemetery, and the smaller area where camels and horses are stabled for those people wishing to ride around the area.

Not too far away, and appearing very small indeed, is the 62-foot tall Sphinx resting quietly in a small ravine. It is easy to see how in the Past blowing sand from the desert had almost completely covered it. Here and now, who could not think of the words of Napoléon Bonaparte saying on July 21, 1798 to the French Army before fighting the Mamelukes at the Battle of the Pyramids: *"Soldats, quarante siècles vous regardent!"*[12] (Soldiers, forty centuries look down upon you!) You can almost smell the smoke of the French cannons; almost hear the thundering hoofs of the Mameluke calvary as they charge the five advancing French phalanxes. As all were thirsty fighting in the blazing sun that day, so you are thirsty now.

Where are you?

You are standing right now on top of the 450-foot tall Great Pyramid at Giza, Egypt, on top of the only survivor of the Seven Wonders of the Ancient

World, built approximately 5,000 years ago for the Pharaoh Khufu. Although thirsty and somewhat tired from the climb, your mind ignores these feelings. You are thrilled to be here, the place where you have wanted to be for two years. You are standing not on an apex but, instead, on a roughly flat surface, approximately 33 feet square but, surprisingly, not square. In the center of this platform are seven stone blocks, each weighing about two tons. Dark brown, and weathered by the centuries. These few blocks of stone are all that remain of what had been the apex, and left there for some unknown reason.

Of the seven blocks, two are resting atop the other five, forming two small additional tiers. As you look at the blocks and the surface on which you standing, you are amazed at what you see. On every surface there are inscriptions of all kinds — names, dates, designs. Most are small, all are interesting. How many different languages are here? you wonder. How many writers?

One inscription grabs your attention. It is much larger than the rest, and is boldly written across one side of the highest block: C O V I N G T O N. Each letter is approximately 3 inches in height, deeply gouged, with the whole roughly 3 feet in length. Who was this COVINGTON? Certainly some tools were involved, not just the handy pocket knife carried by the average tourist. What could have been going through this person's mind as each letter was carefully engraved? Certainly in this arid climate the letters will remain for many lifetimes, for many centuries. Was this person possibly seeking a taste of immortality?

Looking around, you find a bare spot on one of the stone blocks and, using your pocket knife, you add a name to the roster of the faceless others. The stone was much softer than you had expected. Will someone, someday wonder about the name which you inscribed as you wondered today about COVINGTON?[13]

It is your imagination which has taken you to the Future, to the Land-Of-The-One-River, to the Giza Plateau, to the top of the Great Pyramid, and to your name being recorded for centuries to come. There are mental images, actions, feelings, colors, odors, emotions, and context. All this is in your mind, in that domain considered the Future.

As happened in this example, the imagination was directed into the Future. Just as easily, the imagination could have revisited the Past, pondering what might have happened if particular events had or had not occurred, or occurred differently. The same process could be applied to the Present. You could, for example, imagine what someone else is doing right now, in some other part of the world. You could be imagining in the Present what someone else is doing or the occurrence of some other event while you are "travelling" to Giza.

With the imagination, a seemingly infinite number of Futures, each a cluster of images, may be created by our mind. However, there are some obvious differences among these Futures. For example, they may differ according to their: (1) degree of importance to us, (2) time from the Present to the occurrence of the Future event, (3) likelihood of occurrence, and (4) magnitude, or the number of events defining the Future. Clearly, if you had no desire to travel to Egypt, the description given here would be of no interest whatsoever. But, what if you wanted to go to Egypt. Wanted to see for yourself the pyramid of Khufu. Had read everything available. You could find a way to get there. Then, when actually at Giza and examining the stone blocks of the Great Pyramid, you would, in a sense, be doing this for the *second* time. In your mind you had already been there once.

There would seem to be no limitation on the power of our imagination. But is this really so? Casey, a psychologist, has considered this question and his comments are interesting. Think about his comments for a moment.

"It is evident that we cannot imagine absolutely anything we want to... There are some things which cannot be imagined because they are formed from contradictory concepts and thus are logically impossible — e.g., a square circle or a four-sided triangle. Of course, one can attempt to imagine such self-contradictory things and even (as in hallucinated states) come to believe that one has indeed imagined them. But, however far or wide one's imaginary capacity is stretched in this effort, what one does succeed in imagining will not qualify as a bona fide instance of the self-contradictory notion."

163

"Yet this essential restriction upon imaginative powers does not testify to their weakness or failure. For nothing, whether perceived or imagined, can possibly exemplify a conceptually contradictory notion. And where there is no possibility of success, we cannot talk, strictly speaking, of failure. ... It is undeniably the case that, from one person to another, there are discernible differences in the extent to which human imaginative powers are displayed. But these differences are neither so considerable nor so irresolvable as they may seem to be at a glance. In spite of the differences of detail — for example, differences in the degree to which one can visualize or audialize — the general scope of imaginative capacity is remarkably similar from one imaginer to the next. This means that, if one cannot imagine something in one way (say, by visualizing it), one can usually succeed in imagining it in some other way (say, by touching it in imagination). Moreover, a given individual's imagination is capable of being trained, through disciplined exercises in imagining, to overcome marked deficiencies. Thus empirical limitations on a specific imaginer's ability to imagine, though significant, do not serve to curtail human imaginative capacity as such."[14] There are simply limitations to what may be imagined.

Differences Between The Past And The Future

Although both comprise domains of mental images and linkages among these images, the Past and the Future are distinctly different. The Past is the mental domain of what has occurred, been accomplished or achieved, and has taken unalterable form. It is not able to be changed and, for this reason, accounts for our feelings of regret and remorse. The Past is the domain of knowable facts, facts which may be verified as true or false. The phrase "knowledge of the Past (and Present)" is clearly appropriate because it is possible to objectively study the Past and the Present. Although the emphasis of our discussion has addressed mental images, it is important to remember that the Past may include memories of feelings and emotions. These may be recalled equally well.

The Future is the mental domain of what could be. It is what is in progress, still fluid, and capable of ending or being completed in various different ways. This domain may include images of events which have never occurred before and have no historical reality. The domain of the Future is a domain of potential uncertainty. What could be or will be cannot be verified in the same way as a Past event. When forced with two conflicting opinions regarding a Past event, you may try to determine which one is true. However, when faced with two opinions regarding a Future event, you may only determine which of the two is more plausible. There is no way to be certain which will occur. Thinking like this, knowledge of the Future is a contradiction in terms; only knowledge of the Past and Present is possible. What may occur in the Future is a speculation or an opinion on our part. Jouvenal prefers to use the word *conjecture* when referring to Future events.[15] We may conjecture a variety of events occurring in the Future, and very frequently do just this.

Although in our mind the domain of the Past is what is unalterable and the domain of the Future is what could be, both may be subject to continual change. Past events themselves may be unalterable and unchangeable but their value and relevance, as interpreted by our mind, may change over time. And a similar change of interpretation is possible for Future events. From this perspective, the Past and Future may be continually changing for us.

Consider now two or more people. For each, the Past is the mental domain of what has occurred; the Future, the domain of what could be. For these two people, the degree of correspondence between their respective Past domains may range from completely different to identical. This comparison may be applied to their Future domains also. The obvious conclusion is that what two people consider the Past may be completely different, with the same true for the Future. From this perspective, reaching a consensus is seen as the process of reducing the differences among Past domains and Future domains for a group.

Does Tomorrow Already Exist?

This is a challenging question. Answering Yes would certainly mean that any discussion of intentions, possibilities, scenarios, visions of the Future, and the like is a waste of time, stimulating perhaps, but, nevertheless, a waste and appropriately banished to Academia. But is Yes the answer?

Imagine this. You are standing on a high bluff overlooking the ocean. As you look at the ocean, you see only the rolling waves extending to the horizon. Certainly, you see no ships. As you stand there, you are joined by an accomplice who, after briefly scanning the horizon, points to a ship. He sees it. You don't. Clearly, the eyesight of your accomplice is superior to yours.

Is the Future like the ship, existing, but able to be seen only by those with an enhanced degree of visual acuity? Your myopia; their hyperopia? Similarly, is life like a stack of photographs? The Past are those which you have already seen; the Present, the photograph in your hand; and, the Future, the remaining photographs in the stack which you have yet to see. The photographs exist. Are some people better able than you to "see" one or more of the photographs of the Future?

Historically and persistently, the answer to this question is Yes, and all that varies from culture to culture, from time period to time period, is the technique and supporting rationale used to peek at these pictures of the Future. It is merely a question of how it is done. There are many potential analogies. One could propose, for example, that the organization perceived in the planets is a reflection of a larger existing order, with the interactions among men and events on Earth identically ordered but less well understood by the average person.

The Nature Of A Known Event

Assume that the Future exists. Although you may not have the ability to know it, there exists someone more skilled than you and, using his skill, describes a Future event of great importance to you. Unfortunately for you, the event is not one which you desire to have happen. So where does this leave you?

Upon reflection, you realize that if you were to act in a certain way, that is, perform certain actions, the undesired event could be prevented. If fact, this is what you decide to do. Having acted upon this realization, you are relieved to find that, at the appointed hour, the undesired event does not occur. And, you go about your business as usual.

Consider another example. Albert Camus (1913-1960), the famous French writer, was vacationing in the south of France. When returning to Paris, he decided to drive back with his publisher and friend. On the way back, it began to rain, the automobile skidded off the road, and the passenger, Camus, was killed instantly. The driver was only shaken up. An unused railway ticket was found in Camus' pocket. He had been planning to take the train, but at the last moment had been persuaded that it would be a more pleasant trip by automobile. Had Camus been told before getting into the automobile that he would surely die in an accident, he would have decided to take the train instead, attempting to avoid, and in fact avoiding, an untimely death.

But what has happened or, in the case of Camus, could have happened here? Acting on the knowledge of a known event, the known event has been changed. It is no longer known, and wagging its finger at us is a nasty logical contradiction. If the Future is known, it can be changed; therefore, it is not known. If the Future is known, but not able to be changed, the prior knowledge is useless and, in fact, all knowledge is useless.

The answer to the original question "Does the Future already exist?" is No. It is possible that some may not like this answer, thinking that everything which occurred was the known event, that is, your being told of the undesirable event and your subsequent actions to stop it from occurring. The answer to the question is still the same. No. Anything which is known may be changed, making it not known anymore, providing the same logical contradiction. It is this contradiction which provides the uncertainty associated with the Future. It is the knowledge of a Future event which often spurs us to stop it.

Dominating Versus Masterable Events

Thoughts like these lead naturally to considering the extent of our influence on Earth, or in the universe

169

generally. Clearly, there are events which are *dominating* and events which are *masterable* by man. A masterable event is one which may be changed to be different from that expected if no action is taken. By contrast, a dominating event is one which must be endured.

What is important is that, from one person's perspective, an event may be dominating. However, from the perspective of another actor as, for example, another person, group, organization, corporation, army, or nation, the event may be masterable. This relationship holds true for any level of actor. The fundamental concept is the relative degree of power of the actor. Jouvenal addresses this topic and, drawing on his academic education and professional experience in economics, provides the following example:

"Suppose that I am the head of a business and that I see an economic recession coming: all that I can do is to adjust my actions so that my business will suffer as little as possible; I can, for instance, reduce my inventory. For me, the recession is a dominating future, but not so for the government, which has ways of preventing it. The government controls monetary and fiscal policy, public works spending, and so forth, and thus it can master my dominating future."[16]

Some Wise Thoughts

The Future has been written about by many authors, in many countries, and across many centuries. Given below are a few quotations regarding the Future which suggest the range of perspectives on it. You probably have a perspective on the topic too.

"As for the future, your task is not to foresee, but to enable it."
Antoine de Saint-Exupéry (1900-1944) French Writer

"If a man carefully examines his thoughts he will be surprised to find how much he lives in the future. His well-being is always ahead. Such a creature is probably immortal."
Ralph Waldo Emerson (1803-1882) American Poet

"A preoccupation with the future not only prevents us from seeing the present as it is but often prompts us to rearrange the past."
Eric Hoffer (1902-1983) American Writer

"The future, you shall know when it has come; before then, forget it."
Aeschylus (525-456 B.C.) Greek Playwright

"We steal if we touch tomorrow. It is God's."
Henry Ward Beecher (1813-1887) American Clergyman

"The future is like heaven: everyone exalts it but no one wants to go there now."
James Baldwin, American Writer

171

"The empires of the future are empires of the mind."
Sir Winston L. Churchill (1874-1965) British Statesman

"Never let the future disturb you. You will meet it, if you have to, with the same weapons of reason which today arm you against the present."
Marcus Aurelius Antoninus (121-180)
Roman Philosopher and Emperor (161-180)

"But this *long run* is a misleading guide to current affairs. *In the long run* we are all dead."
John Maynard Keynes (1883-1946) British Economist

"The only limit to our realization of tomorrow will be our doubts of today. Let us move forward with strong and active faith."
Franklin D. Roosevelt (1882-1945)
President of the United States (1933-1945)

"Remember this also, and be well persuaded of its truth; the future is not in the hands of Fate, but in ours."
Jules Jesserand (1855-1932) American Philosopher

"For my part, I think that a knowledge of the future would be a disadvantage."
Cicero (106-43 B.C.) Roman Statesman

"The visionary lies to himself, the liar only to others."
Friedrich W. Nietzsche (1844-1900), German Philosopher

"The best way to predict the future is to invent it."
  Peter F. Drucker, American Management Writer

"The present is never our goal: the past and present are our means: the future alone is our goal. Thus, we never live but we hope to live; and always hoping to be happy, it is inevitable that we shall never be so."
  Blaise Pascal (1623-1662), French Philosopher

Creating Futures

There are questions which have been pondered for centuries, indeed, millennia, by man in every culture. These questions will be pondered for as long as man exists in this universe, and they will remain unanswered all the while. Of course, answers have been suggested; each, however, is nothing more than an opinion, regardless of the extent of cultural support at that point in time for that particular opinion.

One of these perplexing questions concerns a basic characteristic of man: Do we act freely? Or similarly, Do we have a free will? Is free will nothing more than an illusion granted to man by a merciful God who realizes how dull life on Earth would be without it? Are we like a fly, riding the trunk of an elephant, who believes he is actually steering it? Of course, this belief in his ability to act independently makes the ride seem interesting, and the elephant presumably does not mind. Or, do we in fact act according to our own volition and create, or attempt to

173

create, through our chosen actions a Future of our choice? What do you really think about all of this?

Interesting though this question may be, the topic will not be considered here any further. In fact, *the* answer is unimportant. We act and think as though we have free will, and the expectations among all men are based on this assumption. Therefore, for all practical purposes, we have free will, and exercise our free will daily in numerous decisions and related actions. Right this moment you could throw this book into the trash, thinking the answer given here to the free will issue is ridiculous. Or, you could put pen to paper and propose a perspective far superior to the one presented here. Or, you could just continue reading. Clearly, there are several scenarios, or alternative Futures possible here. Only you know what you will do this very moment. Regardless of what you do, *you* will have decided to do it.[17]

Nature Of An Intention

Using our imagination, we create images in our mind and cast them into the domain of the Future. We all do this. The process, however, by which we do this is more mysterious than the images themselves. Although most of these images cast into the Future are discarded as fantasies or daydreams, a few are highly valued by us and inspire us to act to make them become a reality. Such images represent what we desire and are referred to here as *intentions*. This notion of an intention is very important. We are much more than *reactors* to what occurs in our environment. We are *actors*, continually seeking through our actions to bring about or cause to happen what is desirable or to cause not to happen what is undesirable. It is the intention which occurs first, followed by actions. Clearly, without an intention, there can be no action on our part, only reaction.

Consider the scaling of a tall cliff by a climber. First he throws a rope with a grappling hook high up the cliff face where it takes hold. Then, tugging on the rope to make sure it is secure, he pulls himself up. The toss of the rope came first; the actual climbing, second. The point at which the grappling hook took hold is like an intention. Once the grappling hook has attached itself to the cliff wall, he has the choice of climbing up or not climbing up.

The intensity associated with the intention is analogous to the amount of energy which we are willing to expend in pulling ourselves up the rope. It is relatively easy to cast ropes up the face of the cliff; more difficult is expending the energy to climb up. From this perspective, the difference between an intention and a daydream or fantasy becomes obvious. An intention has associated with it a level of intensity, or willing, on our part to make it a reality. An intention makes us act. Common synonyms for an intention of some importance are a vision or a desired Future.

The concept of an intention may be considered more broadly as a general orientation toward life or a

175

general way of being. To distinguish it from a specific intention, call it a *general intention*. A general intention describes the rationale for a continuing and long-term series of activities on our part. In this regard, Jouvenal makes an interesting observation:

"The advantage of (the notion of a general intention) is that it helps to bring out the following point — man is not active because he has (intentions), but has (intentions) because he is active. And certainly it is part of the nature of any organism to expend energy."[18] Jouvenal is looking at man as a whole and is saying that because we are active we have intentions. It's a question of what starts the process rolling. To him, it is our general ability to act which is the primary impetus for all intentions. Of course, once we have an intention, we then strive to cause it to happen. Jouvenal is basically getting at the question, What is man? In your spare time, you might think about this.

Concept Of Competing Futures

As we act in the Present to cause our intention to occur, we are attempting to create a Future. Our degree of responsibility and our degree of freedom are at their highest when we act to achieve an intention which we ourselves have created or selected. We are actors and realize that we have at our disposal the means to influence events to varying degrees. We are a cause in and of ourselves. We can make specific events occur to our advantage.

176

The Future is an arena of intentions, because what is true for one person, one organization, one corporation, or one nation (or, more generally, one actor) is true for all. All are casting intentions into the Future and taking actions in the Present to realize these intentions. It is the potential conflict among these intentions which underscores the importance of the *will* of the actor to realize his intention. One example of an intention involving little or no conflict among actors is a person's striving to graduate from college. An example of an intention steeped in conflict is the plan for world domination envisioned by Adolf Hitler in his book *Mein Kampf* (*My Struggle*) published originally in 1925.

Competing Futures may occur in a variety of forms. Starting with one actor, he himself may envision alternative Futures, possibly desirable, and be uncertain as toward which one he should strive. For two or more actors, both may have the same intention, where only one may actually realize it and benefit from it. Alternatively, both actors may envision for the same Future time period two different Futures, only one of which may occur. There are many possible forms of competition.

Although competition is clearly the dominant theme among actors, cooperation is possible.[19] The relative distribution of each in the Past is suggested by Brigadier General John F. C. Fuller (1878-1966), one of the foremost twentieth century writers on the history of warfare.

177

"Whether war is a necessary factor in the evolution of mankind may be disputed, but a fact which cannot be questioned is that, from the earliest records of man to the present age, war has been his dominant preoccupation. There has never been a period in human history altogether free from war, and seldom one or more of a generation which has not witnessed a major conflict: great wars flow and ebb almost as regularly as the tides."[20]

Writing in 1968, Will and Ariel Durant, husband and wife historians, provide some supporting calculations and comments on the causes of war: "War is one of the constants of history, and has not diminished with civilization or democracy. In the last 3,421 years of recorded history only 268 have seen no war. We have acknowledged war as at present the ultimate form of competition and natural selection in the human species. 'Polermos pater panton,' said Heraclitus; war, or competition, is the father of all things, the potent source of ideas, inventions, institutions, and states. Peace is an unstable equilibrium, which can be preserved only by acknowledged supremacy or equal power. The causes of war are the same as the causes of competition among individuals: acquisitiveness, pugnacity, and pride; the desire for food, land, materials, fuels, mastery. The state has our instincts without our restraints. The individual submits to restraints laid upon him by morals and laws, and agrees to replace combat with conference, because the state guarantees him basic protection in his life, property, and legal rights. The state itself acknowledges no substantial restraints, either because it is strong enough to defy any interference with its will or because there is no superstate to offer it basic protection, and no international law or moral code wielding effective force."[21] There can be no doubt that the Future is an arena of competing intentions. To think or hope otherwise is unrealistic.

Creating Your Path In Life

How is a desired Future achieved? Generally what is done? Although the specific Futures which people strive to achieve are large in number and vary widely from person to person, the methods or strategies by which they do it are relatively few in number. In fact, there are only six basic strategies which may be used to create the Future. These six strategies are described below; their titles are:

1. One Path, One Destination.
2. The Process Is Everything.
3. Many Roads Lead To Rome.
4. Somehow Something Good Will Happen.
5. Don't Think About It!
6. What Will Be, Will Be.

Any particular strategy used by an actor as, for example, a person, group, organization, corporation, or nation, will consist of either one of these strategies or a combination of them. As these strategies are paraded past you for your review, you should ask yourself, Which of these strategies am I using? and Why have I selected this strategy or these strategies?

Strategy 1: One Path, One Destination.

Power. Will power. Determination. You will force your will upon the environment. You have a clearly-defined desired Future in mind. You have devised a series of intermediate steps which are to be followed in achieving this desired Future. All resources are focused on accomplishing these intermediate steps exactly in the order in which you originally laid them out. There is to be no deviation from this plan. All of your powers of ingenuity and creativity are focused on devising ways by which these intermediate steps are to be achieved, and in overcoming any and all obstacles which may be in your way. The occurrence of fortuitous events are valued because they shorten the time necessary to achieve your desired Future or because they may allow you to save some of your resources. Such events, however, are not expected. You don't really need them. Your eyes are focused squarely on a particular Future. You know exactly what you want. There is no doubt in your mind. You can make it happen. You will make it happen. It is not you who will bend to the environment; the environment will bend to you. You have the power to do it and you will do it.

Strategy 2: The Process Is Everything.

You do not have in mind a clearly-defined desired Future which you are striving to achieve. However, you do desire to have a good Future, whatever it may be, and are willing to work hard to achieve it. What you do is very simple. You focus your energies on carrying out a particular process. You have the faith that, if this process is followed to the letter, a Future will result which you will find desirable. Your focus is on the process, not the end product. Your only concern is selecting the process which is right for you, and then doing it.

A process is a series of steps which you repeat over and over again. Let's consider a few examples of what is meant by a process. Assume that you are a young man just graduating from college. You will be seeking employment and you sense that you will probably be employed over the next 30 or so years. Although you have no idea of what you will be doing 30 years from now, you have decided on the process you will follow to get there. You will find a job, you will work to the best of your ability on that job, you will learn all that you can while working there, and, at the end of three years, you will find a new and different job. Yes, you will change jobs at the end of three years, regardless of how well you may be performing on your current job. The actual job which you seek next is based on your interests at the end of each 3-year period and what you have learned during those

181

years. You have the faith that adhering to this process will result in a Future, whatever it may be, which you will find desirable.

For our second example, we step into the corporate arena. Assume that you work for a corporation which desires to have a revolutionary and exciting product on the market in the next from seven to ten years. Right now, you have no idea of what this product will be, other than revolutionary and exciting. You do, however, know the process which you will follow in producing it. Research and development. You will assemble a team of experts, identify the general area of interest, provide them with sufficient resources, and charge them with having your new product in hand at the end of five years. You have the faith that a concentration of effort, associated with the learning which will come from repeated trial, error, and revision, will give you what you want.

For our last example, assume that you are the director of a charitable not-for-profit organization. You know that you could do more for those whom you serve if you only had more resources. You decide to continually seek funding from federal agencies. You know that each proposal for funding which you submit will not be funded, but some may be funded. You will seek the reason for why any proposal which you submit is not funded. This is the only way to learn and improve. You have the faith that through your successes and failures that you will learn and gradually over time expand your available resources.

182

Strategy 3: Many Roads Lead To Rome.

You have a specific desired Future in mind. You know exactly what it is. However, you do not know the exact steps which should be followed to achieve it. But you know that you must start. And you do this, by devising a tentative plan of action and, based on this plan, taking the first step. You know what you will be doing now and in the immediate Future.

You expect this plan to change over time. This is not a problem for you. To you, what is important is the end result, and not the particular steps which you will take to achieve it. You know that your desired Future may be brought about in any number of ways, some of which you know nothing about right now. You keep your eyes on the your desired Future and ask yourself each day, Is what I am doing today and planning on doing tomorrow a step toward where I want to be?

Through your ingenuity and resourcefulness, you know that the answer must always be, Yes! You will learn as you incrementally step toward your desired Future, and will take full advantage of any opportunities which present themselves. You believe that you will achieve your desired Future, at a time which may not be exactly known right now, by taking a step toward it each and every day. What is important to you is making certain that every day and tomorrow you take a step, regardless of its size, toward the Future which you desire.

183

Strategy 4: Somehow Something Good Will Happen.

You want to have a good Future. Who wants a bad Future! However, you have no idea of what your good Future might be. There are so many possibilities, and no way of knowing which particular one you should pursue. So, you select several which seem interesting and reasonable to you, and pursue each to some degree. You have the faith that, sooner or later, somehow, something good will happen. One day, one of the Futures which you are pursuing will pay off. You have no idea which one it will be; perhaps none. You keep working every day. "I hope it's soon, whatever it is." you think to yourself.

Strategy 5: Don't Think About It!

Thinking about the Future gives you a headache. Who wants a headache! You have no desired Future, and you do not want to think about one. You become angry when someone asks you about it. You are not striving to achieve any desired Future, and this is because you have chosen not to do so. You know that it is this continual thinking about the Future which causes all the problem, all the frustrations, and all the headaches. If you have to think about the Future, you will do it later, much later. You will concern yourself with doing today what must be done today, and that's all there is to it. You have enough problems just doing that. "Go ask someone else about their desired Future; give them

184

a headache." you say to any inquirer. People should realize that the best they can do is that which they are doing today.

Strategy 6: What Will Be, Will Be.

You know that there will be a Future. You also know that a person may think that he can cause certain events to happen, may think that he is shaping the Future but that is really impossible. What is meant to happen, will happen. If a person is meant to have a good Future, he will have a good Future, and vice versa. This will happen regardless of what the person may think or attempt to do. The Future is "written," that is, what will happen is already determined and will occur regardless of what actions are taken in the Present. People should just relax and go along for the ride of their life. What you do today is what you must do today. You can do nothing else. Whatever happens is acceptable, because nothing else is possible. It is Fate, and every man has a Fate. You don't waste your time trying to change the unchangeable.

Concept Of A Strategy Profile

Our six strategies are distinctly different orientations to the Future. In practice, however, a person may alternate between two strategies or at different times in his life favor a particular strategy. With this in mind, a person's orientation toward the Future is most appropriately considered as a profile consisting of these six strategies. At a particular point in time, each strategy has a relative weight, with one particular strategy being dominant. The relative weight of each strategy is the importance attached to it by the person at that time.

Combinations of strategies are also possible. One interesting example of this is the Vietnamese orientation to life. The following observation illustrates this point very well and was made by some United States military personnel stationed in South Vietnam during the Vietnam War (1957-1975):

"...the Vietnamese often displayed stoicism in the face of personal tragedy and disappointment, and a fatalistic attitude toward life in general, (and this) was a common perception by the American community in Vietnam. But few understood these traits in context. The bamboo plant, a national symbol of the Government of South Vietnam, was frequently adduced as proof of Vietnamese indifference to political fortune. To the Vietnamese, the bamboo is a symbol of the common man's survivability: he bends with the wind."

"This willingness to accommodate external pressures as, for example, defecting from one side to the other, was seen by many Americans as gross opportunism, whereas it actually reflected the belief that since man is forced to react to circumstances beyond his control, then (he) must do everything he can to take advantage of them: *Heaven gives weal or woe / yet from the human heart it also springs / As Heaven shapes our fate we lend a hand.*[22] Paul Berman noted that while belief in the efficacy of individual action, on the one hand, and resignation to destiny, on the other, seem contradictory to the Western mind, it is not so for the Vietnamese. He coined the phrase 'pragmatic fatalism' to describe this trait.[23] Thus, the Vietnamese city dweller who asked an American friend to buy him a watch in the (U.S. military store) so he could sell it on the black market for a profit saw this not as an act of disloyalty or duplicity, but as merely taking advantage of circumstances. Similarly, the villager who woke up with a gun sticking in his face generally did what was ordered, regardless of his private political convictions or who was holding the weapon."[24] This example illustrates a combination of our strategies 3 and 6.

An Alternative Approach

In the context of planning and change, management theorist Ackoff describes four different orientations to the Future: reactive, inactive, preactive, and proactive.[25] The most famous and frequently quoted is the last. Each orientation is briefly summarized below. Ackoff stresses that there are strengths and weaknesses associated with each of his four orientations. To his way of thinking, one is not clearly superior to another.

Reactive Orientation. Reactivists like the Past. They like the way things once were, and seek to return to a time in the Past by undoing the relevant intervening changes. They are nostalgic about the Past and ro-

187

manticize it. Reactivists enter the Future facing the Past; they have a better view of where they have been than of where they are going. Their goal is changing the Present to be like the Past.

Inactive Orientation. Inactivists like the Present. They are unwilling to return to the Past and they do not like any change from the Present. They try to prevent change. Inactivists may not believe that the Present is the best, but they believe that it is good enough or as good as can reasonably be expected. Inactivists are generally satisfied with the Present and want to keep it that way.

Preactive Orientation. Preactivists are unsatisfied with both the Past and the Present. They seek to identify and exploit new opportunities which will occur only in the Future. They strive to predict what opportunities will occur in the Future, and to be the first to capitalize on them. Preactivists do not seek to change the Future; they want to take advantage of what will happen.

Proactive Orientation. Proactivists are not willing to return to the Past, or to accept the Present, or to settle for the Future that appears to confront them. They do not believe that what occurs in the Future is largely uncontrollable. Proactivists believe that what happens in the Future depends at least as much on what happens in the Present as it does on what has happened in the Past. They believe that the Future may be created, and strive to create a Future which is desirable to them.

The Future Influences Your Present

You, like us, create intentions which are cast forward into the Future. Then, in the Present, you make decisions and act to achieve these intentions. What is true for you, as an actor, is true for other actors, whether a team, organization, corporation, army or a nation. All have intentions cast into the Future which shape the decisions and actions of their Present. So, it is easy to see how your desired Future influences what you do in the Present. The Present, however, is more complicated than that. Others are also acting to achieve their desired Futures. The stage is set for the occurrence of competing intentions and competing actions. What you are trying to accomplish may be constrained, restricted, or made impossible by what another is doing to achieve their desired Future. Here, their desired Future may be influencing your desired Future. Ackoff must have had this notion in mind when he added to his book *Creating The Corporate Future* the subtitle *Plan Or Be Planned For.*[26] Clearly, the Future is an arena of competing intentions which has the potential to influence in the Present the actions of each and every actor.

It is difficult to argue that intentions do not influence actions taken in the Present. What can be argued, however, is the usefulness of an intention whose realization lies in the long-term as, for example, 10 to 15 years from the Present. Is the Future so unpredictable as to make such intentions completely unrealistic? If you think that it is difficult to predict what will happen next month, is it not more difficult to predict what will happen 10 to 15 years from now? Is it realistic to think that we can envision a desired Future, strive to achieve it, and actually achieve it? Is this possible? We consider this issue in the next chapter.

Chapter VI

The Alternative Is Unthinkable

The only way to predict the future is to
have power to shape the future.[1]

Is striving to achieve a desired Future realistic when it
may only occur in the long-term, say, 8 to 10 years
from the Present? We think the answer is Yes; there
are others who think No. Although both perspectives
will be considered here, the general nature of the con-
test is suggested by the dialogue given below between
two Greek seamen, Dimitris and Yannis, two men who
have grown up together and been friends all the while.
It is the year 336 B.C.

*So, Dimitris, you think that you are the captain
of your own ship but, in reality, your ship only goes
where the currents and winds allow. To attempt to go
otherwise is a waste of your energy. You should study
the moods of the great Neptune. Let him guide your
ship. You have no choice, you know. Besides, he may
take your ship to some interesting destination, a destination beyond your current imagination. Study Neptune,
Dimitris; study Neptune. It is to your advantage to
learn from him.*

*Yannis, my friend, we have known each other
since we were boys. Your advice has always been
sound. Then and now. But, my friend, you are, perhaps, too cautious in this matter. Is it not true that, by*

191

the set of my sail and the position of my rudder, my ship may be maneuvered to wherever I so desire? Regardless of which way the winds may blow and the currents run. Would not the mighty Neptune himself be pleased that I am using so well the wonderful gifts which he has given us both? My destination will be what I choose it to be.

We shall see, Dimitris; we shall see.

Everyone has a desired Future, but is it realistic to think that it may actually be achieved? Before we jump into the debate, let's consider a few examples which we can hold in our hand while thinking about the question.

Imagine this. You are a counselor in a high school in the United States. One day you are talking with a 17-year-old boy about his plans for after high school graduation. While you are reviewing various career options, he suddenly looks you right in the eyes and says, "What I really want to do is be the President of the United States. Tell me what is the career path for that job!" You sit there for a few seconds and then begin to tell him what you think he must do. This is your job. But, what do you really think, deep in your heart? Do you think there is no way that he could be President! There are just too many unknowns, too many variables! Or, do you think, "Well, I've always wondered how someone becomes President. Perhaps it starts just like this. With one person saying, 'I want to do it!'" What do you really think?

Now, let's travel to France. The year is 1801. Your son, Jean-Francois Champollion, 10 years old, tells you one afternoon, "I swear that I will be the first person to read the Egyptian hieroglyphics." He's serious! It seems that he has just finished reading a story about the discovery of the Rosetta stone in Egypt in 1799. You know that some of the greatest minds in the world have been struggling with the decipherment of the writing on this stone for several years now. As you recall, there are three kinds of writing on the stone: one is ancient Greek, the second is Egyptian hieroglyphics, and the third is some other language. You would probably tell him to study and some day he may be able to do it. But, what do you really think? Do you think it is really possible for your son to be the first person in 1,500 years to correctly translate the formal writing of the ancient Egyptians?[2]

Now, let's travel back to the Present. You and your partner have just started a corporation. It's small. One day your partner tells you that he has a great idea for a revolutionary product, a product which will take about 10 years to develop, but, once developed, will dominate its market. As he describes it, what he wants to develop does, in fact, seem revolutionary and exciting. It's hard not to be caught up in his logic and enthusiasm. But, what do you really think? Do you think that 10 years is a long time, and who knows what the clients, those people who will purchase your revolutionary product, will want to buy then? Will what seems revolutionary now really be revolutionary in 10 years? Or, do you think, "You know, I think we can do it. It's going to be rough, and there will undoubtedly happen some things that we don't know about right now, but we can do it. Let's do it!" What do you really think?

For our last example, imagine that you are a single mother with two young sons, the one is age 5 and the other age 7. Life has been hard, and you have worked hard and will work hard. That will be your life and you don't doubt it. You are poor now and you will probably always be poor. But, your sons. They will not be poor; they will be trained and educated, somehow. They will have good jobs. They will be happy! But, what do you really think? Do you really think it's possible? Are you just dreaming? Can you make it happen? What do you really think?

We consider next both sides of the debate about the feasibility of achieving a desired Future when that Future lies in the long-term. Although our examples have focused on the individual, our question applies equally well to the desired Future of a group, whether it be a family, team, organization, corporation, or nation.

For one of these groups, the corporation, our question has received some attention in the literature on management and leadership, in the context of the role played by the corporate vision. Here, the question is asked, Is a vision of a desired Future necessary for a corporation? Several authors believe that a properly constructed and properly communicated vision is essential for success, and that all activities of the corporation should be directly focused on achieving it. However, a few believe that a corporate vision is not only worthless but potentially detrimental to the corporation.[3]

The question which corporations are asking themselves is the same one which a person may ask of his own desired Future. Why has this question been debated in the corporate arena and not the more general arena of life? Perhaps it is more professionally prestigious and financially rewarding with the former.

Unpredictable Versus Manageable

The arguments both for and against the feasibility of achieving a desired Future are given here. All are interesting and merit your consideration. A person's opinion regarding the arguments is directly related to his orientation toward the Future and his choice of a dominant strategy (of the six presented in the last chapter) for creating a Future. Everyone does in fact create a Future for himself. What differs among people is the strategy or strategies by which this is done.

Arguments Against Achieving A Future

There are two arguments against achieving a desired Future. The first is that the Future is unknowable and, therefore, unpredictable. The second is that a successful person is creative, and creativity cannot be planned, controlled or predicted. The conclusion of each is that a vision of a desired Future is unrealistic.

The premise of the first argument is that *The future, in the long-term, is basically unknowable*. It follows then that the long-term consequence or effect of any action taken in the Present is unknown and cannot be predicted. Therefore, it is impossible to identify in advance the specific steps or activities which will bring about the desired Future. The person may know what he would like to achieve in the Future, but there is simply no way to know what steps should be taken to bring it about.

The premise of the second argument is that *Future success depends primarily on creativity*. It follows then that the specific activities in which a person will be involved in the Future are unpredictable because the creative process is an unpredictable process. Therefore, any planning which involves the creative process is useless. A creative person cannot be expected to achieve a predetermined desired Future.

Some additional comments which serve to buttress these arguments are: (1) Envisioning a desired Future simply gives the illusion of having control over Future events. This is a soothing fantasy, a psychological opiate, for relieving the stress associated with facing what is, in fact, an unknowable Future. People should accept the fact that they really have no idea of what will happen in the long-term. They must learn to function effectively in an environment where both the long-term Future and the forces operating within it are unknowable. Suggesting that a person should create a vision of a desired Future will only result in frustration and bewilderment. (2) Large groups are very complex and no one really understands how they operate. Such groups change and evolve incrementally as a result of a multitude of individual actions and interactions which are very difficult, if not impossible, to identify, control, or predict. (3) Attempting to develop a meaningful vision for a group places a tremendous and unrealistic burden on its leader. Additionally, it perpetuates the myth that large groups must rely on a few unusually gifted people to determine what is best for the whole group. (4) When a group is striving to achieve its vision, group-think, in which everyone accepts without question a single idea, may result. In a rapidly changing environment, this may prove fatal.

Arguments For Achieving A Future

There are three arguments for achieving a desired Future. The conclusion of each is that striving to achieve a desired Future is realistic. The premise of the first argument is that *An individual or group evolves incrementally from their current state to a future state as a result of decisions and actions made daily*. It follows then that any process which affects the decisions made daily by a person shapes his Future state. Therefore, to change from the Present state to a desired Future state, it is necessary to know only (a) the current state, (b) the relevant forces operating presently within and with-

197

out the current situation, and (c) the desired Future state. The Present can be transformed incrementally from what it is currently to any desired Future.

The premise of the second argument is that *The appropriate concentration of effort and resources can produce any desired Future.* It follows then that any possible Future may be achieved if the force is sufficient. If a person has neither the appropriate resources nor the determination to succeed, a desired Future is nothing more than a daydream. But, given resources and a concentration of effort, the desired Future becomes an achievable goal.

The premise of the third argument is that *Through the power of the human spirit, everyone has the potential to achieve more than what they might consider to be realistically achievable.* It follows then that the potential for greatness resides in the spirit of everyone. Therefore, it is reasonable for a person or group to aspire to achieve what may seem to be challenging or beyond their currently perceived capabilities.

A few additional observations are: (1) It is obvious that, in striving to achieve their vision of a desired Future, the person or group will take advantage of opportunities in the environment whenever possible. These opportunities, however, are means to a predetermined end. (2) When a group vision is shared by all, one member, working in one subgroup or team within the group, is able to act, guided by the vision, in a way which will benefit the whole group, even though the person may be unaware of specific activities in other parts of the group. (3) A vision provides the impetus for asking questions. Why am I doing this? Why is the group doing this? The answer to questions such as these must be that it is a step toward achieving the vision. If this is not the answer, the activities must be changed.

Challenging, But Possible

There is no final or absolute answer to our question, Is striving to achieve a desired Future realistic? The debate will continue for as long as man exists. Although we do acknowledge the challenges associated with achieving a desired Future, we believe that a desired Future may be achieved and that man has the necessary abilities to do just this. We find very compelling the argument that any Future may be created by incrementally shaping the Present.

History is ennobled with examples of one man or a group achieving their desired Future. History is also littered with examples of the failure to achieve a desired Future. This suggests to us that the concept of achieving a desired Future is valid, but that it may be implemented with varying degrees of success. Clearly, there are prerequisites for attempting to achieve a desired Future. The first prerequisite is relevant knowledge; the second, resources; the third, a plan for managing the resources; and, the fourth, personal determination to succeed.

Attempting to achieve a desired Future is, in many cases, a challenging task. The comment attributed to Calvin Coolidge (1872-1933), thirtieth president of the United States (1923-1929) inspires us and seems very appropriate here: "Nothing in the world can take the place of persistence. Talent will not; nothing is more common than unsuccessful men with talent. Genius will not; unrewarded genius is almost a proverb. Education will not; the world is full of educated derelicts. Persistence and determination are omnipotent. The slogan 'press on' has solved and always will solve the problems of the human race."[4]

It is interesting to consider for a moment one particular scenario: What if everyone believed that it is impossible to create a desired Future and therefore made no attempt whatsoever to do so? What kind of a world would this be? Think about it.

Having a vision of a desired Future and achieving it are not the same. Whether or not a desired Future is achieved is primarily determined by the nature of the competition in the environment. If we assume that a person or group has the necessary prerequisites (that is, knowledge, resources, a plan, and determination to succeed), why is it that a desired Future is not always achieved? Of course, if the prerequisites do not exist, it is easy to see how failure may result. However, when this is not the case, and there exists a serious effort to achieve the desired Future, it is the nature of the competition which determines success or failure. Remember that there are many individuals and groups attempting to achieve their desired Futures at the very same time. Some of these Futures are complementary; others are contradictory. Only *one* Future will occur.

With competition playing a critical role in achieving a desired Future, what advice is there to give someone attempting to achieve their vision? Good advice there is, and it is gleaned from the best classroom on Earth: the battlefield. War. It is here, amid the clash of armies, the smoke of battle, the dead, the dying, the survivors, the pain, the suffering, and the spilt blood of many, that our lessons are found. Looking elsewhere is only a detour to the battlefield. We agree with John Stuart Mill that "All principles are most effectively tested by extreme cases."[5] For us, speaking of the "battlefield of life" is not an analogy but a reality, a reality which must be accepted by everyone. It must be accepted by you.

Battlefields Of Life

The one activity in which man has been engaged from the beginning is competition. Man generally competes to live, be it with the environment, with other men, or with himself. For man, the ultimate form of competition is warfare and he has been developing this art for the past 3,000 years, over approximately 160 generations. In fact, for the last 3,421 years, only 268 days have been free of war in the world.[6] Lessons learned in this arena have been well learned and speak directly

201

to man striving to achieve his vision. Although we may not like to think of life as a battlefield, it is exactly that.

Although the topic of warfare is not pleasant, there is clearly much to be learned from the battlefields of the world. Before discussing what has been learned from the battlefield, the definition of war provided by the famous military theorist Carl von Clausewitz (1780-1831) is helpful:

"I shall not begin by expounding a pedantic, literary definition of war, but go straight to the heart of the matter, to the duel. War is nothing but a duel on a larger scale. Countless duels go to make up war, but a picture of it as a whole can be formed by imagining a pair of wrestlers. Each tries through physical force to compel the other to do his will; his immediate aim is to throw his opponent in order to make him incapable of further resistance. War is thus an act of force to compel our enemy to do our will. ... Force — that is physical force, ...is thus the *means* of war; to impose our will on the enemy is its *object*."[7]

Fortunately, we do not have to review the successes and failures of 3,000 years worth of battles. Others have done that for us over the last few hundred years. We merely have to take advantage of the tremendous amount of work and thinking which has already been done. The distillation which we value is called the principles of warfare. They are applicable today and tomorrow because the nature of man has not changed.

Historical Development Of The Principles

The development of modern warfare has been strongly influenced by the thinking of two men: Carl von Clausewitz and Antoine-Henri Jomini (1779-1869). Clausewitz wrote *Vom Kriege* (*On War*) published posthumously in 1831; and Jomini, *Précis de l'Art de la Guerre* (*Summary of the Art of War*), published in 1838. Clausewitz and Jomini were contemporaries and both studied under the great master of warfare, Napoléon Bonaparte I (1759-1822). No man in the history of war has exerted a greater influence on the strategy and tactics of war during his life and on modern warfare than Napoléon.

The ideas of Clausewitz and Jomini have much in common. "Many of the concepts popularly attributed to the mind of Clausewitz find their counterparts in the words of Jomini. The fundamental difference between Clausewitz and Jomini is that while the Prussian (Clausewitz) roamed in the psychological and philosophical domains of battle, (addressing the) intangible but nevertheless omnipresent components of combat, Jomini was more concerned with the more immediate character of war as it *exists*, and dealt more with the tangible, less with the philosophic."

"And yet when Jomini considered the intangible factors of war he was surprisingly close to Clausewitz, and when Clausewitz wrote of battle methods he was often on common ground with Jomini. Both wrote of tactics and strategy, and each appreciated the great importance of morale; they were aware that battle was something fluid, changing, and subject to chance. Clausewitz advocated simplicity of plans and emphasized the friction (unanticipated problems and complications, or incidents attributed to chance) of war. Likewise, to Jomini simplicity in battle planning was a cardinal virtue, for he postulated that 'the more simple a decisive maneuver is, the more certain will be its success.' Jomini's discussions of battlefield difficulties indicated that he was thoroughly aware of the fact that friction was an ever-present combat factor. It is significant that Jomini as well as Clausewitz frequently referred to the 'drama' of war."[8]

That principles of war do exist was, for Jomini, beyond question: "There have existed in all time fundamental principles on which depend good results in warfare...these principles are unchanging, independent of the kind of weapons, of historical time and place."[9] A particular strength which Clausewitz brought to the art of warfare was an understanding of the individual soldier.

According to the military historian Sir Basil H. Liddell-Hart (1895-1970): "Clausewitz's greatest contribution to the theory of war was in emphasizing the psychological factors. Raising his voice against the geometric school of strategy, then fashionable, he showed that the human spirit was infinitely more important than operational lines and angles. He discussed the effect of danger and fatigue, the value of boldness and determination, with deep understanding."[10]

Before turning to the principles of warfare, it is interesting to review Napoléon's opinion about such principles. Remember that Napoléon fought more battles than all those fought by the "great captains" whom he cites next. Now, the words of the Emperor:

"The principles of war are those which have regulated the great captains whose deeds have been handed down to us by history: Alexander, Hannibal, Caesar, Gustaphus Adolphus, Turenne, Prince Eugene (of Savoy) and Frederick the Great. ... The history of these eighty-eight campaigns, carefully written, would be a complete treatise of the art of war; the principles which ought to be followed, in offensive and defensive war, would flow from it spontaneously.[11] Read and re-read the campaigns of Alexander, Hannibal, Caesar, Gustaphus Adolphus, Turenne, Eugene and Frederick; take them as your model; that is the only way of becoming a great captain, to obtain the secrets of the art of war."[12]

The principles of warfare evolved over time, and their historical development has been well documented by Alger.[13] His analysis shows clearly the dominant influence of the writings of Clausewitz and Jomini on the principles of warfare taught currently in the military academies of the major nations of the world. We now turn to the principles of warfare adopted by two major nations: the Unites States of America, and to what was formerly called the Union of Soviet Socialist Republics. We will find that their principles have much in common.

Unites States Army Principles Of Warfare

The nine principles of warfare given below are those published in 1954 in the *Field Service Regulations* of the United States Army.[14] Every military officer is well-acquainted with these principles.

Principle Of The Objective. Every military operation must be directed toward a decisive, obtainable objective. The destruction of the enemy's armed forces and his will to fight is the ultimate military objective of war. The objective of each operation must contribute to this ultimate objective. Each intermediate objective must be such that its attainment will most directly, quickly, and economically contribute to the purpose of the operation. It must permit the application of the maximum means available. Its selection must be based upon consideration of means available, the enemy, and the area of operations. Secondary objectives of any operation must contribute to the attainment of the principal objective.

Principle Of The Offensive. Only offensive action achieves decisive results. Offensive action permits the commander to exploit the initiative and impose his will on the enemy. The defensive may be forced on the commander, but it should be deliberately adopted only as a temporary expedient while awaiting an opportunity for offensive action or for the purpose of economizing forces on a front where a decision is not sought. Even on the defensive the commander seeks every opportunity to seize the initiative.

Principle Of Simplicity. Simplicity must be the keynote of military operations. Uncomplicated plans clearly expressed in orders promote common understanding and intelligent execution. Even the most simple plan is usually difficult to execute in combat. Simplicity must be applied to organization, methods, and means in order to produce orderliness on the battlefield.

Principle Of Unity Of Command. The decisive application of full combat power requires unity of command. Unity of command obtains unity of effort by the coordinated action of all forces toward a common goal. Coordination may be achieved by direction or by cooperation. It is best achieved by vesting a single commander with requisite authority. Unity of effort is furthered by willing and intelligent cooperation among all elements of the forces involved.

Principle Of Mass. Maximum available combat power must be applied at the point of decision. Mass is the concentration of means at the critical time and place to the maximum degree permitted by the situation. Proper application of the principle of mass, in conjunction with the other principles of war, may permit numerically inferior forces to achieve decisive combat superiority. Mass is essentially a combination of manpower and firepower and is not dependent upon numbers alone; the effectiveness of mass may be increased by superior weapons, tactics, and morale.

Principle Of Economy Of Force. Minimum essential means must be employed at points other than that of decision. To devote means to unnecessary secondary efforts or to employ excessive means on required secondary efforts is to violate the principles of both mass and the objective. Limited attack, the defensive, deception, or even retrograde action are used in noncritical areas to achieve mass in the critical area.

Principle Of Maneuver. Maneuver must be used to alter the relative combat power of military forces. Maneuver is the positioning of forces to place the enemy at a relative disadvantage. Proper positioning of forces in relation to the enemy frequently can achieve results which otherwise could be achieved only at heavy cost in men and material. In many situations maneuver is made possible only by the effective employment of firepower.

Principle Of Surprise. Surprise may decisively shift the balance of combat power in favor of the commander who achieves it. It consists of striking the enemy when, where, or in a manner for which he is unprepared. It is not essential that the enemy be taken unaware but only that he becomes aware too late to react effectively. Surprise can be achieved by speed, secrecy, deception, by variation in means and methods.

Principle Of Security. Security is essential to the application of the other principles of war. It consists of those measures necessary to prevent surprise, avoid annoyance, preserve freedom of action, and deny to the enemy information of our forces. Security denies to the enemy and retains for the commander the ability to employ his forces most effectively.

Soviet Army Principles Of War

Similar to the nine principles of warfare adopted by the United States Army are the seven principles of warfare espoused by Soviet military doctrine. These fundamental principles, presented below, are considered applicable to all levels of combat.[15] Marshal of the Soviet Union Vasiliy D. Sokolovskiy (1897-1963) has stated that "In the land theaters, the mission of an armed conflict will be resolved primarily by the offensive." and this perspective has not changed in the intervening years.[16] The Soviets consider the offensive to be essential for achieving a decisive victory. The aim of the offensive is twofold: the complete destruction of the enemy in the shortest possible time, and the occupation of his vital regions. The Soviets recognize defense only as that done by the enemy, or as a temporary measure used by them when preparing for a successful offensive.

Mobility And High Tempo. The rapid movement of combat forces, including all supporting units, is to be achieved and sustained. High tempo is the relentless prosecution of an operation without pause. Applying constant pressure keeps the enemy off balance and prevents his forming an effective defense.

Concentration Of Effort. This principle applies to the deliberate attack and to the employment of artillery.[17] An essential feature of the deliberate attack is the concentration of troops and weapons on relatively small frontages to achieve superiority at the point of attack. A deliberate attack should be used only when the success of a hasty attack cannot be foreseen. A deliberate attack is inevitably more costly in men and equipment and, because of the time required for planning and execution, must result in loss of momentum.

Surprise And Security. Strategically, surprise is achieved through the integration of military, political, and psychological operations. Tactically, surprise comes from undertaking an action when and where least expected. It is not essential that the enemy be taken wholly unaware, but only that he become aware too late to react effectively.

Combat Activeness. All combat operations should be characterized by boldness and decisiveness. Taking the offensive is the basic form of combat action. There must be a constant attempt to seize and maintain the initiative.

Preservation Of The Combat Effectiveness Of Friendly Forces. The minimum force necessary to accomplish a specific task should be employed. This principle applies also to: (a) conserving the fighting strength of military units through the use of sophisticated combat vehicles and equipment, and (b) having a medical system geared to returning casualties to combat duty rapidly.

Conformity Of The Goal. The goal or purpose of a military operation must conform realistically to the actual combat situation. A realistic estimate of the situation is essential if two hazards are to be avoided. The first hazard is over-estimating friendly forces and under-estimating the enemy; this leads to impossible missions. The second hazard is under-estimating friendly forces and over-estimating the enemy; this leads to losing an opportunity to defeat the enemy. Clarification and understanding of the combat goal is essential at all operational levels.

Coordination Of Effort. Coordination allows rapid exploitation of success. It requires the coordination of commanders both in planning the initial attack and in carrying through to the depths of enemy defenses. Coordination of effort entails: (a) reviewing the strong and weak points of combat and supporting units, (b) reviewing the extent of mutual assistance between these and adjacent units, and (c) continuous teamwork for the duration of the battle.

Applying The Principles To Life

War is horrible. This fact, however, should not blind us to the lessons to be learned. At the very least, we pay tribute to the bravery of the combatants by taking seriously the lessons which they have written with their lives and their deeds. War is a method of achieving a desired Future. As an orientation to the Future, war is akin to our strategy number 1, One Path, One Destination, given in Chapter V. The principles of warfare developed over the years to guide armies are appropriate guides for individuals as well. Given below are our adaptations of the U.S. Army's principles of warfare for the battlefield of life.

Principle Of The Objective. Always have clearly-defined objectives to be achieved. Keep the number of objectives small and manageable. Select objectives which, when achieved, will significantly improve your current position. Do not select objectives which are easily achieved but of little importance to you.

Principle Of The Offensive. Always take the initiative. Act; avoid reacting. Take the lead; let others follow.

Principle Of Simplicity. Always take the simplest possible actions which will achieve your objectives. Make plans as simple as possible. Complexity should be avoided.

Principle Of Unity Of Command. If a group is performing an activity, each person must know and adhere to his role and responsibilities. Each group must have one, and only one, leader.

Principle Of Mass. Concentrate resources on achieving the objectives, at the right time and the right place. This is the most important principle and one which should always be followed in each and every struggle.

Principle Of Economy Of Force. Resources should be focused primarily on achieving the objectives, and secondarily on all other activities. Use the minimum possible resources on secondary activities.

Principle Of Maneuver. Learn faster and be able to change faster than the competition. Exploit available technology whenever possible. Know both yourself and the strengths and weaknesses of the competition. You must know the competition well.

Principle Of Surprise. Do the unexpected. Act boldly. Force the competition to react to you.

Principle Of Security. Tell people only what they need to know to effectively help you. There is no reason to divulge your plans, objectives, and level of resources to those having no reason to know.

Concentrate! Concentrate! Concentrate!

The Principle Of Mass is the fundamental or central principle of warfare. The other eight operate in support of this one principle, and numerous authors have stressed this point over the years. According to Jomini, "One great principle underlies all the operations of war — a principle which must be followed in all good combinations. ...to throw by strategic movements the mass of an army, successively, upon the decisive points of a theater of war...to maneuver to engage fractions of the hostile army with the bulk of one's forces. ... On the battlefield, to throw the mass of the forces upon the decisive point, or upon that portion of the hostile line which it is of the first importance to overthrow. To so arrange that these masses shall not only be thrown upon the decisive point, but that they shall engage at the proper times and with ample energy."[18]

Clausewitz expresses the same point of view: "After everything we have so far said on the subject, we can identify two basic principles that underlie all strategic planning and serve to guide all other considerations. The first principle is that the ultimate substance of enemy strength must be traced back to the fewest possible sources, and ideally to one alone. The attack on these sources must be compressed into the fewest possible actions — again, ideally, into one. Finally, all minor actions must be subordinated as much as possible. In short the first principle is: act with the utmost concentration."[19]

The lesson to be learned for those attempting to achieve a desired Future is very simple: Concentrate your resources, both material and psychological, on achieving your objectives. Concentrate your resources on achieving your desired Future. You must concentrate. When this principle is violated, the probability of failure increases and the probability of success decreases. Concentration is essential. This is the fundamental principle which is so easily explained and frequently difficult to practice.

Principles Of War Applied To Corporations

The principles of warfare are readily applied to corporations. The corporate battlefield is not an analogy; it is a description of what actually occurs. The principles given below are merely another application of the principles of warfare applied to a different arena, the corporate arena. If you listen carefully, you can hear in the background the echoes of Clausewitz and Jomini as they read their texts to us.

In 1985, Kuhn reported the results of his extensive analysis of the performance of mid-sized corporations in the United States.[20] His goal was identifying factors associated with high performance and those associated with relative poor performance. He compared hundreds of successful and relatively unsuccessful mid-sized corporations, matching by pairs similar in size and product markets. The result of this analysis was the identification of ten principles of success or, as he prefers to call them, critical success strategies. These strategies, according to him, are responsible for outstanding and consistently high corporate performance. Kuhn's ten critical success strategies are given here, and are listed in their relative order of importance, that is, 1 is more important than 2, etc. To Kuhn's way of thinking, his results apply both to mid-sized corporations and to aspiring small corporations and divisions of major corporations. We look now at his ten critical success strategies:[21]

1. Dominate your market niche. Identify smaller segments of the market, and tailor the products of the corporation to these markets. Achieve and sustain maximum market share within these smaller market segments. This segmentation may be according to, for example, specific item, customer, price, quality, brand, distribution, geography, or service. Do anything to segment. Seek control through perceived superiority. Be a big fish in a little pond.

2. Be product-oriented. Give primary importance to company output. Stress product focus, es-

215

sence, name, reliability, and service. Visualize products from the customers' viewpoint. Never make the products of the corporation subservient to executive desire or financial comfort. See each product in its broadest sense; understand the needs it fills and the desires it satisfies.

3. Be different. Make the corporation overtly dissimilar to its competitors. Strive for originality; find something to set the corporation apart in the eyes of the customer. Make an impact on the client or customer. Seek differentiation in each functional area affecting customers. Cater to customers and service them well. Be noticed and remembered.

4. Align resources with goals. Establish goals, objectives and strategies with clarity of thought and coherence of content. Build new businesses on the central skills, resources, facilities, or competencies of old businesses. Build on managerial strengths. Consider corporate cohesion and business focus as a means to an end, not as an end in and of itself.

5. Have a committed leader. The Chief Executive Officer (CEO) should be more than a CEO. Personal charisma, profound dedication, pulsating presence are what counts. The CEO should project high levels of commitment and radiate intense auras of energy. There should be a desire, even a compulsion, on the part of the CEO to be involved in every aspect of the business.

6. Satisfy and fulfill personnel needs. Exploit the comparative advantage of smaller corporations to attract entrepreneurial people. Offer corporate executives and managers greater job content and individual satisfaction. Be people-oriented. Give employees a real sense of self-worth and personal participation, both emotionally and financially. Develop meaningful stock ownership programs. Get the right executives, then give them what they want both on the job and in the bank.

7. Develop new products, services and methods. Develop and market new technologies. Exploit the comparative advantage of smaller firms to introduce new products sooner and swifter than major corporations. Encourage creative employees to be creative. Attack market leaders if they protect current positions by withholding innovation — as often happens. Emphasize efficiency in research; optimize development for rapid, cost-conscious results. Never attack broadside; focus research and development efforts for maximum effectiveness. Use rifles, not shotguns.

8. Know the market environment. Monitor all market opportunities and threats, both current and potential. Stay attuned to market conditions and customer needs. Know your customers; develop personal relationships. Have a keen sense of your competitors. Understand well the concepts of market share, concentration ratios, growth patterns and trends, powers of suppliers and buyers, threats of new entrants and substitute products. Study long-term forecasts, and watch them change. Be prepared for sudden breaks in the apparent trends and be ready to exploit them.

9. Strive for profitability. Avoid growth for growth's sake, but seek growth for business's sake. Market products forcefully. Visualize longer time-horizons for profit return. The bottom line is what counts. Billion-dollar corporations have gone bankrupt, while many very small firms have made their owners and executives very rich. Weaker mid-sized companies should strive for profits, not growth. Stronger mid-sized firms should not fear sacrificing short-term profits for long-term growth. When top corporations establish a strong market position, ultimate profits become much greater and more secure.

10. Be able to change direction and move quickly. Develop dynamic decision-making. Be prepared to react rapidly to changes in products or markets. Be ready to change quickly and beat larger competitors to new opportunities. Retreat when the enemy attacks. Attack when the enemy retreats. Weaker mid-sized firms should emphasize flexibility and opportunity more so than stronger firms.

Kuhn offers some advice to managers contemplating these ten strategies: "These (strategies) may seem obvious and easy; do not allow the former to discourage you or the latter to fool you. The points are powerful and pragmatic; they were derived from hundreds of contemporary companies... On the other hand, any simplistic advice — of which (these strategies) can be considered classic — should not be used as a magic wand. Smooth aphorisms are no panacea for confused executives. Such platitudes often appear when management consultants, who usually haven't run real businesses, spout traditional wisdom. Generalized prescription, never forget, is one thing; realistic recommendation quite another. ... Observing management principles in current combat is vital. The struggle of company units on industrial battlefields is the ultimate touchstone. Each (strategy) must be field tested in hard fighting. "[22]

Are these strategies generally applicable only to mid-sized corporations? The comments of Jack Welch, Chief Executive Officer of the General Electric Corporation, suggest strongly that they also generally apply to large corporations:

"Trying to define what will happen three to five years out, in specific quantitative terms, is a futile exercise. The world is moving too fast for that. What should a company do instead? First of all, define its vision and its destiny in broad clear terms. Second, maximize its own productivity. Finally, be organizationally and culturally flexible enough to meet massive change. The way to control your destiny in a global environment of change and uncertainly is simple: Be the highest-value supplier in your market-place. "[23]

The More Stubborn Conquers

Although the Future resides in the mind of man and the minds of men are many and varied, one and only one Future will occur. Man, acting as either an individual, group, organization, corporation, or country, decides upon his Future and then competes every day to achieve what he has selected. Stated rhetorically with Yes the answer, Preismeyer asks: "Can we not simply decide what is wanted (in the Future) and then control the forces to get there? Are we not able to create any reality if we make the proper incremental changes that lead to that reality?"[24]

Of course, the answer is Yes, providing the actor has the ability to control the relevant forces in the context of a hostile and competitive environment. Remember that the desired Future of one actor may be repugnant to another. On the battlefield of life, there is no formula for success. There are principles, however, which provide general directions, the primary being concentration, concentration of resources both physical and psychological on achieving clearly-defined objectives. The psychological force involves the will and determination of man, the actor, to succeed, and its importance should never be underrated because its nature is generally intangible.

Ferdinand Foch (1851-1929), the French Marshall during World War I, relates an interesting story about a Prussian general touring Silesia, a region of central Europe, now chiefly within southwestern Poland, probably around the year 1790: "(General) Von Brack...was passing by an old castle in Silesia. A coat of arms stood on the door: two stags fighting each other and the motto *The more stubborn conquers*. 'Here is the true source of success,' said that man of arms. 'Victory means will.'"[25]

If the environment is generally unchanging and few if any opposing forces exist, a vision of a desired Future would be meaningless. Fortunately, we are not in such an environment. We are in a continually changing environment and it is this reality which gives us the opportunity to shape the Future to our desires. What is true for us is true for others. All change fosters competition. Approving or disapproving of this condition is analogous to attempting to stop the wind by pushing it back with your hand. Although competition is stressful, it can also be a source of vitality.

It is impossible for us to think of an environment alternative to competition which would be better suited to our seeking the awareness which we need. This statement is true for the individual and for the group. Competition is the best of worlds. It is what is best for man. It is what is best for us. It is what is best for you.

Is striving to achieve a desired Future realistic? The answer is Yes. Yes, it is possible to achieve the Future which you desire. What is essential is knowing your current status, the forces at play, how these forces may be manipulated, and then manipulating these forces. Conceptually, the process is very simple. We are well aware that drive, determination, and perseverance are essential requirements. The Future, your Future, is the result of the competitive forces at play, and what is most important is your ability to compete, now and in the Future. You are a force. You are a competitor.

221

Eric Hoffer was absolutely correct when he said that "The only way to predict the future is to have power to shape the future." Think about what Hoffer has said.

Chapter VII

Choose Your Principles

> General principles are not the less true or
> important because, from their nature,
> they elude immediate observation; they
> are like the air, which is not the less
> necessary because we neither see nor feel
> it.[1]

Yes, it is realistic to strive to achieve a desired Future
which lies in the long-term. To us, the alternative is
unthinkable. Taking each day as it comes and hoping
for the best is not for us. We have never said that it is
an easy process, and have continually referred to the
struggle to achieve as being a necessary requirement.
Creativity and ingenuity are required, as well as will
and determination to succeed.

What guidance did we offer? The principles of
warfare. We selected one set of nine principles from
among the very large number which have been developed by man in all cultures over the centuries. Why
did we select the principles of warfare? Why did we
not, for example, turn to the Bible and the nine
Beatitudes given in the Gospel according to Matthew
5:1-12? One beatitude which comes immediately to
mind is "Blessed are the meek, for they shall inherit
the earth."[2] Is not your desired Future a part of the
Earth? Why not just be meek? If we are meek, when
will we inherit the Earth? But why did we select the

principles of warfare instead? This question is worth considering in some detail and we will provide an answer in the penultimate section of this chapter. Between here and there we will address the nature and purpose of principles, their origins, and the relationships among principles, values, ideals and a desired Future. We begin with a closer look at what is a principle.

Principles Predict

We often hear the word principle in conversation, but what exactly is a principle? A principle is nothing more than a relationship inferred among classes of events considered important. This relationship exists only in our mind. To demonstrate the meaning of our definition, consider an example to which parents may easily relate. Assume that the following events occurred to a young son in the order indicated below:

1	Studies 4 hours for math test
2	Studies 3 hour for science test
3	Receives satisfactory score on math test
4	Receives satisfactory score on science test
5	Does not study for language test
6	Receives unsatisfactory score on language test
7	Studies 3 hours for math test
8	Receives satisfactory score on math test
9	Studies 3 hours for language test
10	Receives satisfactory score on language test

11   Does not study for history test
12   Receives unsatisfactory score on history test

Pairing each preceding event with its resultant event we have two classes of events.

Studies 4 hrs math   → Satisfactory score
Studies 3 hrs science   → Satisfactory score
Studies 0 hrs language   → Unsatisfactory score
Studies 3 hrs math   → Satisfactory score
Studies 3 hrs language   → Satisfactory score
Studies 0 hrs history   → Unsatisfactory score

A few repetitions of sequences of this kind would only add more events to each class. Fairly soon, most parents would conclude that: (a) to receive a satisfactory score on a test, study for it, or (b) to receive an unsatisfactory score on a test, don't study for it.

In their mind, they have formed two classes of events: (studying for tests) and (receiving satisfactory scores) or, conversely (not studying for tests) and (not receiving satisfactory scores) and have created a mental link or causal relationship between the two. If A, then B; if not-A, then not-B. They have developed a *principle* about how students may receive a satisfactory score on a test in school. It is a relationship important to them as parents. There is no doubt about what two classes of events are involved here. The first class consists of all *studying for tests* events; and, the second, of all *receiving satisfactory scores* events.

225

We now know how to perform satisfactorily on tests. We have a principle to guide us: *To receive a satisfactory score on a test in school, study for it*. If we study for a test, our prediction for our Future is that we will receive a satisfactory score. If we do not study, we predict that we will not receive a satisfactory score.

Now, think more broadly. What if we observed that applicants who did well on employment interviews had prepared well for them? They dressed neatly, read descriptions of the company and were familiar with its operations, and, through considering what questions might be asked of them, rehearsed their answers.

Given these results, we can create another principle: *To do well on an employment interview, prepare for it*. Were we to replicate this logic in other areas, we could create a set of principles having the general form: *To perform satisfactorily on X, prepare for X*. — where X refers to any activity. Here, the numbers of events in our two classes have increased dramatically from those in our test score example.

Thinking that *To perform satisfactorily on X, prepare for X* sounds unnecessarily academic, we could paraphrase and say: *Always be prepared*. Who could possibly forget a two-word principle which applies to all activities in life. Certainly not the Boy Scouts of America; it's their motto. Our examples show how a principle is the product of experience. This is the source of most principles in the world, but not all principles.

A principle is nothing more than a relationship inferred to exist among classes of events considered important. Its purpose is to predict the Future occurrence of something important to someone. Every principle is important to someone; only a few of them are important to everyone.

In the next section, we will be examining the origins of principles, looking at the possible ways by which they come to be. We, of course, are not the first nor will we be the last to consider principles. It is interesting to note some observations which others have made about them.

"It is easier to fight for one's principles than to live up to them."

Alfred Adler (1870-1937) Austrian Psychiatrist

"It is easier to produce ten volumes of philosophical writing than to put one principle into practice."

Leo Tolstoy (1828-1910) Russian Novelist

"A man who prides himself on acting upon principle is likely to be a man who insists upon having his own way without learning from experience what is the better way."

John Dewey (1859-1952) American Philosopher

"A man may be very sincere in good principles, without having good practice."

Samuel Johnson (1709-1784) English Essayist

227

"Honesty is largely a matter of information, of knowing that dishonesty is a mistake. Principle is not as powerful in keeping people straight as a policeman."
Edgar Watson Howe (1835-1937)
American Journalist

"Men of principle are sure to be bold, but those who are bold may not always be men of principle."
Confucius (551-479 B.C.) Chinese Philosopher

"In practice, such trifles as contradictions in principle are easily set aside; the faculty of ignoring them makes the practical man."
Henry Adams (1838-1918) American Historian

"Expedients are for the hour, but principles are for the ages."
Henry Ward Beecher (1813-1887)
American Clergyman

"Manners with fortunes, humors turn with climes
Tenets with books, and principles with times"
Alexander Pope (1688-1744) English Satirist

"Amid the pressure of great events, a general principle gives no help."
Georg Friedrich Hegel (1770-1831)
German Philosopher

"Everywhere the basis of principle is tradition."
Oliver Wendell Holmes, Jr. (1841-1935)
American Jurist

"Prosperity is the best protector of principle. Principles have no real force unless one is well fed."
Mark Twain (Samuel Clemens, 1835-1910)
American Writer

"Man cannot make principles; he can only discover them."
Thomas Paine (1737-1809) English Writer

"When a fellow says, 'It ain't the money, but the principle of the thing,' it's the money."
Kin Hubbard (1868-1930) American Writer

In these quotations, three different meanings of principle are used. Some authors used the word in the sense of a value; others, in the sense of a principle as we have defined it above; and, still others, in the sense of an ideal, a standard of excellence to be achieved. We will disentangle these three distinctly different concepts later in this chapter. We turn now to what it is that principles actually address.

In The Beginning

Over the centuries and in every culture, people have created principles to help them understand what is oc-

229

curring in their environment and, most importantly, to predict the occurrence of Future events of importance to them. Principles address every aspect of man's three major environments: his physical environment, his mental environment, and his spiritual environment. They address the person himself, the behavior of groups, what occurs in nature, and the relationships between God and everything which is. In short, principles as a whole address everything. There are principles which are the same in many cultures; there are principles which are unique to a particular culture. But, they are all principles which man uses to predict the occurrence of one or more events in an environment which is important to him. It is the development of principles which most clearly distinguishes man from all else.

Considering principles generally, what are the sources of the relationships which they embody? How do they come to be? There are generally four basic sources for principles: Experience, Logical Analysis, Intuition and Divine Revelation. Undoubtedly everyone in every culture is familiar with each of these. We will merely give some interesting examples of each.

Experience

The Bedouin tribes of Saudi Arabia continually wage war on one another. During the period 1929-1936, a sociologist studied the life of the Bedouin and described one particular aspect of this warfare which il-

230

lustrates a principle created by experience. "Should a camp be suddenly raided and overrun by a horde of screaming enemy horsemen, the Bedouin woman has absolutely nothing to fear for herself. The laws of the desert hold her inviolable. Her men may be killed, her sons may have to scatter and flee for safety, but the women of the tent are safe."

"On such occasions they sit about in their tents, moaning and crying softly, but they know that the victors will not touch a hair on their heads. The carrying-off of women is impossible in Arab warfare. The victorious raiders, having rounded up and driven off the camels and sheep, are allowed by definite laws to seize certain articles of property, and these only, from the tents. This legitimate loot includes carpets, coffee-pots and spare tents, if a family has more than one. They may also take food-stuffs if there is a plentiful supply, but they must leave one tent overhead for the mistress of each family and sufficient food to see her provided for a definite period of time. No part of the personal clothing which the women are wearing may be taken, and not a finger must be laid on any woman. It follows that any article of jewelry which a woman is wearing is entirely safe, and so also is her camel saddle. These rules are all very explicitly and minutely laid down. To break them would be to bring dishonor to the attackers, and no one can afford to risk such dishonor in the desert."

"... This inviolability of women in war evolved during years and centuries of raid and counter-raid.

231

Men always knew that today they might be the victorious but, tomorrow, the beaten. It was wise and natural to declare women sacred. The Bedouin world valued wives and daughters above all other possessions, so the principle 'You let my womenfolk alone, and I will not harm yours' gradually became established."[3]

Logical Analysis

From the time of Aristotle to the end of the sixteenth century, people generally believed that if two bodies of different mass were dropped from the same height at the same time, the heavier one would hit the ground first. The Italian astronomer and physicist Galileo Galilei (1564-1642) thought differently. His mental gymnastics provides one example of a principle created through logical analysis. Galileo reasoned, as you yourself might have done, that if two bricks of the same mass fall at the same speed, side by side, they ought to fall at the same speed even when cemented together. Therefore, a single brick would fall just as fast as the heavier two bricks cemented together. However, Galileo's fellow scientists were not persuaded by his logic.

As legend has it, he proved his theory in the year 1590 through an experiment at the Leaning Tower of Piza, Italy. Galileo is supposed to have gone to the top of the tower with two cannon balls, one large and one small. He dropped them both at the same instant, and they reached the ground at nearly the same time.

232

There was a small difference, but not nearly so great as the difference between their weights. Galileo concluded correctly that it was the resistance of the air which caused the difference in time of fall between the two cannon balls. In 1650, his conclusion, that *falling bodies descend at the same rate* was shown to be correct by a procedure which eliminated air resistance. It was shown that if the air were pumped from a long tube, and a feather and a coin dropped down the tube at the same instant, they would fall side by side and reach the bottom together.

Intuition

Intuition is acquiring knowledge and understanding without logical analysis or reasoning. It simply "falls in" to your awareness. How many of us, like the great English scientist Sir Isaac Newton (1642-1727), could be drinking tea in a garden one day, see an apple fall from a tree, and suddenly realize that the same force which just pulled the apple to the Earth keeps our moon in its orbit and all the other planets revolving as they do? Although our intuitions may not be of the magnitude of Sir Isaac Newton, each of us has intuitively solved problems on occasion.

The German-born American physicist Albert Einstein (1879-1955) made the following comment on the discovery of natural laws in general and the formulation of his Theory of Relativity in particular: "There are no logical paths to these laws, only intuition resting on sympathetic understanding of experience can reach them."[4] In a similar vein, the English economist John Maynard Keynes (1883-1946) tells us Sir Isaac Newton's secret: "It was his intuition which was preeminently extraordinary. So happy in his conjectures that he seemed to know more than he could have possibly any hope of proving. The proofs were...dressed up afterwards; they were not the instrument of discovery."[5] Sir Isaac Newton invented a new system of mathematics (the integral calculus and the differential calculus), developed a new theory of optics to explain why anything appears to be the color that it is, and devised a theory of gravitation and laws of motion — all during an eighteen-month period, from 1665 to 1667. Does this account for the popularity of drinking tea in England?

We turn now to a more detailed example of principles acquired through intuition. Our example involves the Indian philosopher Siddhartha Gautama (the Buddha), the Enlightened One, the founder of Buddhism.[6] Born in 563 B.C. in northern India, Gautama led the life of a young prince and had every luxury which his father could possibly provide for him. He was spoiled. His father knew, however, that there was a little black cloud on the horizon. Shortly after the birth of his son, astrologers predicted that, if the child ever saw the four signs of illness (old age, sickness, death, or a recluse), he would renounce the life of royalty and exchange it for the poverty of a homeless monk. Well, as you might suspect, his son saw the

234

four signs, decided to seek for mankind the ultimate deliverance from suffering, left his home secretly, and became a wandering beggar.

After several years of self-inflicted hardship which reduced him to a mere skeleton, one day he fainted. When he recovered, he understood clearly that all his penitence and self-mortification had been useless; he had achieved no increase in knowledge or awareness. He decided then and there that a middle course for life was more appropriate and began to eat. A few days later, he sat down at the foot of a bodhi tree in Gaya, India.

Gautama had now reached the climax of his inner struggle for knowledge; he had to have an answer. He sat cross-legged before the bodhi tree and made a solemn vow: "Let my skin, my sinews and bones dry up, likewise my flesh and blood, but until I have achieved the Supreme Enlightenment I will not leave this posture."

The question he wanted answered was, In what way should a person live to decrease the pain and suffering in his life, bring an end to his unwise desires, and finally experience the joy of being free from suffering? He remained firm in his determination and, by the end of the night, the answer to this question came to him all at once in a thought. The answer which came to Gautama (now the Buddha) was the Doctrine of the Middle Path which consists of the Four Noble Truths and the Eight-Fold Path. These are the Four Noble Truths.

The Noble Truth Of Suffering. Birth is suffering; decay is suffering; illness is suffering; death is suffering. Presence of objects we hate is suffering; separation from objects we love is suffering; not to obtain what we desire is suffering.

The Noble Truth Of The Cause Of Suffering. Thirst, that leads to rebirth, accompanied by pleasure and lust, finding its delight here and there. This thirst is three-fold, namely, thirst for pleasure, thirst for existence, and thirst for prosperity.

The Noble Truth Of The Cessation Of Suffering. Suffering ceases with the complete cessation of this thirst, a cessation which consists in the absence of every passion, with the abandoning of this thirst, with the doing away with it, with the deliverance from it, and with the destruction of desire.

The Noble Truth Of The Eight-Fold Path. The path which leads to the cessation of suffering is eightfold, that is to say, Right Belief, Right Aspiration, Right Speech, Right Conduct, Right Means Of Livelihood, Right Endeavor, Right Mindfulness, and Right Meditation.[7]

He got up, stretched his legs, and began teaching. There was much to be done.

Divine Revelation

There are many recorded instances where a person has received knowledge by supernatural means. Those receiving this knowledge believe that it was given to them by God or a being closely associated with God. Our first example of principles obtained through divine revelation is that of Moses receiving the ten commandments; the second, Muhammad, the Prophet of Allah (God), receiving instructions on how to live one's life. We turn first to Moses.

After leaving Egypt, Moses and the tribe of Israel wondered in the Sinai desert for three months, finally camping at the foot of Mount Sinai. The year is approximately 1500 B.C. God is on Mount Sinai and calls down to Moses, who then proceeds up the mountain alone. God appears as a thick cloud and asks Moses to tell the tribe of Israel that He will return in three days. God also tells Moses that He will appear as a thick cloud so that the people may hear when He speaks with Moses and believe him forever.

"Then it came to pass on the third day, in the morning, that there were thunderings and lightnings, and a thick cloud on the mountain; and the sound of the trumpet was very loud, so that all the people who were in the camp trembled. And Moses brought the people out of the camp to meet with God, and they stood at the foot of the mountain."

"Now Mount Sinai was completely in smoke, because the Lord descended upon it in fire. Its smoke ascended like the smoke of a furnace, and the whole mountain quaked greatly. And when the blast of the trumpet sounded long and became louder and louder, Moses spoke, and God answered him by voice. Then the Lord came down upon Mount Sinai, on the top of

237

the mountain. And the Lord called Moses to the top of the mountain, and Moses went up. God then instructed Moses to return to his people and tell them to not touch or climb the mountain. To do so is very dangerous, and they will die."

"And God spoke these words, saying: I am the Lord your God, who brought you out of the land of Egypt, out of the house of bondage. You shall have no other gods before Me. You shall not make for yourself a carved image (to worship). You shall not take the name of the Lord your God in vain, for the Lord will not hold him guiltless who takes His name in vain. Remember the Sabbath, to keep it holy. Honor your father and your mother, that your days may be long upon the land which the Lord your God is giving you. You shall not murder. You shall not commit adultery. You shall not steal. You shall not bear false witness against your neighbor. You shall not covet anything (which belongs to your neighbor)."

"Now all the people witnessed the thunderings, the lightning flashes, the sound of the trumpet, and the mountain smoking; and when the people saw it, they trembled and stood far off."[8]

We turn now to Islam and to the person of Muhammad (570-632), the Prophet of Allah. It is with Muhammad that the religion of Islam began and, as revealed to him, that the Koran, the sacred book of Islam, was written.[9] How the contents of this book came to be is our second example of principles obtained through divine revelation. Our description begins with the selection of Muhammad to be The Prophet of Allah (God). It is the year 610. "It was his (Muhammad's) practice to retire with this family for a month of every year to a cave in the desert for meditation. His place of retreat was Hira, a desert hill not far from Mecca, and his chosen month was Ramadan, the month of heat."

"It was there one night toward the end of his quiet month that the first revelation came to him when he was forty years old. He was asleep or in a trance when he heard a voice say: Read! He said: I cannot read. The voice again said: Read! He said: I cannot read. A third time the voice, more terrible, commanded: Read! He said: What can I read? The voice said: Read: In the name of thy Lord Who createth. Createth man from a clot. Read: And it is thy Lord the most bountiful. Who teacheth by the pen. Teacheth man that which he knew not."

"Nay, but verily man is rebellious, that he thinketh himself independent! Lo! unto thy Lord is the return. Hast thou seen him who dissuadeth, a slave when he prayeth? Hast thou seen if he (relieth) on the guidance (of Allah) or enjoineth piety? Hast thou seen if he denieth (Allah's guidance) and is forward? Is he then unaware that Allah seeth? Nay, but if he cease not. We will seize him by the forelock — the lying, sinful forelock — then let him call upon his henchmen! We will call the guards of hell. Nay! Obey not thou him. But prostrate thyself, and draw near (unto Allah)."[10]

"When he awoke the words remained as if 'inscribed upon his heart.' He went out of the cave on to the hillside and heard the same awe-inspiring voice say: O Muhammad! Thou are Allah's messenger, and I am Gabriel. Then he raised his eyes and saw the angel, in the likeness of a man, standing in the sky above the horizon. And again the dreadful voice said: O Muhammad! Thou art Allah's messenger, and I am Gabriel. Muhammad stood quite still, turning away his face from the brightness of the vision, but whithersoever he might turn his face, there always stood the angel confronting him. He remained thus a long while till at length the angel vanished..."[11]

In the following years, the angel Gabriel spoke repeatedly to Muhammad in his dreams and his visions. In the year 652, twenty years after Muhammad's death, the revelations were assembled into the Koran. The Koran speaks of a day of judgment when each person shall stand before God to account for his life on Earth. It contains many specific teachings designed to regulate Muslim daily life. It requires daily prayers, and stresses charity and brotherly love among Muslims. The Koran teaches that a person should be humble in spirit, temperate, brave, and just. Note the word brave.

The Power Of The Story

Stories have been used for thousands of years and in all cultures to communicate knowledge and principles.

People understand stories; people enjoy stories; people remember stories; people enjoy telling stories. All great teachers have used stories to communicate, educate, and cause people to think. And principles are very often taught through stories. The following centuries-old story is just one example of this:

There was once a Sage who had sixty disciples. He had taught them as well as he could, and the time had come to undergo a new experience. He called his disciples together and said: "We must now go on a long journey. Something, I am not sure what, will happen on the way. Those of you who have absorbed enough to enter this stage will be able to accompany me. But first you must all memorize this phrase, 'I must die instead of the Sage.' Be prepared to shout this out at any time, whenever I raise both my arms." Some of the disciples started muttering among themselves, now highly suspicious of the Sage's motives. No less than fifty-nine of the sixty deserted him, saying "He knows that he will be in danger at some time, and is preparing to sacrifice us instead of himself." They said to him, "You may even be planning some crime — perhaps even a murder; we can never follow you on terms like that."

The Sage and his sole remaining companion started the journey. Now a most terrible and unjust tyrant had seized the next city shortly before they entered it. He wanted to consolidate his rule with a dramatic act of force, and called his soldiers together. He said to them: "Capture some wayfarer of meek aspect and bring him for judgment in the public square. I propose to sentence him as a miscreant." The soldiers said: "We hear and obey!" and went into the streets, pouncing upon the first travelling stranger they met. He happened to be the disciple of the Sage. The Sage followed the soldiers to the place where the king sat, while all the citizens, hearing the drums of death and already trembling with fear, collected around. The disciple was thrown down in front of the throne, and the king said: "I have resolved to make an example of a vagabond, to show the people that we will not tolerate unconformity or attempted escape. You are to die at once."

At this, the Sage called out in a loud voice: "Accept my life, O Mighty Monarch, instead of the life of this useless youth! I am more blameworthy than he, for it was I who induced him to embark upon a life of wandering!" At this point he raised both arms above his head, and the disciple cried out: "Munificent King! Please allow me to die — I must die instead of the Sage!""

"The king was quite amazed. He said to his counsellors: "What kind of people are these, vying with one another to taste death? If this is heroism, will it not inflame the people against me? Advise me as to what to do." The counsellors conferred for a few moments. Then they said: "If this is heroism there is little that we can do about it, except to act more viciously until people lose heart. But we have nothing to lose if we ask this Sage why he is anxious to die."

When he was asked, the Sage replied: "Imperial Majesty! It has been foretold that a man will die this day in this place; and that he shall rise again and thereafter be immortal. Naturally, both I and my disciple want to be that man." The king thought, "Why should I make others immortal, when I myself and not?" After a moment's reflection, he gave orders that he should be executed immediately, instead of the wanders. Then the worst of the king's evil accomplices, eager for immortality, killed themselves. None of them rose again, and the Sage and his disciple went their way during the confusion.[12]

This story about the Sage and his disciple is a classic teaching story, and nowhere are the principles addressed by it explicitly stated. You just read it and think about it. And then read it again. And think about it again. The more you do this, the more you understand. With these kinds of stories, there are several levels of understanding possible.

Not to be ignored are *morals*, principles which are communicated through a story and designed to teach appropriate behavior or communicate an insight. In Western civilizations, for example, the stories or fables of Aesop, attributed to an obviously very intelligent slave of ancient Greece, have been popular since the Middle Ages. The style of Aesop's fables is simple and direct. They are told in a language that is unpretentious. Each is designed to teach a moral. All told, there are 579 of them, one of which is the story of *The Old Woman And The Doctor*: "An elderly woman who

243

was having eye trouble called in a doctor. Every time he came to see her, he would apply some ointment, and while her eyes were still closed, he would carry off some of her household utensils. When he had carried off all she had and successfully completed his treatment, he asked her for the fee they had agreed on. She would not pay it, and he took her before the magistrates. She said that she had promised to pay the fee if he restored her sight, but that now, as a result of the treatment, she was in a worse condition than before. 'As it was,' she said, 'I could see all the utensils in my house, but now I can't see them at all.'"[13]

Fables parallel to Aesop's Fables exist in all cultures. We note that *proverbs* or *maxims* are principles, stated more succinctly. What is interesting about proverbs is that they are few in words — in the English language they are almost always one sentence in length — and easily remembered. Here are some examples of proverbs. *An apple a day keeps the doctor away. The best things in life are free. If at first you don't succeed, try, try, again. Misery loves company. Strike while the iron is hot. A slave is a slave even if he owns great pearls. Knowledge acquired as a child is more lasting than an engraving on stone. Why concern yourself with a tree and its existence. Blessed is the man whose opponent is wise. Deceit of the heart is often shown by the slip of the tongue.* There are many, many proverbs, from all cultures and all countries. Asking how many proverb are there is similar to asking how many stars are there.

Principles As A Whole

There is a seemingly countless number of adages, proverbs, aphorisms, fables and the like which have been created by all cultures over the centuries. They are certainly interesting and, as you study them, you will find many which strike you as particularly insightful. Frequently you will be able to recall something which has happened in your life which is an instance of a particular one.

Proverbs add a sparkle to the history of man. However, after you have browsed through several books on proverbs, adages and aphorisms, you start to wonder about the whole. You wonder if they all sum to some hierarchy of knowledge, with each being a brick, collectively forming a solid wall of wisdom. Could this be the case? If proverbs about the behavior of people are any indication, the answer is No.

Imagine this. You have been romantically involved with another person for some time. This other person has just told you that they are going on a trip and will be gone for three months. You will not be able to see or talk to each other until their return. What will happen to your relationship during these three months? Will you and your friend still be speaking? Will your relationship be the same or better than it has always been? If you could only predict the outcome! Don't worry, the accumulated wisdom of the ages will come to your aid. Let's see what help there is for you.

Proverb 1: *Absence makes the heart grow fonder*.
Proverb 2: *Out of sight, out of mind*.

Although you probably hope that the first proverb is the one for you, you sense that predicting the outcome will be difficult. Which of the two conflicting proverbs is the answer? If man has learned so much over the ages, why can't this accumulated body of wisdom answer your simple question? Other people over the centuries must have been in this same predicament. The wisdom of the ages does not seem to be very helpful here. Let's move on to another example. Now, imagine this. You have a specific job to do and you know that you will need help from others to do it. How many people should you ask? Well...

Proverb 1: *Many hands make light work*.
Proverb 2: *Too many cooks spoil the broth*.

So, do you ask several people to help you, or ask only a few? We are starting to sense that the nature of the situation might determine which proverb is more appropriate. Perhaps we need more information. Assuming that this is the case, we could create a new principle. It might be that, when the work is dull and monotonous, many people may be used effectively; however, when the work requires a large amount of creativity and innovation, a few people are better. With this in mind, our new principle might be: *Pull a load with many, but think with a few*.

246

These two slightly humorous examples merely suggest that there are competing principles. Each principle is undoubtedly valid in a particular situation, but obviously not in all situations. This suggests that those principles which are relevant to you are dictated by either the situation in which you find yourself or by that toward which you aspire. It is not immediately obvious which principles are applicable to a particular situation. Some knowledge and judgment are clearly required.

As there are competing principles, there are also complementary or similar principles. One interesting example of this is the principle of reciprocity found in the scriptures of nearly every religion. More commonly known as the Golden Rule, it says in effect that you should treat others as you would like to be treated yourself. An African proverb words it as *One going to take a pointed stick to pinch a baby bird should first try it on himself to feel how it hurts*; in the Koran, *Not one of you is a believer until he loves for his brother what he loves for himself*; and, in the Bible, *Whatsoever you wish that men would do to you, do so to them.*[14] So, as we consider principles as a whole, we find that there are both contradictory and complementary principles.

We assume that each principle is valid for a particular situation. The question is, What is the situation? And what principles are appropriate for this situation? Thinking like this places the burden on our shoulders to decide which principles are appropriate

247

for us and for what we are trying to do with our lives. The culture in which we live helps us make many of these decisions, particularly regarding which values and ideals are appropriate.

Principles, Values And Ideals

Why did Colonel Travis and King Leonidas, and the men with them, choose to die rather than live? In each case, they could have postponed death to another day, another place. Why did they not appeal to the principle *He who fights and runs away, shall live to fight another day*? The answer is that they were acting in a manner which embodied the values and ideals which they considered important. In the same way that their actions were guided by their values and ideals, so are many of the actions which you take.

What is the difference between a principle and a value, and a principle and an ideal? A principle is a relationship inferred to exist among classes of events considered important. The key word is relationship. A value, by contrast, is an inferred characteristic of a class of events. And, an ideal is a standard of excellence or achievement. The differences among the three concepts are shown through an example involving honesty. *Honesty* is a value; it is a potential characteristic of a class of events. *Honesty is the best policy* is a principle; it relates being honest to some form of success. *Honesty in every business transaction* is an ideal; it is a standard of excellence which states how much honesty is acceptable. Frequently an ideal can never be fully achieved, but only approximated to some degree. As another example, consider freedom. *Freedom* is a value; *If you desire freedom, prepare for war* is a principle; *Freedom forever* is an ideal.

Our definition of a value is the general definition applicable to all classes of events. Accordingly, hot, long, red, and weight are examples of potential values of classes of events. However, in the arena of human behavior, a value is typically defined more narrowly as a concept of the desirable, or a concept of the desirable which tends to act as a motivating determinant of behavior. From this perspective, some examples of values are: Courage, Cowardice, Deceit, Honesty, Loyalty, Passivity, Prudence, Self-Reliance, Thrifty, Vengeance, and Vigilance. Those values which a particular culture considers important are, for that culture, *virtues*; their opposites, *vices*. And, what is a virtue in one culture may be a vice in another. Both vices and virtues are values, and all are inferred characteristics of a class of events.

To demonstrate that a value is an inferred characteristic of a class of events, let's consider loyalty. If someone were to ask you what is meant by loyalty, you could provide an answer. Your immediate response would probably involve the synonym faithful. However, you would quickly realize that to explain what is meant by loyalty, you must cite an example or two. You must describe something which has happened. You must describe an event. You must tell a story. You might, for example, tell the story of the 189 men who fought to the death at the Battle of the Alamo in 1836. They were loyal to each other, to Colonel Travis, and to the concept of freedom. After two or three of these stories, most people would infer what is meant by the word loyalty. Here, loyalty is a characteristic of a class of events which you have inferred.

Socrates (470-399 B.C.), the Greek philosopher, is reputed to have said that "The unexamined life is not worth living." We extend this admonition to values: the unexamined value is not worth holding. With this in mind, we take a more careful look at values, if only briefly. The essential point to keep in mind is that values do not exist *in the world*. They, like principles, are creations of the mind and exist only in that realm. Each event, action, or object acquires value only when we go through the process of assigning value to it.

We turn now to why a person considers a value to be good or right. The English philosopher and writer Hodgkinson has considered this question and has proposed four reasons for why a person holds any value or a particular value.[15] The first reason is preference. A value is held because it is liked or preferred. The second is consensus. A value is held because the majority of the group to which he is affiliated likes it. The third is consequence. A value is held because the consequences of holding it are liked. The fourth and final reason is ideal. A value is held because it is associated with an ideal which is liked.

When considering these four reasons, it is important to note that a particular value may be held for any one of them, or for all of them. One implication here is that different people may hold the same value for quite different reasons.

Who Likes Your Desired Future?

Everyone has a desired Future. Taken as a whole, they are like snowflakes, each having much in common, but each unique in some ways. If we were to stand back a few paces and consider a desired Future more abstractly, this is what we would see. A series of events, one following the other, forming a chain of events. One of these events would be the first action taken by a person in striving to achieve his desired Future. A later event in this chain would be the achievement of his desired Future. But the desired Future is just one event in this chain of events. Other events will still occur and, because they follow the desired Future event, are considered consequences of it. Other people may be affected or influenced by these consequences, these subsequent events.

This is certainly a very sterile description of something which is important to you. It is values and ideals which change this, adding life and meaning to what you are trying to do. Regardless of what you do in struggling to achieve your desired Future, one or more values may be inferred from your actions. Whether they are virtues or vices is an assessment

251

made by the person inferring the values. Similarly, the ideal which your desired Future may embody is a function of the observer or evaluator, as is also the degree to which your desired Future embodies these ideals. So, when you ask yourself, Who likes my desired Future?, the answer is that it all depends on who you are asking. If you ask yourself, you will get one answer. If you ask the society in which you live, you will also get an answer. If you ask *posterity*, you will also get an answer. If you infer an answer from the writings associated with the divinity which you consider important, you will get an answer. There is an answer for each point of reference. What you actually do and accomplish may mean different things to different people. In practice, you merely select one point of reference as being the most important to you, and proceed. Knowing of other possible evaluations adds to your understanding of the struggle in which you are involved.

As you consider your desired Future, there is one ideal which we would like to bring to your attention. This is not a surprise, and you are aware of it already. This is the ideal of striving to achieve that which extends beyond yourself. Your desired Future may do just this. It sounds noble and it is noble. It refers generally to the number of people influenced by your striving to achieve and achieving your desired Future. It is helping other people. Each time that an action which you take primarily helps someone else and only secondarily, if at all, helps yourself, you have

252

extended beyond yourself. To us, this is the fundamental ingredient for adding meaning to your life.

Your desired Future should involve a striving to achieve that which extends beyond yourself. We believe that everyone has the capability of doing exactly this to some degree. You may be able to extend yourself to only one other person; to help only one person. You may be able to extend yourself to a nation. The important point is to extend beyond yourself. By contrast, helping only yourself is relatively easy.

In Warfare And Life

We have finally arrived at the question presented at the start of this chapter, Why were the nine principles of warfare selected as those most appropriate for a person striving to achieve a desired Future? We will answer this question now, cutting to the heart of the matter.

We see life as a competitive arena, not as a Garden of Eden. To achieve anything, we must compete, and it is only a question of against whom or what are we competing. We compete to survive; we compete more so to achieve what is desired beyond mere survival. It has been this way for thousands of years and there is not the slightest hint that this will change in the Future. But, what is the source of this competition? It is the fundamental nature of man himself. Man is a competitor; it is in his very fiber.

What we find particularly interesting is that, amidst the many changes in the environment and tech-

253

nology over the many years and generations, man as a being has remained so constant through it all. Basically, man has not changed.[16] He is no different now than he was, for example, as an ancient Egyptian. He has the same general shape, the same needs, same desires, passions, angers, loves and so on. He was a competitor then and he is a competitor now. He will be a competitor in the Future. In fact, competition and warfare are the dominant themes throughout all history. Warfare is only an extreme form of competition. As we mentioned in a previous chapter, only 268 days of the preceding 3,000 years have not seen war somewhere on the planet Earth.

Why is that? Can you think of anything, anything realistic, which will bring about the cessation of war among man? Can you think of anything which could happen which would cause no war to occur on Earth during the next 1,000 years, or even the next 100 years? The only way for this to possibly happen would be for the fundamental nature of man to change. We do not believe this will ever happen. Ever. The arena of life is the arena of man, and it is a competitive arena. Cooperation is merely a short-term expedient to enhance a competitive position. It will remain this way.

The principles of warfare are more generally considered as principles of competition. It matters little what is the nature of the competition. The competition can be against ourself, another group, with the environment, or with a concept. It is all competition. The principles of warfare are a summary of what has been learned from the experience of man over the many centuries. They have stood the test of time. All that differs is the time, the place, and what is in our hands. The concepts addressed by these principles may be adapted to any competitive situation — which is almost every situation in which we find ourselves. There are, of course, levels of competition. With this in mind, there is much to be learned from the principles of warfare.

We have defined a principle as an inferred relationship among classes of events considered important. We have also said that the focus of a principle is on the Future, and its utility is its ability to predict the occurrence of Future events. In the context of your striving to achieve a desired Future, that to be predicted is your degree of success or achievement. We believe that the principles of warfare do this very well, and are superior to any others which might be used instead.

Lastly, we acknowledge that we are not totally free to follow or be guided by any principles which we might consider appropriate or relevant. We are in fact competing with the society with which we choose to affiliate ourselves. Part of the price paid for remaining with and being supported by that society is adhering to its virtues and ideals. If we choose to remain within that society, we must accept what the society considers acceptable. Within this context, we see the principles of warfare, considered more generally as

255

principles of competition, as being in tune with the virtues and ideals of the society in which we find ourselves and in many societies in the world. There are restrictions, however, placed primarily on the methods and tools used in the competition. Generally, competition is approved and sanctioned. There really is no other choice for any society composed of human beings.

We close this section with an interesting example of competition taken from the automotive parts retail industry in the United States. The following is an excerpt from an article entitled "How To Murder The Competition" appearing in *Fortune* magazine.

"Mitchell Leibovitz, (Chief Executive Officer) of Pep Boys — Manny, Moe & Jack, wants to annihilate other auto parts retailers. When intense competition from Pep Boys forces chains like Auto Zone, Western Auto, or Genuine Parts to abandon a location, he adds a snap-shot of the closed-down store to his collection. He burns and buries baseball caps bearing their corporate logos and videotapes the ritual to show his 14,500 employees. 'I don't believe in friendly competition,' he says. 'I want to put them out of business.' An accountant who got his MBA at Temple University at night, Leibovitz, 47, treats retailing like war. He says consolidation is under way in the $125-billion-a-year aftermarket for parts and servicing, so survival demands that Pep Boys be a killer. That means offering superior selection, price, and service. ... With Leibovitz behind the wheel, Pep Boys continues to accelerate. Its success demonstrates that unswerving dedication to a single concept, no matter how homely, can create a dynamic, growing business. Since Leibovitz became president in 1986, he has more than doubled the number of stores, to 358, and doubled sales to over $1.1 billion for the fiscal year ended February 1 (1993). For the first nine months of 1992, comparable store sales grew 13%, and earnings per share increased 35%. With (more planned) expansion, Leibovitz expects to double sales again and to triple profits by the end of 1997. Says he: 'If you want to have ho-hum results, have ho-hum goals.' No doubt more baseball caps will get trashed in the process."[17]

We challenge you to think of a set of principles more appropriate than the principles of warfare. As you try this, keep in mind the fundamental nature of man. Ask yourself why it is that man has remained so constant throughout history. Try to separate what you hope is the case from what is the case.

The Proverb Test

We have talked about principles in general, but we have not presented many of them. There are, in fact, many of them, developed by every culture in the world. What we present next are most commonly referred to as proverbs — short, concise statements of principles. On the next four pages you will find eight sets of proverbs, with five proverbs in each set. Your challenge is very simple: Identify the cultural group which created each set of proverbs. Do different cultures create different kinds of proverbs? Are certain proverbs peculiar to a certain culture? Is it easy to identify the proverbs created by a particular culture? We shall see. The answers are given in the Notes.[18]

Proverb Set 1

Cultural Group: _____

<small>(American, Arabic, Burmese, Chinese, German, Greek, Japanese, Russian, Spanish)</small>

If a camel gets his nose in the tent, his body will soon follow.

If the sailors become too numerous, the ship sinks.

Live together like brothers and do business like strangers.

It may be fire today; tomorrow it will be ashes.

A wise man who associates with the vicious becomes an idiot; a dog traveling with good men becomes a rational being.

Proverb Set 2

Cultural Group: _____

<small>(American, Arabic, Burmese, Chinese, German, Greek, Japanese, Russian, Spanish)</small>

One cannot manage too many affairs; like pumpkins in the water, one pops up while you try to hold down the other.

A journey of a thousand miles begins with a single step.

Fuel is not sold in a forest, nor fish on a lake.

The path of duty lies in the thing that is nearby, but men seek it in things that are far off.

To forget one's ancestors is to be a brook without a source, a tree without a root.

259

Proverb Set 3

Cultural Group: _____

(American, Arabic, Burmese, Chinese, German, Greek, Japanese, Russian, Spanish)

If you take big paces, you leave big spaces.

Great desire obtains little.

A full gut supports moral precepts.

Sparrows who emulate peacocks are likely to break a thigh.

The more violent the love, the more violent the anger.

Proverb Set 4

Cultural Group: _____

(American, Arabic, Burmese, Chinese, German, Greek, Japanese, Russian, Spanish)

What is the use of running when we are not on the right road?

Everybody knows good counsel except him that has need of it.

Noble and common blood is of the same color.

One beats the bush, the other catches the bird.

Where might is master, justice is servant.

Proverb Set 5

Cultural Group: _____

(American, Arabic, Burmese, Chinese, German, Greek, Japanese, Russian, Spanish)

Act quickly, think slowly.

A miser and a liar bargain quickly.

The net of the sleeper catches fish.

Don't hear one and judge two.

Marriage is the only evil that men pray for.

Proverb Set 6

Cultural Group: _____

(American, Arabic, Burmese, Chinese, German, Greek, Japanese, Russian, Spanish)

Too many boatmen will run the boat up to the top of a mountain.

Unless you enter the tiger's den you cannot take the cubs.

He is poor who does not feel content.

Wisdom and virtue are like the two wheels of a cart.

A statement once let loose cannot be caught by four horses.

Proverb Set 7

Cultural Group: _____

(American, Arabic, Burmese, Chinese, German, Greek, Japanese, Russian, Spanish)

Long whiskers cannot take the place of brains.

He who digs a hole for another may fall in himself.

Gossip needs no carriage.

When money speaks, the truth keeps silent.

Pray to God but continue to row to the shore.

Proverb Set 8

Cultural Group: _____

(American, Arabic, Burmese, Chinese, German, Greek, Japanese, Russian, Spanish)

A man who prides himself on his ancestry is like the potato plant, the best part of which is underground.

It is better to weep with wise men than to laugh with fools.

An ounce of blood is worth more than a pound of friendship.

Every hair makes its shadow on the ground.

Life without a friend is death without a witness.

Chapter VIII

All Roads Don't Lead To Rome

The winds and the waves are always on
the side of the ablest navigator.[1]

In 1668, the French writer Jean de La Fontaine (1621-
1695) published his *Fables*, a book similar in style and
content to the popular fables attributed to the legendary
Greek slave Aesop. A line taken from one of La
Fontaine's fables is *All roads lead to Rome*, a sentence
which over the years has assumed the stature of a lesser adage.[2] Although it probably has different meanings
depending upon the context in which it is used, the adage seems to suggest that regardless of what you do,
the result will be the same. For example, you might
say of a particular person that, for him, all roads lead
to Rome, in that regardless of what he does, he seems
to be quite successful. For him, his success is his
Rome.

Now let's focus this adage on your desired
Future. For you, is your desired Future like Rome?
Will you achieve it regardless of what you do? Of
course the answer is No. Your experience tells you
that both success and failure are possible, and that is
exactly why you must and do strive to succeed. Failure, that is, a road which doesn't lead to your Rome,
is a road on which you know that you could find yourself traveling, and is a road to be avoided if possible.
But what would be the best situation as you begin the

journey toward your desired Future? To know, at the start, what roads on which you most likely could find yourself and, of these roads, which lead to Rome, which lead away from Rome, and which come close to Rome.

If you had such a map, you could while en route continually ask yourself, "Where am I?" and "Am I on a road which leads to my Rome?" If you were not on the right road, your map would give you an idea of the necessary change in direction which you must make. Your map would also show some potential, and un-desirable, destinations other than Rome. With your desired Future now clearly in mind, it is possible to build such a map.

Your new map will consist of several scenarios, perhaps four or five, each of which will be a series of events beginning in the Past and Present and extending into the Future. Each will end at a different Future, with only one or two of them being your desired Fu-ture. Your new map will not be perfect and it may be revised as you travel, but it will certainly be better than no map at all. How you build and use these sce-narios in your journey toward your desired Future are described in this chapter. You will find scenarios to be a very powerful tool to help you face the Future and to make decisions. They do, however, require some effort on your part. You should consider this effort to be an essential component of your striving to achieve. If you had no desired Future, there would be no need to de-velop scenarios.

Before starting our discussion of scenarios, we shall consider a hypothetical situation and some scenarios which might be developed from it. Our initial situation is humorous in nature and one where a variety of scenarios are possible. You most certainly will be able to devise some scenarios which we have not considered. Following this situation, we will describe four others for which you can develop scenarios should you choose to do so. These four additional situations are not humorous, just as many facets of your life are not humorous. Now, for our first situation.

Imagine this. You are a successful rancher and have a large ranch, several thousand acres in fact. One night you hear a loud explosion not far from your house and, quickly looking from your front door, you see smoke and some flashes of fire. It seems to be about a mile away. You race over to the place in your truck. The fire has stopped, but there is still some smoke. It looks like some strange and technically very sophisticated aircraft has crashed. No identification marks are on its sides. There is a large hole torn open in one of its sides. Getting as close as you dare, you look at the inside, and spy three small bodies, the likes of which you have never seen before on this Earth. Right then and there you are absolutely certain that this craft is a spaceship from another planet and that the beings inside are inhabitants from that planet. What do you do right now? What could you possibly do? What should you do? What will you do? These thoughts race through your head:

Scenario 1: Great Humanitarian. Perhaps there are more of these beings, inside and alive. You could try to befriend them. In time they might share with you some of their advanced knowledge. You could be the funnel by which this information could be passed on to the people of Earth. Through your being friendly to these beings right now, over time you could help everyone on Earth, and be a hero in the process.

Scenario 2: Savior Of The World. This spaceship obviously came from another planet. Who knows what germs and viruses there may be on it or inside it. Everything must be burned immediately. Nothing must escape to pollute the Earth. Nothing! This is what you must do right now. Burn everything. When this is all over and done, people for years to come will thank you for saving their lives and the lives of their children. Indeed, the whole Earth will thank you.

Scenario 3: Traveler To The Unknown. You immediately get into your truck, drive home as quickly as you can and call the local police. They arrive and place a rope barricade around the crash site. Shortly after this, representatives from the U.S. Department of Defense arrive. They question you repeatedly about everything you heard and saw. As you look out the window of your house, you see soldiers and large trucks with no marking on their sides. Everything at the crash site is being removed. It looks as though all traces of the crash are being removed. As though it never happened. The person from the Department of Defense tells you and your family to pack some clothes and a few personal effects. You are going on a trip right away. Where? you ask. There is no answer.

Scenario 4: Television Celebrity. You immediately get into your truck, drive home as quickly as you can and call the local police. The police arrive and place a rope barricade around the crash site. As you watch them do this, you see several large trucks speeding toward your house. It's the news media. Almost immediately you are looking into a battery of cameras and microphones. What happened? What did you see? What did you do? Are there really beings from another planet here? It goes on and on. Day after day. Soon you are scheduled to appear on several nationally televised news programs. You tell your story over and over. The same story. You don't spend much time at your ranch anymore. Your wife tells you that the nearby town has turned into a tourist center, as has the crash site on your ranch. Everyone wants to see where the spaceship landed. You have no idea when you'll be able to be a rancher again. Perhaps never.

Scenario 5: Gone In A Flash. As you stand there looking into the hole in the side of the spaceship, you can still see the three bodies. The smoke is almost gone now. They don't seem to be moving. There are no sounds. Everything is very, very quiet. You slowly walk closer, and closer. Now you are standing by one side of the hole. You shine your flashlight inside. You see other beings, five or six, and they are moving. You hear a strange sound, like a humming, getting louder and louder. Louder and louder. There is a brilliant flash before your eyes. This is your last sensation on the planet Earth. You are no more.

What would you do? In your mind you can see clearly each of these five scenarios. What is your decision? Will you be a great humanitarian, a savior of the world, a traveler to the unknown, a television celebrity, or gone in a flash?

Our spaceship example was meant to be humorous. It was easy to think of alternative scenarios. There was no pain or suffering. Our life was not at stake. It was more like a child's game. Now consider the following incidents. These are serious, like your life and the lives of those about whom you care. You will find it easier to create scenarios for other people than for yourself. You might ask yourself why this is true. Now, consider these four incidents. What would be some realistic scenarios for each?

Situation 1. You are an attractive young woman, single, age 26 give or take a few years, and you have just been informed by a medical specialist that you will be unable to bear children. You have always wanted to be married and raise a family.

Situation 2. You have just married a person whom you love very much. Shortly after your honeymoon, you receive a very attractive offer for a job in a foreign country. It would be a fantastic opportunity for you. Your know that your spouse is very attached to where you are currently living and to your friends and neighbors. Your spouse often talks about how great it is where you currently live.

Situation 3. You have just started a new business. It is all so small right now and the competition is keen. A few of your friends have suggested that you take on some partners who have some large amounts of money to invest.

Situation 4. Your great grandfather, grandfather, and father have all been in the military. You too have enlisted and for the last two years have been trained. Tomorrow, you and your company will be airlifted to a hot spot in a foreign country. It will be the first time that you have been in combat. It will be the first time that you will look at the enemy through your rifle sights.

War Games Came First

We shall be discussing scenarios which are descriptions of possible Futures, some of which are desirable, others undesirable. The goal, of course, is bringing about the desirable and avoiding the undesirable. Before doing this, however, it is worthwhile to briefly consider the origin of scenarios. How did they come to be? What started it all? Are scenarios a relatively recent invention, a part or symptom of the new technological age in which we find ourselves?

The answer is that the concept of scenarios is very old; the term scenario may be a recent addition to the language and literature. There can be little doubt that the origin of scenarios is warfare, man's primary preoccupation for at least the past three thousand years. In the context of warfare, a scenario is an alternative plan of attack envisioned by a commander which assumes a particular action or response taken by the opposing enemy force. In war, a commander orders a particular attack, but the selection of that attack is made by considering the relative merits of alternative and potential attacks. In short, scenarios.

The popularity of warfare goes hand in hand with an emphasis on training for warfare. To train, you must practice, and an effective way of practicing is using war games. In a war game, there are opposing forces, rules of conduct, and each side responds to a move initiated by the other. And there is an outcome. One side wins; the other loses; sometimes there is a tie. It is like the game of chess which, perhaps, was an early war game for kings.

In 1824, the first real war game appeared. George von Reisswitz was an artillery lieutenant in the Prussian army when he developed it. Reisswitz called his game *Kriegsspiel* (literally wargame) and based its design on a game his father had originally developed for King Friedrich Wilhelm III during the Napoleonic wars. His father's game used a large and awkward sand table, while his new game used a detailed topographical map instead. Small metal strips were used to represent different combat units. Taking turns, players maneuvered their combat units across the map in moves. Kaiser Wilhelm I, then a young prince, arranged for Reisswitz to demonstrate his game to General von Müffling, chief of the Prussian army general staff. Despite the general's initial skepticism, he quickly recognized the potential value of the *Kriegsspiel*. To him, it was not a game but training for war. He recommended that every army unit play the game. Soon, the Prussians were developing their own war games for training and exploring new military strategies.

After the stunning Prussian victories in the Austro-Prussian (1866) and Franco-Prussian (1870-1871) wars, European and world military opinion became enamored of all things Prussian. Some military experts attributed the Prussian victories to their use of *Kriegsspiel* to play through their plans.

In 1905 the British became concerned that war could erupt between Britain and Germany if the Germans went through Belgium to attack France. To explore this possibility, the newly-formed British general staff played a war game that became the basis of British army planning for the next decade. One of the most important (and distressing to the British) insights derived from playing the game was the time it would take to transport any substantial British force across the English Channel. The army staff soon developed new plans to speed up the process.

Even more importantly, playing the game convinced the British that France could not resist a German invasion that marched through Belgium. Although the British and French knew this, they were unable to stop the Germans from invading France and marching to Paris at the beginning of World War II.

271

During World War II, the United States, Germany and Japan all used war games extensively. A comment made by U.S. Admiral Chester Nimitz, summarizing his experience with war games, is an example of comments made generally about such games: "The war with Japan had been re-enacted in the game rooms at the Naval War College by so many people and in so many different ways, that nothing that happened during the war was a surprise...absolutely nothing except the kamikaze tactics[3] toward the end of the war; we had not visualized these."[4]

A variety of other examples could be cited in which the relative merits of alternative scenarios were estimated through war games. Before attacking Pearl Harbor in 1941, the Japanese built a huge model of Pearl Harbor and used it to study the merits of alternative attacks. Similarly, the Germans used war games before and during World War II. War games are in fact used currently by all armies of the world.

The value of these games lies in the opportunity to define relevant scenarios and the actions and reactions which should be taken in each case. The goal is to triumph in the competitive arena of life, through the learning which has been acquired from playing the game. So, a scenario is not some dusty, academic topic. It is a topic ennobled by the struggle and striving of man over centuries past and centuries to come.[5] If we listen carefully, we can hear the ancient Greek philosopher Heraclitus (540-470 B.C.) whispering in our ear that war is the father and king of all.

Power Of Scenarios

In 1931, the Australian explorer and scientist Sir George Hubert Wilkins (1888-1958) tried unsuccessfully to reach the North Pole by submarine. On the eve of Wilkins' expedition under the polar ice, he was asked about his feelings regarding the potential hazards he would have to face, and what his actual feelings and thoughts would be when facing them.

"Do you experience fear when you are face-to-face with a great emergency, perhaps death?" and, according to the interviewer, "I shall never forget the quiet expression of amusement with which Sir Hubert greeted my query." This was the great explorer's answer: "I have never known the sensation of fear when I have been undergoing a dangerous or perilous experience. This is because before leaving on an expedition I have fought and overcome my fears of everything possible that might happen. I have looked ahead and tried to anticipate mentally everything that might go wrong. One fears only that which he cannot understand or for which he feels himself to be unprepared. I make it my duty to prepare for every conceivable emergency. I try to foresee the bad breaks which might be physically impossible to prevent, and to work out a plan for overcoming and surviving these breaks when and if they happen. As a result, when I am on my expedition and suddenly find myself in a tight place, my mind immediately leaps to the solution of the problem — taking complete mental and physical command so that any fear emotions don't have a chance. In others words, I have visualized myself meeting any and all situations successfully, and fear, as a consequence, has no hold upon my consciousness. It simply does not and cannot exist."[6]

Although Sir Hubert did not specifically say that he had developed various scenarios which defined what could happen to him, that was, in fact, exactly what he had done. Scenarios have been used by man throughout history to cope with the potential uncertainties of the Future. To act with confidence, you must be willing to look ahead and consider what might happen.

Developing scenarios is a powerful tool for planning and making decisions. Their use was formally introduced to the literature on planning by Kahn and Wiener in 1967. This is how they explained the use and value of scenarios:

"Scenarios are hypothetical sequences of events constructed for the purpose of focusing attention on causal processes and decision-points. They answer two kinds of questions: (1) Precisely how might some hypothetical situation come about, step by step? and (2) What alternatives exist, for each actor, at each step, for preventing, diverting, or facilitating the process? 'Alternative futures' can be used for generating additional scenarios, for setting forth and discussing criteria, for the systematic comparison of various alternative policies (or alternative combinations of assumptions and objectives), or for the analysis and examination of specific issues. They are also of interest in

274

making assumptions and contexts explicit, as should be done, for example, in any analysis of 'directions and destinations.' With a set of alternative futures and scenarios that lead to them by alternative routes, one may see better what is to be avoided or facilitated, and one may also gain a useful perspective on the kinds of decisions that may be necessary, and the points in time after which various branching-points will have been passed."[7]

Consistent with Kahn and Wiener, management theorist Schwartz provides two alternative definitions of scenarios: "A tool for ordering one's perceptions about alternative future environments in which one's decisions might be played out." and "A set of organized ways for us to dream effectively about our own future."[8]

For us, *a scenario is a narrative description of related Future events occurring in a given timeframe which cause a particular Future environment to exist.* Although the events described in a scenario relate to the Future, they must also relate to the Past and the Present. A particular scenario is not a prediction of the Future but is, instead, a description of one possible Future.

A scenario describes *a Future*, not *the Future*. A *scenario set* consists of two or more scenarios, developed for the same timeframe, which are related to the achievement of your desired Future. The product of scenario development is not an accurate forecast of the Future but, instead, better decisions about the

Future. Scenarios allow you to see different Futures in the Present. According to Schwartz: "Scenarios allow a manager to say 'I am prepared for whatever happens.' It is this ability to act with a knowledgeable sense of risks and rewards that separates the business executive and the wise individual from the bureaucrat or gambler."[9] Although his comment is addressed to managers of corporations, it applies to everyone. The major concept behind scenarios is this: Scenarios help you maximize the actions you choose to make while minimizing the reactions you are forced to make.

If the occurrence of a desired Future were certain, there would be no need to develop scenarios. This is also true if you have no desired Future.

Considering The Undesirable

Developing scenarios is hopefully an eye-opening process. It forces us to overcome one of our primary limitations: to deny the possibility that the undesirable may occur. It is simply much easier for us to not think about it than to come to grips with it. This is all the more true as the event becomes increasingly more undesirable in our eyes.

Consider the following dialogue between you and a wise, old gentlemen:

"That's impossible!" was your only response.
"Is that what you think will happen, or is that what you hope will happen?" said the old gentlemen.

"But," he continued, "if there's one lesson I've learned about man it's that he won't believe what doesn't fit with his plans or suit his likes. To put it bluntly, he just won't see what he doesn't want to see. Find a problem with my logic, debate the information, develop different chains of events, but don't just sit there and say, 'That's impossible!' Say something to me which shows that you have at least spent some time thinking about and pondering over these matters, all of them, and perhaps some others. Don't just tell me what you hope is the case."

The inclination to avoid thinking about the possible occurrence of an undesirable Future is difficult to overcome. You must force yourself to think about the undesirable. This may not be enjoyable; it may be quite unpleasant. If your mind is at all open to the undesirable, the process of developing scenarios provides some help. A scenario set will usually contain from four to six scenarios. One of these scenarios must be the scenario by which your desired Future is achieved. At least one of the remaining scenarios must be a realistic scenario which results in failure, that is, not achieving your desired Future. Not only must this scenario be your worse case, it must be a failure. Through devising a scenario for failure, you hopefully will acknowledge that failure is a possibility, and then guard against it to the extent of your ability. However, don't forget that, if you have a realistic scenario for success, success is also a possibility.

Scenario Building Blocks

The building blocks of a scenario are *events* and *relationships* among events. But what is an event? An event is an occurrence in the environment which has a beginning and an end. An event exists only in your mind and is what you consider it to be. The concept of an event is a mental tool used by man to analyze and understand the environment in which he finds himself. From this perspective, the temporal orientation (Past, Present, Future) of an event is a minor qualification. You can easily consider any one of these, or all three simultaneously. Also, a particular event, existing as it does in your mind, may be what has never occurred.

It is interesting to consider some examples of events, as they show the versatility of the mind. In the mind of a historian, the Egyptian dynastic civilization, spanning approximately 3,000 years, might be an event in the civilization of the planet Earth. In the mind of a classroom teacher, administering an algebra examination one week from today might be an event in the academic year. Attending your place of employment today undoubtedly is an event in the mind of your employer.

An event acquires relevance in the context of other events. In the same way that events exist in your mind, mental linkages or relationships among events are also created by your mind. These relationships are very important to your survival. Consider two events, labeled A and B, with B always occurring after A, and

278

B never occurring unless A occurs first. A relationship may be conceptualized as existing between events A and B. This abstraction acquires added importance if Event A is *Eating food* and Event B is *Decrease in stomach pains.*

Clearly, conceptualizing relationships among events is an essential survival skill of man. Because events may be nested within events, equally important, but seldom recognized as such, is the skill of learning what constitutes a meaningful event, that is, a meaningful unit of analysis. It is important to recognize also that every event is always linked to a preceding event; there is never an isolated event.

This way of thinking about events and their relationships generally follows from considering time as a continuum, coming from the Past, to the Present, and going into the Future. Western civilizations generally consider time in this manner. We mention this because, if a different perspective of time were used, our discussion of events and relationships among events would be considered silly. If you are interested in alternative ways of thinking about time, you should read the observations reported by Hall.[10]

Your Desired Future Must Be One Scenario

The set of from four to six scenarios which you construct must have a clearly-defined theme or focus. That theme or focus is the achievement of your desired Future to varying degrees. One of these scenarios,

279

then, must be the scenario by which your desired Future may be achieved completely. The remaining scenarios are those in which your desired Future is partially achieved or not achieved at all. One of these remaining scenarios must relate to your failure to achieve your desired Future.

If a particular scenario is unrelated to your desired Future, it is at best interesting, but generally useless. If you are unable to devise a realistic scenario by which your desired Future may be achieved, then you must discard your desired Future and devise another. If you are unwilling to discard your desired Future, then you must enlist the help of others in devising the scenario by which it may be achieved.

Your scenarios are nothing more than tools to help you make better decisions when striving to achieve your desired Future. Scenarios are not an end in themselves; they are only the beginning. Remember this. You don't want to consider the undesirable as possible. Scenarios may help overcome this.

Building A Scenario

A scenario is a description of an unfolding series of events which, at a particular time in the Future, will result in the occurrence of a particular environment. Each scenario should identify important Future events. What will happen? When will it happen? These future events must be related to what has happened in the Past and the Present. These events in your scenario may be those which you will cause to happen, or those which are the products of others, or both.

The scenario should also describe the relationships among the major events, going from the Past, to the Present, and into the Future, with the emphasis on what will happen in the Future. These relationships should describe a plausible chain of events. The hypothetical relationships among events must be logical. How are the events related? What events precede other events?

The scenario must identify the driving force behind the chain of events. What will cause, and continue to cause, the specific chain of events to occur? Also, the scenario must have a timeframe, when it begins and when it ends. Depending on the situation, the timeframe may be hours, days, years or decades.

The chain of events defined by the scenario will at any point in time produce a particular environment. What environments will be successively produced as the scenario unfolds? Each of these anticipated environments will have an effect on you. What are these effects? What are the consequences? Finally, each scenario should identify the early warning signs for its potential occurrence.

Some Suggestions

A scenario set should contain from four to six scenarios. You should avoid assigning probabilities to scenarios as, for example, saying that a particular scenario has a sixty percent chance of occurring. When this is done, you may only take seriously either the scenario having the highest probability of occurrence or those scenarios with the highest probabilities of occurrence. Although unexplainable incidents have occurred not infrequently in the Past, avoid creating scenarios involving or requiring the occurrence of miracles.

Some Causes Of Failure

Why might your desired Future not occur, even though you have carefully devised a set of relevant scenarios? One answer is suggested by the notions of the friction of war and the fog of battle mentioned repeatedly by the military theorist Clausewitz. Friction refers to the effects of unforeseen and potentially unforeseeable events in the Present, events generally described as chance events; and fog, to the absence of accurate, meaningful, or relevant information as to what is actually happening in the Present or what has happened in the immediate Past. By definition, a chance event may facilitate or inhibit the occurrence of a desired Future; a chance event is not always detrimental. An important idea related to the fog of battle is that the available information may be sufficient for some people to take appropriate action, and completely insufficient for others. Clearly knowing what is happening and knowing how to act based on this information are two different skills. Both types of skills are important and needed.

Added to these two notions is the conflict among desired Futures. As you attempt to bring about your desired Future, others are also involved in the very same process. They are striving to achieve their desired Future. As these desired Futures become increasingly similar, so also increases the potential for teamwork and cooperation. As the desired Futures become increasingly different, so increases the potential for competition and conflict. The answer to the question at the start of this section is that what occurs in the Present is the result of forces existing in the Present, and the dominant force, in the context of competing forces, will prevail. You may not think of yourself as a dominant force but, if you are to achieve your desired Future, that is what you must be.

Example Of Alternative Futures

We turn now to a hypothetical incident and to the four scenarios which have been developed for those involved. This particular example involves a physical trauma to a family member following a serious traffic accident. Although a particular physical trauma is cited here, the scenarios are very similar to those which would be appropriate for anyone receiving a serious physical injury, where the extent of the recovery is unknown.

Whether the scenario developer is a person, family, organization, corporation, or nation, all scenarios are ultimately personal in nature, involving the

283

emotions, desired, fears, and hopes of the individual. Following the four scenarios, we consider several decisions which are relevant to the family involved in the example. Scenarios as a whole are merely tools for making decisions. To devise scenarios but not use them for making decisions is to have missed the point entirely.

Imagine this. You live in the United States of America, are married, with one eight-year-old son. Both you and your husband are college graduates and have good jobs. One afternoon you receive a telephone call at your office from the local police. Please come immediately; your husband has been involved in a serious automobile accident and has been taken to a hospital. You rush to the hospital. Your husband is in the operating room and will be there for several hours. Somehow you answer the administrative aide's questions and the necessary paperwork is completed. The police officers who accompanied your husband to the hospital talk to you. More paperwork, but you find out what happened. Your husband stopped at the traffic light at a busy 4-way intersection, a drunken driver struck his automobile from behind, pushing him into the traffic, where his automobile was struck again by two other automobiles. After about two hours, one of the doctors from the operating room talks with you. Your husband is alive and will survive. The damage he received was serious, his spinal chord has been damaged, and he is currently paralyzed from the waist to his toes.

ALL ROADS DON'T LEAD TO ROME

As you and your husband talk with several medical specialists in the following days, the unavoidable conclusion is that he is paralyzed from the waist down and will remain that way for some time. The doctors tell you that recovery is possible to some unknown degree through physical therapy and the natural healing power of the body. But it will take time and the extent of recovery is unknown. As you sit by your husbands's bedside you wonder what will happen to him over the next several years. What will life be like for you, your son and your husband? For the family? What could life be like? As you think about it, four different Futures take shape in your mind.

Scenario 1: Speedy Recovery.

Through extensive physical therapy and the healing power of the human body, lost functions in his legs gradually return. The wheelchair used for the first several months after the operation is no longer needed. He then walks with the help of crutches for a few months; then he walks with only a cane. Now he's able to walk without any support. He walks with a limp, but he walks. Each week he is able to do more than the previous week. He is getting stronger each day and knows that he will continue to improve. Although the cane is no longer needed, he carries it just as an added precaution. The limp is barely noticeable now. He returns to his old job. At first, it's one day a week; then two days a week; and, then, three days a week. At the end of a few months, it's back to his job full-time. It's very tiring for the first few weeks. But after a few months, it's like he never left. He has much more energy now. It almost seems as though the accident never happened.

Scenario 2: Cane And Able.

Through extensive physical therapy and the healing power of the human body, lost functions in his legs gradually return. The wheelchair used for the first several months after the operation is no longer needed. He then walks with the help of crutches for a few months; then he walks with only a cane. He walks with a cane, but he walks. Weeks pass and he practices every day. The cane is indispensable. He wishes that he could walk faster and more steadily, but that just isn't possible. He has resigned himself to walking with a cane, and walking slowly, for a long time to come. The cane has become a part of his life, an irreplaceable part of his life. He returns to his old job. At first, it's one day per week; then two days per week; and, then, three days per week. At the end of two months, it's back to the job full-time. It's obvious that the best job for him is one where he does little walking. Of course, there are such jobs where he works. He is retrained and can do his new job very well. It's not the same as his old job, but it's a job. It's hard not to think about what he would be doing if he hadn't been in an automobile accident.

Scenario 3: Only With Crutches.

Through extensive physical therapy and the healing power of the human body, some functions in his legs return. The wheelchair used for the several months after the operation is not really needed. He can move about on his crutches. However, his legs are not steady enough to support his weight with only a cane. Try as he will, the legs simply do not improve. He is resigned to walking with crutches. He walks with his crutches, but he does walk. He returns to his old job. At first, it's one day per week; then two days per week; and, then, three days per week. At the end of two months, it's back to his job full-time. It's obvious that the best job for him is one where he does little walking. Of course, there are such jobs where he works. He is re-trained and can do his new job very well. It's not the same as his old job, but it's a job. It's hard not to think about what he would be doing if he hadn't been in an automobile accident.

Scenario 4: The Unthinkable.

Through extensive physical therapy and the healing power of the human body, some slight feeling does return to his legs. He has no control of his legs and his condition has not changed in the 8 to 12 months since the accident. He tries and he tries, but his legs just do not improve. It is a wheelchair for him. There is simply no other way for him to get about on his own. He

287

has resigned himself to this reality — life in a wheel-chair. Some adaptations are made to his automobile so that it may be operated only with his hands. After practicing automobile driving for a few weeks, he returns to his old job. At first, it's one day per week; then two days per week; and, then, three days per week. At the end of two months, it's back to the job full-time. It's obvious that the best job for him is one where he can remain in one location. Of course, there are such jobs where he works. He is retrained and can do his new job very well. It's not the same as his old job, but it's a job. Sometimes he thinks about quitting his job; it's just too difficult to get about. It's hard not to think about what he would be doing if he hadn't been in an automobile accident.

Making Decisions

A scenario set provides a framework for making decisions and evaluating potential decisions. An example is given below, where the questions are some which you and your husband might ask yourselves. The S1, S2, S3 and S4 refer respectively to Scenarios 1, 2, 3 and 4. The ? indicates that the answer is not known.

Question 1: Will my husband need constant assistance? S1: No; S2: No; S3: No; S4: ?; Decision: No.

Question 2: Will the house need to be modified to adapt to his physical condition? S1: No; S2: No; S3: No; S4: Yes; Decision: No.

288

Question 3: Will he be able to take part in family activities? S1: Yes; S2: Yes; S3: Yes; S4: Yes; Decision: Yes.

Question 4: Will his mental attitude be OK? S1: Yes; S2: Yes; S3: ?; S4: ?; Decision: Uncertain.

Question 5: Will he be able to continue working? S1: Yes; S2: Yes; S3: Yes; S4: ?; Decision: Yes.

The scenario set provides the rationale for why a particular decision is made. It also forces you to answer each question in the light of each scenario being true. A less desirable alternative is living day-by-day, and deciding each day only what must be decided that day. Our example also suggests the difference between a dominating environment and a masterable environment. In a dominating environment, the individual is generally powerless to change the situation; that which cannot be changed must be endured. In an environment which is masterable, the individual is able to make a wide variety of changes, and the challenge is making the most appropriate change. Obviously, a masterable environment is preferred to a dominating environment.

Scanning The Horizon

A scenario set, once developed, is continually being evaluated and revised as necessary. An essential activity is continually collecting and evaluating information about each scenario. This information is used to verify

289

the selection of major events and the assumed relationships among them, and to evaluate the degree to which a particular scenario is still relevant. The result of this process over time is a revision of the scenario set, a revision which may involve the deletion, modification, or addition of one or more scenarios. The process of acquiring information related to each scenario is referred to as *scanning*. Of particular importance is detecting the early warning signs for the occurrence of a scenario, particularly when the outcome associated with the scenario is undesirable. The more effort devoted to environmental scanning, the greater is your capacity to survive and to achieve. Scenarios provide the rationale for scanning the horizon of the Future.

Management theorist Nanus has made some interesting observations on scanning as applied to organizations. He believes that there are two important time horizons for an organization's Future. The first he refers to as *commitment time*; the second, as *scanning time*. Commitment time is that time over which decisions can reasonably be made to allocate resources, design and implement programs, or complete an important transition as, for example, the introduction of a new product or the opening of a new facility. For most corporations, Nanus believes that the commitment time is generally from 3 to 5 years.

Scanning time is that time beyond the commitment time that the organization must understand if it is to make intelligent choices. For most organizations, Nanus believes that the scanning time is generally from

5 to 20 years or more.[11] Nanus gives an example and issues an important caution to industrial corporations in the United States:

"...commitment time is the time it takes to implement a major change while scanning time is the time it takes to realize the benefits of that change. If a steel manufacturer decides to build a new plant, it could take five years or more to complete site selection, gain zoning approvals, design the buildings and actually finish the construction. So far, the plant has had no impact on the firm's revenues. Now in the fifth year, it is ready to open and is expected to pay back its investment over the subsequent 5 to 20 years."

"The world will have changed significantly over this period. Regulations might differ, the technology could change, and new materials, say ceramics, might steal markets the plant was designed to serve. So if today's decision is to be a wise one, it must be taken in light of informed anticipation of circumstances 5 to 25 years hence, the scanning time horizon. A future-oriented organization, therefore, is constantly scanning the distant horizon to learn what might work and how to proceed. By studying trends and possible developments, it hopes to anticipate threats and opportunities with sufficient lead time for appropriate action."

"Such an organization promotes broad participation in this search for useful images of the future, with great stress on creativity and the sharing of responsibility. To promote flexibility, people are encouraged to experiment and to take risks as part of the

291

THE FIFTH DIMENSION

price of successful adaptation over the long-term. Thus organizations that aspire to leadership must move from being present-oriented to being future-oriented."

"The differences are profound...and characterize the opposite of how many organizations have been behaving in the past few years. Goodyear Tire and Rubber (Corporation), for example, cut their operating, plant investment, and research budgets to increase short-term profits and weakened themselves against the long-term challenge of foreign tire makers. In the name of becoming 'lean and mean,' many U.S. firms have cut the very heart out of their long-term ability to lead their industries."[12]

You Are An Actor

A scenario set defines two categories of future environments: those conducive and those not conducive to the achievement of your desired Future. Within this context, you are not merely an observer of the environment, waiting for events to happen. To the contrary, you are actively involved in attempting to bring about or cause to happen that scenario which will allow you to achieve your desired Future. Those events over which you have direct control will be controlled. Those events over which you have indirect influence will be indirectly influenced. Those events which must be endured will be endured. Clearly, you are more than an observer of events, a collector of information, or a learner. You are an actor.

292

It is probably true that you prefer a unique prediction of the Future instead of from 4 to 6 possibilities. Each representation of a possible Future requires an effort of the mind, an effort which you want to avoid making if possible. Clearly, working within the context of scenarios is both a mental and physical burden.

The primary value of scenario development is that the process, which is on-going, causes you to frequently think about the Future and the potential forces at play in your relevant environment. More specifically, however, scenarios force you to acknowledge the possibility of undesirable Futures. These undesirable Futures might otherwise be denied or overlooked.

Scenarios indicate the nature and range of decisions which you may have to make in the Future. When decisions are based generally on a particular scenario which proves to be inappropriate, changing to another scenario, and using it as the basis for action, is more readily accomplished because it is one with which you are already familiar.

Scenarios provide a means of rehearsing for alternatives Futures. Through rehearsing, you become emotionally and psychologically prepared for the Future.

Scenarios provide a framework for determining what information is relevant to you. If you want to become a learner, what is to be learned — as opposed to everything which you could possibly learn — should be directly related to a better understanding of your scenarios. Your scenarios provide a focus for what should be studied and the basis for your actions.

Epilogue

Leave Some Footprints

Life, misfortunes, isolation, abandon-
ment, poverty, are battlefields which
have their heroes; obscure heroes, sometimes greater than the illustrious heroes.[1]

Our goal is increased awareness, awareness of ourselves and the relationship between ourselves and the
whole of which we are a part. It is our intuition which
must instruct us. But intuition cannot be nurtured directly; it must be nurtured indirectly. We do this by
striving and struggling to bring about a Future which
we have consciously and rationally selected. What is to
be achieved we envision and this image in our head
motivates us to act, and to act with persistence and
determination. Emotions play an important role here.
Meaning to ourselves and to our life comes directly
from what we are struggling to achieve and our perception of its effect on others. It is in the process of
acquiring meaning that the stage is set for our intuition
and the potential for increased awareness on our part.
We must learn to pay attention to our intuition.

Be A Hero

Lying on the slopes of Mount Parnassus high above the
Gulf of Corinth and situated approximately 75 miles as
the crow flies northwest of Athens, Greece, lies the

295

ancient site of Delphi. This was one of the most famous sites in ancient Greece, for here was the sanctuary of the god Apollo and his oracle. It is on the
sanctuary walls that Thales of Miletus (640-546 B.C.),
one of the legendary seven wise men of ancient
Greece, is said to have had inscribed the phrase *Gnothi
Seauton* or, in English, *Know Thyself.* There is no
doubt that the phrase was inscribed somewhere on the
sanctuary walls. Other sayings are thought to have
been included there; each having the same structure: a
very short phrase, consisting of from 3 to 5 words.[2]
Apparently 2,500 years ago there was a need, or perhaps a pressure, for a person to express or compress
their knowledge into a few choice words. For Thales
it was: Know Thyself. The same pressures which were
felt by the ancient Greeks we feel ourselves today, as
we are often asked to summarize what we are saying
in a few simple words or at most a sentence. For us,
the gist of what is contained in this book is captured by
the phrase: Be A Hero. From our perspective, the key
to acquiring meaning for your life and for yourself,
and for setting the stage for your intuition, is summed
up in these three words.

A Perspective On Heroism

Everyone has the potential to be a hero in some arena
of life. The process or journey for everyone is the
same; what differs among people is the magnitude of
the project. And, the process is simply stated: One

man, using the abilities and resources at his disposal, strives to overcome an obstacle which he has chosen to overcome so as to achieve that which he values. In doing this, he demonstrates a moral or mental strength to venture, persevere, and withstand danger, fear, or difficulty. The by-product of the struggle is an awareness of the meaning of his life. From this perspective, two people, each involved in quite different projects, may be acting equally heroically. What is important is the process, not the magnitude of the project. A person who endures a great physical pain instead of committing suicide because he believes that his behavior will inspire others having similar problems is as much a hero as the researcher who labors long and hard to devise a cure for a deadly disease. A person who struggles to keep his family healthy and together because he believes in the value of the family is as much a hero as the person who commands soldiers during time of war in pursuit of the goals of his country. The American psychologist and philosopher William James (1842-1910) made this same point when he said: "The solid meaning of life is always the same eternal thing — the marriage, namely, of some...ideal...with some fidelity, courage, and endurance; with some man's or woman's pains. And, whatever or wherever life may be, there will always be the chance for that marriage to take place."[3]

Ideals in and of themselves are barren; hard work by itself is mere activity. It is the conceptual linking of the two which is all important. Every culture

297

generally defines the boundaries for projects which it considers acceptable. The themes for these potential projects are found in the values and ideals of the culture at a particular point in time.

Meaning Of The World Comedy

We have said to the best of our ability what we have wanted to say. Our comments have not been designed to persuade you to adopt our particular perspective on the issues addressed here. We know that the ideas which are important to you are your own ideas. We only hope that some phrase or some sentence which we have written will cause you to think or wonder about something or other, perhaps even to begin "dancing." In our first chapter we described the reaction of G. Bernard Shaw to the interviewer who asked him for his perspective on the meaning of life. Shaw very pointedly told him that the question could not be answered, and brushed the interviewer aside. However, just a few years after this particular incident, Shaw did proclaim rather well the nature of life:

"This is the true joy in life, the being used for a purpose recognized by yourself as a mighty one; the being thoroughly worn out before you are thrown on the scrap heap; the being a force of Nature instead of a feverish selfish little clod of ailments and grievances complaining that the world will not devote itself to making you happy. And also the only real tragedy in life is the being used by personally-minded men for purposes which you recognize to be base. All the rest is at worst mere misfortune and mortality; this alone is misery, slavery, hell on earth..."[4] To us, this is the prescription for the hero.

Longfellow's Psalm Of Life

We close with a poem by the great American writer Henry W. Longfellow (1807-1882). It was startling to see that he had captured so well and so simply many of the themes over which we had painstakingly labored and smothered with prose. So few words, yet so powerful. We can think of no better way to close than for you to read for yourself his *A Psalm Of Life*.[5]

> Tell me not, in mournful numbers,
> Life is but an empty dream! —
> For the soul is dead that slumbers
> And things are not what they seem.
>
> Life is real! Life is earnest!
> And the grave is not its goal;
> Dust thou art, to dust returnest,
> Was not spoken of the soul.
>
> Not enjoyment, and not sorrow,
> Is our destined end or way;
> But to act, that each tomorrow
> Find us farther than today.

Art is long, and Time is fleeting,
And our hearts, though stout and brave,
Still, like muffled drums, are beating
Funeral marches to the grave.

In the world's broad field of battle,
In the bivouac of life,
Be not like dumb, driven cattle!
Be a hero in the strife!

Trust no Future, howe'er pleasant!
Let the dead Past bury its dead!
Act, — act in the living Present!
Heart within, and God o'erhead!

Lives of great men all remind us
We can make our lives sublime,
And departing, leave behind us
Footprints on the sands of time.

Footprints, that perhaps another,
Sailing o'er life's solemn main,
A forlorn and shipwrecked brother,
Seeing, shall take heart again.

Let us then be up and doing,
With a heart for any fate;
Still achieving, still pursuing,
Learn to labor and to wait.

Notes

Chapter I: Finding Life's Meaning

1-1.   This is line 3, section IV from the *Meditations* of Marcus Aurelius Antonius (121-180).

1-2.   Platt (1989), page 91.

1-3.   Simmons (1946), page 326.

1-4.   Tolstoy (1983), pages 26 through 35.

1-5.   Tolstoy died at age 82 on November 20, 1910, approximately 30 years after having written *Confession*. The following is his description of the outcome of his struggle: "...I turned to a study of the very (religious) theology that at one time I had contemptuously rejected as unnecessary. Then it had struck me as so much useless nonsense; then I had been surrounded by life's phenomena, which I thought to be clear and full of meaning. Now I would have been glad to free myself of everything that did not foster a healthy mind, but I did not know how to escape. Rooted in this religious teaching, or at least directly connected to it, is the one meaning of life that has been revealed to me. No matter how outrageous it might seem to be in my old stubborn intellect, here lies the one hope of salvation. It must be examined carefully and attentively in order to be understood, even if I do not understand it in the way I understand the position of science. I do not and cannot seek such an understanding of it due to the peculiar nature of the knowledge of faith. I shall not seek an explanation of all things. I know that the explanation of all things, like the origin of all things, must remain hidden in infinity. But I do want to understand in order that I might be brought to the inevitable incomprehensible; I want all that is incomprehensible to be such not because the demands of the intellect are not sound (they are sound, and apart from them I understand nothing) but because I perceive the limits of the intellect. I want to understand, so that any instance of the incomprehensible occurs as a necessity of reason and not as an obligation to believe. I have no doubt that there is truth in the doctrine (religious teaching); but there can also be no doubt that it

301

harbors a lie; and I must find the truth and the lie so I can tell them apart. This is what I set out to do. What I found that was a lie, what I found that was the truth, and the conclusions I came to are presented in the subsequent portion of this work, which, if someone should find it useful, will probably be published someday, somewhere." (Tolstoy, 1983, pages 90-91.) The work to which Tolstoy refers is *An Investigation of Dogmatic Theology* which, although obviously planned, was never published.

1-6. King Solomon describes his feelings very well in *Ecclesiastes*, Chapters 1 and 2.
1-7. Tolstoy (1983), pages 49-50.
1-8. Tolstoy (1983), page 52.
1-9. Frankl (1992), pages 84-85 and page 87.
1-10. Deuteronomy, 8:3.
1-11. The authors' understanding of these two questions has profited from reading Singer (1992) and Stern (1971).
1-12. Shaw (1949), pages 90-91.
1-13. Stern (1971), pages 1 and 3.
1-14. Stern (1971), page 6, labels this category the critical answer; Comte (1974) initially uses the terms scientific and positive, but favors positive.
1-15. Comte (1974), pages 25-26.
1-16. The four functions were proposed by Carl Jung (1875-1961) and are described in von Franz and Hillman (1971).
1-17. Emerson (1979), page 37.
1-18. Govinda (1960), page 74.
1-19. Mill (1960), pages 93-94.
1-20. Mill (1960), pages 99-100.
1-21. Ballou (1888), pages 1058-1059.
1-22. Lanier (1987), pages 348 and 350.
1-23. Carter (1992), page 7.
1-24. Paul (1885), pages 46-47.

Chapter II: Moving Mountains

2-1. Thoreau (1902), page 362.

2-2.   Thomas (1976), pages 246-247.
2-3.   Fenn (1973), pages 105-106.
2-4.   Washington (1986), pages 217-220.
2-5.   Lacey (1986), page 93.
2-6.   Eade (1952), Volume I, pages 180-181.
2-7.   Cannadine (1989), pages 155-156.
2-8.   Boorstin (1973), page 596.
2-9.   Boorstin (1973), page 596.
2-10.   Kumar (1987), page 133.
2-11.   In English, this title is potentially confusing. The title in Russian is *My*; the English translation is *We*. A good review of Zamyatin's works is given by Richards (1962).
2-12.   *Chutzpah* is Yiddish referring to supreme self-confidence.
2-13.   Nanus (1992), pages 33-34.
2-14.   Adams (1978), pages 18-22.
2-15.   From Madigan and Elwood (1983), pages 12-13.
2-16.   Waterman (1987), pages 222-225.
2-17.   Howard (1961), pages xiv-xv.
2-18.   *Correspondance de Napoléon Ier* (1862), Volume X, (Item No. 8908), page 536.
2-19.   Lecestre (1897), Volume I, page 270.
2-20.   *Correspondance de Napoléon Ier* (1870), Volume XXX, page 264.
2-21.   Masson and Biagi (1895), Volume II, page 396.
2-22.   Howard (1961), page xvi.
2-23.   *Correspondance de Napoléon Ier* (1864), Volume XV, (Item No. 12379), page 73.
2-24.   Howard (1961), page xvii.

Chapter III: The Force Is With You

3-1.   Attributed to Martin Luther (1483-1546).
3-2.   As given in *Time* magazine, September 12, 1960.
3-3.   Titus Livius (1872), Book II, Section 10, pages 91-92.
3-4.   Titus Livius (1872), Book II, Sections 12-13, pages 93-96.
3-5.   Bradford (1980), page 34.
3-6.   Herodotus (1972), pages 518-519

3-7.   The Alamo was a Spanish Franciscan mission which had been converted into a fortress. The Battle of the Alamo began on February 23, 1836 and lasted 12 days.

3-8.   McAlister (1990), pages 160-161.

3-9.   Boyd (1986), page 160.

3-10.   Colonel James W. Fannin and a small army of Texans occupied a presido in the town of Goliad, Texas. On March 20, 1836 they were attacked and overrun by the Mexican army under the leadership of General Jose Urrea. Approximately 300 Texans were taken prisoner. On March 26, the prisoners were executed, and the wounded were shot, bayoneted, or sabered. The number of prisoners massacred at Goliad was more than twice the number massacred at the Alamo. A good description of the battle is given by De Bruhl (1993) and Long (1990).

3-11.   Liddell-Hart (1944), page 80.

3-12.   *Correspondance de Napoléon Ier* (1865), Volume XVI, (Item No. 14276), page 469.

3-13.   Mill (1946), page 117.

3-14.   Clausewitz (1984), page 189.

3-15.   As reported in Alger (1982), page 259.

3-16.   Reported by Collins and Lazier (1992), page 84.

3-17.   Reported by Collins and Lazier (1992), page 86.

3-18.   Collins and Lazier (1992), page 85.

3-19.   DuVal (1968), pages 337-338.

3-20.   The Shaolin Temple and Monastery was located in what is now the city of Cheng-Chou, the capitol of the province of Honan, located in east-central China. (Lewis, 1987, pages 18-19.)

3-21.   Tatum (1984), pages 17-19.

Chapter IV: Casting Your Net Upon The Waters

4-1.   Shaw (1947), page 5. This quotation is from Shaw's play *In The Beginning*, Act I. The scene is the garden of Eden, and the serpent is speaking to Eve.

4-2.   Germany's assault on the West began on May 10, 1940 with the Battle of Flanders (the Netherlands and Belgium) in which the Allied armies (British, French, Belgium) were subjected to a stunning defeat. On May 29, 1940, the remains of the Allied armies had been pushed to Dunkirk (France) where, from May 29 through June 4, approximately 338,000 troops were evacuated by ship to England. Approximately 30,000 troops were left on the beach at Dunkirk, either dead or as prisoners. In this 26-day battle, the Allies lost more than one million men in prisoners alone, with the total German casualties being 60,000. On June 5 and after this over-whelming victory, the German armies, led by tanks, 140 divisions strong (approximately 2,240,000 troops), turned south and attacked France. In a series of battles, the French army was totally defeated. On June 11, the French government declared Paris an open city and fled to Bordeaux. On June 14, 1940, the German Eighteenth Army under General Georg von Kuechler marched into Paris.

4-3.   Crosscup (1993), pages 86-87. This particular speech also appeared in the *New York Times*, Wednesday, June 19, 1940.

4-4.   *Correspondance de Napoléon Ier* (1860), Item No. 2710, pages 182-183.

4-5.   Peters (1987), pages 406-407.

4-6.   Nutt (1992), page 258.

4-7.   The authors would like to thank Dr. Phillip Meddings for raising this question about the Vision Pyramid.

4-8.   Graves (1992), page 110.

4-9.   Forisha-Kovak (1984), page 42.

4-10.   Neave (1990), page 338. The quotation is attributed to Myron Tribus.

4-11.   Kotter (1990), page 104.

4-12.   Bennis (1989), pages 45-46.

4-13.   Hickman (1990), page 7.

4-14.   Hersey and Blanchard (1988), page 5.

Chapter V: The Future Is In Your Mind

5-1.   Attributed to John Galsworthy (1867-1933), English writer.

5-2.   The complete play is given in Seltzer (1917). An exciting description of the career of Andreyev is given by Woodward (1969). His life and career makes for interesting reading.

5-3.   This quotation is taken from the *Confessions* written by St. Augustine, Book XI, Chapter XX, paragraph 26. An English translation (the original being written in Latin) is given by Chadwick (1991), page 235.

5-4.   Chadwick (1991), page 194. The material is from Augustine's *Confessions*, Book X (Memory), Chapter XVII, paragraph 26.

5-5.   Jouvenal (1967), page 5.

5-6.   Chadwick (1991), pages 230-231. The material is from Augustine's *Confessions*, Book XI, Chapter XIV, paragraph 17.

5-7.   Steiner (1975), page 139.

5-8.   Steiner (1975), page 139.

5-9.   Steiner (1975), page 139.

5-10.   In *My* (*We*), the dystopian novel written by Zamyatin, the authorities concentrate on destroying imagination in the individual.

5-11.   Aristotle. *De anima*. Book III, Chapter 3, Bekker Reference 427-b-16. Given in Barnes (1984), Volume 1, page 680.

5-12.   *Correspondance de Napoléon Ier* (1870), Volume XXIX, page 450. A good description of the scene is given by Herold (1962), pages 95-96.

5-13.   The COVINGTON inscription was undoubtedly made by Lorenzo Dow Covington. At the top of the Great Pyramid is a large beam of wood extending upwardly from the center point of the platform to what was the height of the pyramid when originally built. The structure was put there in 1874 by a team of scientists studying the transit of the planet Venus from atop the Great Pyramid. (Petrie, 1885, page 12.) An interesting description of climbing to the top of the Great Pyramid is given by Karl Baedeker in his 1902 *Handbook For Travellers*. See Baedeker (1902), pages 117-118.

5-14.   Casey (1991), page 44.

5-15.   As Jouvenal (1967, page 17) explains it, "...the reason why the word 'conjecture'...(is used)...is precisely that it is opposed to the term 'knowledge.'"

5-16.   Jouvenal (1967), page 52.

5-17.   Regarding free will, the Dutch philosopher Baruch Spinosa (1632-1677) argues that "in the mind there is no absolute, or free, will. The mind is determined to this or that volition by a cause, which is likewise determined by another cause, and this again by another *ad infinitum*. The mind is a definite and determinate mode of thinking and thus it cannot be the free cause of its actions: that is, it cannot possess an absolute facility of willing and non-willing. It must be determined to will this or that by a cause, which likewise is determined by another cause, and this again by another, etc. In the same way it is proved that in the mind there is no absolute faculty of understanding, desiring, loving, etc. Hence it follows that these and similar faculties are entirely fictitious or nothing more than metaphysical entities or universals which we are wont to form from particulars. So intellect and will bear the same relation to this or that idea, this or that volition, as stoniness to this or that stone, or man to Peter and Paul." (Spinoza, 1982, page 95.) An entirely different orientation is stated in *Ecclesiasticus*, Chapter 15, lines 11 through 20: "Do not say, 'The Lord is to blame for my failure'; it is for you to avoid doing what he hates. Do not say, 'It was he who led me astray'; he has no use for sinful men. The Lord hates every kind of vice; you cannot love it and still fear him. When he made man in the beginning, he left him free to make his own decisions; if you choose, you can keep the commandments; whether or not you keep faith is yours to decide. He has set before you fire and water; reach out and take which you choose; before man lie life and death, and which ever he prefers is his."

5-18.   Jouvenal (1967), page 29.

5-19.   Hitler (1971), pages 349-351, presents an interesting perspective on the value of competition.

5-20.   Fuller (1954), Volume I, page xi.

5-21.   Durant and Durant (1968), page 81.

5-22.   Nguyen Du (1983), lines 2655-2657.

5-23.   Berman (1974), pages 35-36.

5-24.   Lanning and Cragg (1992), pages 34-35.

5-25.   Ackoff (1981), pages 52-65.

5-26.   Ackoff (1981), page 51, comments on the subtitle of his book: "An even more fundamental difference exists between those who believe in planning and those who do not, whatever concept of it. To plan or not seems always to have been a matter of temperament... Some people refuse to plan, at least consciously; they prefer just to let things happen. Nevertheless, these anti-planners cannot avoid being affected by the planning of others, and they are often victimized rather than benefitted by it. *Plan or be planned for.* It is a matter of elementary justice that people be permitted to plan for themselves."

Chapter VI: The Alternative Is Unthinkable

6-1.   Hoffer (1954), page 78.

6-2.   Jean-Francois Champollion (1790-1832) is considered the Father of the Decipherment of Hieroglyphs. His letter to Baron Joseph Dacier, Secretary of the French Acadamie Royale des Inscriptions, written in September 1822, outlined the method by which hieroglyphs could be translated. Champollion wrote, "I have now reached the point where I can put together almost a complete survey of the general structure of these two forms of writing (that is, Coptic and Hieroglyphic), the origin, nature, form and number of signs, and the rules of their combination...thus laying the first foundation for the grammar and dictionary of these scripts which are found on the majority of monuments." The publication of his grammar, however, was to elude him, for in 1832, at the age of 42, he died unexpectedly after suffering a stroke. Ceram (1994), page 90, describes Champollion's pledge as follows: "...Jean-Baptiste Fourier, the famous mathematician and physicist, had a conversation with the lad (Champollion) who knew so much about languages. Fourier had accompanied (Napoleon's) Egyptian expedition and later served as secretary of the Egyptian Institute in Cairo. ... During a school inspection he entered into a little debate with Francois (Champollion) and was so taken by his superior intelligence that he invited him to his home, where he showed him his Egyptian collection. The dark-skinned little boy was enchanted by his first sight of papyrus fragments and hieroglyphic inscriptions on stone tablets. 'Can anyone read them?' he asked. Fourier shook his head. 'I am going to do it,' little Champollion announced with absolute certainty. 'In a few years I will be able to do so. When I am big.' In after years he himself often referred to this incident." This anecdote calls to mind the other "little boy," Heinrich Schliemann (1822-1890), German archaeologist and discoverer of ancient Troy, telling his father, "I will find Troy."

6-3.   Some examples of authors whose recent books support the importance of a corporate vision for success are Peters (1987), Senge (1990), Nanus (1992), Collins and Lazier (1992), Puccino and Shoemaker (1992), Quigley (1993), and Wick and Leon (1993). The perspective opposing the use of a corporate vision and long-term planning activities in general is well articulated by Stacey (1992). The tenor of Stacey's comments is suggested by the following excerpt: "Everyone admits that the future is basically unknowable, particularly in the case of an innovative product or course of action. This prospect, however, makes many managers uncomfortable, and they then ease their discomfort by assuming that even innovative futures are nonetheless approximately knowable. One can at least, they say, have a vision or make some assumptions about the long-term future. One can give shareholders, or others in a controlling position, meaningful information on future rates of return and risk levels. I argue that this is a soothing fantasy that distracts attention from, and weakens the resolve to deal with, the real world. Instead of sidestepping the issue of unknowability, managers must learn to face it head on. That means accepting that you really have no idea what the long-term future holds for your organization; forming visions and making assumptions are not realistic possibilities. It means accepting that no individual or small group can be in control of an organization's long-term future and that securing uniformity by damping out differences between people is harmful. It also means sustaining contradictory positions and behavior within the same organization: SONY (a Japanese corporation) has budgets and hierarchies with power concentrated at the top, yet individuals and groups lower down in the hierarchy can pursue new ideas in relative freedom without having to keep justifying what they are doing to those much higher up. In the new way of thinking about management, a key concept is that of sustaining, rather than trying to resolve, this paradox of control and freedom." (Stacey, 1992, page 7.)

6-4.   Platt (1989), page 255. This is an unverified quotation attributed to Calvin Coolidge (1872-1933).

6-5.   Mill (1946), page 90.

6-6.   Durant and Durant (1968), page 81.

6-7.   Clausewitz (1984), page 75.

6-8.   Hittle (1958), pages 14-15.

6-9.   Hittle (1958), page 9. The primary interest of Clausewitz and Jomini is land warfare. The concepts of warfare developed by Jomini, in particular, were applied to sea warfare by U.S. naval officer Alfred T. Mahan (1840-1914). Although he wrote many books, his most influential was *The Influence Of Sea Power Upon History, 1660-1783* published in the United States in 1890. At that time, naval history consisted chiefly of narratives and anecdotes. There had been no systematic treatment of wars and campaigns, of sea battles, with analysis showing the strength or weakness of opposing forces and an explanation of success or failure. Mahan's book did exactly this. A good overview of his contribution to sea warfare is given by Alden (1943).

6-10.   Liddell-Hart (1967), page 353.

6-11.   *Correspondance de Napoléon Ier* (1870), Volume XXXI, page 347.

6-12.   See Phillips (1985), *Military maxims of Napoleon*, pages 401-441. That quoted is Napoléon's Maxim 78 given on page 432.

6-13.   In the Preface of his book, Alger tells an interesting story: "As a student at the United States Military Academy in the early 1960s, I, like every other cadet presumably since the founding of the academy in 1802 (in the minds of most cadets, little, if anything, had changed since the academy's founding, and certainly not the principles of war), was required to learn nine principles of war. ... My classmates and I quickly learned that it was important for examination purposes to memorize this list, and the farsighted among us possibly realized that there was some connection between the memorization of the list and success in future military endeavors. ... After learning the principles, or at least learning to recall them with the help of an acronym, in tactics courses, we found that as first classmen in the very popular History of the Military Art course that the principles were used extensively to judge and evaluate military operations from the time of the early Greeks to the present. It was somehow presumed, at least by the students, that those nine principles had prevailed throughout history and therefore that they must have been at least as well known to Alexander the Great as they were to us. Imagine my surprise when I learned as a graduate student that the list of nine principles first appeared in the U.S. Army *Field Service Regulations* of 1949." (Alger, 1982, pages xi-xii.)

6-14. As given in Alger (1982), pages 260-262. The principles of warfare which will be presented here revolve around such terms as strategy, tactics and logistics. According to Antoine-Henri Jomini (1779-1869), a military theorist and contemporary of Clausewitz, "*strategy* is the act of making war upon the map, and comprehends the whole theater of operations. Grand *tactics* is the art of posting troops upon the battle field according to the characteristics of the ground, of bringing them into action, and of fighting upon the ground, as opposed to planning upon a map. *Logistics* comprises the means and arrangements which work out the plans and tactics. Strategy decides where to act; logistics brings the troops to this point; grand tactics decides the manner of execution and the employment of the troops." (Hittle, 1958, pages 66-67.) The explanation of the military historian Lt. Colonel Theodore A. Dodge joins a variety of relevant terms: "The words campaign and battle cover the same ground as strategy and tactics. ... A campaign consists in the marching of an army about the country or into foreign territory to seek the enemy or inflict damage on him. Strategy is the complement of this term, and is the art of so moving an army over a country, — on the map, as it were, — that when you meet the enemy you shall have placed him in a disadvantageous position for battle or other maneuvers. One or more battles may occur in a campaign. Tactics (or grand tactics, to distinguish the art from the mere details of drill) relates only to and is coextensive with the evolutions of the battle-field. Strategy comprehends your maneuvers when not in the presence of the enemy; tactics, your maneuvers when in contact with him. Tactics has always existed as common military knowledge, often in much perfection. Strategy is of modern creation, as an art which one may study. But all great captains have been great strategists. To say that strategy is war on the map is no figure of speech. Napoléon always planned and conducted his campaigns on maps of the country spread out for him by his staff, and into these maps he stuck colored pins to indicate where his divisions were to move. Having thus wrought out his plan, he issued orders accordingly. To the general, the map is a chessboard, and upon this he moves his troops as you and I move queen and knight." (Dodge, 1889, pages 2-3.)

6-15. These principles are a summary of those presented by Erickson *et al.* (1986), pages 52-56.

6-16. Sokolovskiy (1968), page 341. Cited in Erickson *et al.* (1986), page 51.

6-17. Soviet military doctrine distinguishes between a *hasty* attack and a *deliberate* attack. A hasty attack is an attack rapidly mounted off the march against a stationery defender, and may be mounted by a division within about one hour. A deliberate attack against a well-prepared position is staged from an assembly area. A deliberate attack is heavily supported by artillery and is organized into echelons. (Erickson *et al.*, 1986, pages 81, 228 and 231.)

6-18. Hittle (1958), pages 67-68.

6-19. Clausewitz (1984), pages 617 and 624.

6-20. Kuhn (1985), page 70, defines *mid-size* as follows: "The independent criteria are bounded by three dimensions: *Assets* represent capital size; *revenues* represent market size; number of *employees* represents organizational size. Numerical ranges chosen are broad, since industry-specific criteria will narrow them: assets, $10 million to $500 million; revenues, $10 million to $500 million; employees, 100 to 10,000. These ranges may seem excessively wide. The reason is the wide variability of mid-sized criteria between different industries, between, say, original airframe manufacturing and wholesale jewelry. What's 'small' in the former would be 'large' in the latter."

6-21. Kuhn (1985), pages 12-16.

6-22. Kuhn (1985), page 16.

6-23. Tichy and Sherman (1993), page 245.

6-24. Priesmeyer (1992), page 179. In his Chapter 8 *Forecasting and Visioning*, pages 173 through 191, Priesmeyer argues in favor of visioning as a procedure for creating a future. What follows is the context for this quotation taken from his chapter. "Visioning is synonymous with discernment, foresight, insight, imagination, and dreaming. It is the process of defining the future. The concept flows from an understanding that the state of a system in the past, at the present, and in the future is deterministically defined by its initial condition and the forces that act on it. Consider this. The final position of a cue ball is defined by its initial position before the opening break and all the forces that act on it during the game of pool. To forecast the cue ball's final position is unthinkable. One would have to consider not only the force of the opening break, but also the force and direction of every stroke of the game. One would have to estimate with absolute precision the deflection of every bumper and the momentum of every collision on the table. One would even have to project the order in which each ball would be played. One simply cannot forecast the final resting place of the cue ball. But one can vision it. You simply would have to decide where you want it to be at the end of the game — 'corner pocket, that end' — and you could put it there. Or if you don't have control of the ball at the end of the

313

game, your partner could put it there. If your competitor has control of the ball, you may be able to show how it is to his or her advantage to put it there. The ability to know the future greatly increases when we vision it. Rather than trying to estimate all the forces that act on a system in order to forecast the future behavior of that system, we can vision the future and then act on the forces to create the visioned condition. ... This is not forecasting. It is not projecting and estimating. It is the process of choosing and creating a future. It is a technique of planning that emerges from an understanding that all that is important is the current state of the system and the way in which it evolves incrementally. Control over the current state, combined with control over the system's evolution, allows us to take it anywhere. Don't degrade this concept as simply another form of goal-setting. This is a non-quantitative approach based on a new understanding of dynamic systems. ... If we knew the underlying equations that describe the observed system, as we do with the solar system, we could simply compute the future behavior for the system. ... However, there seems to be no precise way of determining the generating equation. Further, intervention with free will allows us to change the behavior of the system; therefore, visioning is more important to our future than any method that would reveal an underlying equation."

6-25.   Foch (1920), page 286.

Chapter VII: Choose Your Principles

7-1.   Attributed to William Hazlitt (1778-1830), English essayist.
7-2.   The Gospel according to Matthew, chapter 5, lines 1 through 11, reads as follows: "And seeing the multitudes, He (Jesus Christ) went up on a mountain, and when He was seated His disciples came to Him. Then He opened His mouth and taught them, saying: Blessed are the poor in spirit, for theirs is the kingdom of heaven. Blessed are those who mourn, for they shall be comforted. Blessed are the meek, for they shall inherit the earth. Blessed are those who hunger and thirst for right-

eousness, for they shall be filled. Blessed are the merciful, for they shall obtain mercy. Blessed are the pure in heart, for they shall see God. Blessed are the peacemakers, for they shall be called sons of God. Blessed are those who are persecuted for righteousness' sake, for theirs is the kingdom of heaven. Blessed are you when they revile and persecute you, and say all kinds of evil against you falsely for My sake." A passage, similar in content, is found in the Gospel according to Luke, chapter 6, lines 20 through 38.

7-3.   Dickson (1949), pages 124-125.

7-4.   Goldberg (1983), page 21.

7-5.   Goldberg (1983), page 21.

7-6.   Our description of the life of the Buddha is taken generally from the description provided by Morgan (1956).

7-7.   Noss (1971), page 140, describes The Eight-Fold Path of Buddhism: "The first step in the Eight-Fold Path is Right Belief, that is, belief in the Four Noble Truths and the view of life implied by them. The next step, Right Aspiration or purpose, is reached by resolving to overcome sensuality, have the right love of others, harm no living being, and suppress all misery-producing desires generally. The third and fourth steps, Right Speech and Right Conduct, are defined as not giving in to loose or hurtful talk or in ill-will; a person must love all creatures with the right sort of love in word and deed. Right Means Of Livelihood, the fifth step, means choosing the proper occupation of one's time and energies, obtaining one's livelihood in ways consistent with Buddhist principles. The sixth step, Right Effort, implies untiring and unremitting intellectual alertness in discriminating between wise and unwise desires and attachments. Right Mindfulness, the seventh step, is made possible by well-disciplined thought habits during long hours spent in attention to helpful topics. Lastly, Right Meditation or absorption refers to the climax of all the other processes, the final attainment of the trance states that are the advanced stages on the road to sainthood and the assurance of passage at death into Nirvana."

7-8.   Holy Bible: The Book of Exodus, 19-20.

315

7-9.   In Arabic, the meaning of the word Koran is *the reading* or
        the lecture. As a book, the Koran consists of 114 Surahs or
        chapters, varying in length from a few lines to several hundred
        lines.

7-10.   Koran, Surah XCVI.

7-11.   Pickthall (No Date), pages x-xi.

7-12.   Shah (1972), pages 15-17.

7-13.   Daly (1961), page 117.

7-14.   International Religious Foundation (1991), pages 114-115. The
        ethic of reciprocity is identified in 14 current religious texts of
        the world.

7-15.   Hodgkinson (1983), pages 36-41.

7-16.   The observation that the fundamental nature of man has re-
        mained unchanged over the centuries has been made before.
        For example, Colonel Ardant Du Picq (1821-1870), author of
        the classic French military text *Etudes sur le combat* (Battle
        Studies), says in his Preface that "...the human heart...is then
        the starting point in all matters pertaining to war. Let us study
        the heart... Centuries have not changed human nature. Pas-
        sions, instincts, among them the most powerful one of self-
        preservation, may be manifested in various ways according to
        the time, the place, the character and temperament of the race.
        Thus in our times we can admire, under the same conditions
        of danger, emotion and anguish, the calmness of the English,
        the dash of the French, and that inertia of the Russians which
        is called tenacity. But at the bottom there is always found the
        same man. ... Let us then study man in battle, for it is he who
        really fights." (Du Picq, 1987, pages 65-67)

7-17.   Taylor (1993), pages 87-90.

7-18.   Answers to the Proverb Test: (1) Arabic, (2) Burmese, (3)
        Chinese, (4) German, (5) Greek, (6) Japanese, (7) Russian,
        (8) Spanish.

Chapter VIII: All Roads Don't Lead To Rome

8-1.   Attributed to Edward Gibbon (1737-1794), English historian.

8-2.   La Fontaine published 240 fables in twelve books. The line *All roads lead to Rome* is taken from his fable *The Judge, The Hospitaler, And The Hermit* which is fable XXIV in book XII.

8-3. The *kamikaze* tactic used by the Japanese during World War II involved sending a Japanese pilot in an airplane loaded with explosives to dive directly into certain targets, usually American warships. It was a suicide mission for the pilot. In Japanese, the word *kamikaze* means divine wind. It originally referred to a typhoon that destroyed a fleet sent by the Mongol conqueror Kublai Khan to attack Japan in 1281.

8-4. Allen (1987), page 127.

8-5. The examples of war games presented here were taken from Allen (1987) and given in his Chapter 6 *Playing Pearl Harbor and Other Games*, pages 115-140. Similar information is presented by Perla (1994).

8-6. Sherman (1966), pages 84-85.

8-7. Kahn and Wiener (1967), page 6.

8-8. Schwartz (1991), page 4.

8-9. Schwartz (1991), page 6.

8-10. Hall (1983) presents several alternative conceptualizations of time developed by other cultures. He cites an interesting quotation from the psychologist Carl Jung: "We cannot visualize another world ruled by quite other laws, the reason being that we lie in a specific world which has helped to shape our minds and establish our basic psychic conditions... Our concepts of space and time have only approximate validity, and there is therefore a wide field for minor and major deviations." (Hall, 1983, page 191.) The source for this quotation is Jung (1973), page 300. That different groups of people conceptualize time differently should come as no surprise. The noted anthropologist and sociologist Benjamin Whorf (1897-1941) hypothesized that language influences thinking. Whorf has proposed that the commonly-held belief, that the cognitive processes of all human beings possess a common logical structure which operates independently of languages, is erroneous. It is Whorf's view that the linguistic patterns themselves determine what the individual perceives in this world and how he thinks about it. Since these patterns vary widely, the modes of

317

THE FIFTH DIMENSION

thinking and perceiving in groups utilizing different linguistic systems will result in basically different world views. Whorf makes two cardinal points: (1) all higher levels of thinking are dependent upon language, and (2) the structure of the language one habitually uses influences the manner in which one understands his environment. The picture of this universe shifts from tongue to tongue. (Carroll, 1956, pages 214-215.)

8-11.   Nanus (1989), page 128.
8-12.   Nanus (1989), pages 128-129.

Epilogue: Leave Some Footprints

E-1.   Attributed to Victor-Marie Hugo (1802-1885), French poet and novelist.
E-2.   According to legend, the following maxims were produced by the Seven Wise Men of ancient Greece and inscribed somewhere on the walls of the sanctuary of Apollo at Delphi:

> Know thyself.
> Nothing in excess.
> Seize the occasion.
> Nothing is impossible to industry.
> Keep thine eyes fixed upon the end of life.
> Haste, if you would fail.
> Most men are bad.

A comprehensive description and history of the Delphic oracle is given by Parke and Wormell (1956).
E-3.   James (1976), pages 90-91.
E-4.   Shaw (1934), pages 163-164. This quotation is taken from the Preface of Shaw's play *Man and Superman*.
E-5.   Cook (1958), page 123.

References

Ackoff, R. *Creating the corporate future: Plan or be planned for*. New York: John Wiley, 1981.

Adams, R., Jr. *King C. Gillette: The man and his wonderful shaving device*. Boston, Massachusetts: Little and Brown, 1978.

Alden, C. *Makers of naval tradition*. New York: Ginn, 1943.

Alger, J. *The quest for victory: The history of the principles of war*. Westport, Connecticut: Greenwood Press, 1982.

Allen, T. *War Games: The secret world of the creators, players, and policy makers rehearsing World War III today*. New York: McGraw-Hill, 1987.

Baedeker, K. *Egypt: Handbook for travellers*. (Fifth Edition) London: Dulau, 1902.

Ballou, A. (Ed.) *History and genealogy of the Ballous in America*. Rhode Island, Connecticut: Freeman, 1888.

Barnes, J. (Ed.) *The complete works of Aristotle: The revised Oxford translation*. (Volumes 1 and 2). Princeton, New Jersey: Princeton University Press, 1984.

Bennis, W. *On becoming a leader*. Reading, Massachusetts: Addison-Wesley, 1989.

Berman, P. *Revolutionary organization, institution-building within the People's Liberation Armed Forces*. Lexington, Massachusetts: Lexington Books, 1974.

Boorstin, D. *The Americans: The democratic experience*. New York: Random House, 1973.

Boyd, B. *The Texas revolution: A day-by-day account*. San Angelo, Texas: San Angelo Standard, 1986.

Bradford, E. *The battle for the West: Thermopylae*. New York: McGraw-Hill, 1980.

Cannadine, D. (Ed.) *Blood, toil, tears and sweat: The speeches of Winston Churchill*. Boston: Houghton-Mifflin, 1989.

Carroll, J. (Ed.) *Language, thought, and reality: Selected writings of Benjamin Lee Whorf*. Cambridge, Massachusetts: M.I.T. Press, 1956.

Carter, R. *Becoming bamboo: Western and Eastern explorations of the meaning of life*. Montreal, Canada: McGill-Queen's University Press, 1992.

Casey, E. *Spirit and soul: Essays in philosophical psychology*. Dallas, Texas: Sprint Publications, 1991.

Ceram, C. *Gods, graves and scholars: The story of archaeology*. (Translated by E.B. Garside and Sophie Wilkins) (Second Edition) New York: Wings Books, 1994.

Chadwick, H. *Saint Augustine: Confessions*. (Translated by Henry Chadwick) New York: Oxford University Press, 1991.

Clausewitz, C. *On war*. (Translated by Howard and Paret) Princeton, New Jersey: Princeton University Press, 1984.

Collins, J. & Porras, J. "Organizational vision and visionary organizations." *California Management Review*, 1991, 34 (1), 30-52.

Collins, J. & Lazier, W. *Beyond entrepreneurship: Turning your business into an enduring great company*. Englewood Cliffs, New Jersey: Prentice Hall, 1992.

Comte, A. *The positive philosophy*. (Translated by Harriet Martineau) New York: AMS Press, 1974. (Reprint of the 1855 edition published by Calvin Blanchard of New York City)

Cook, R. *One hundred and one famous poems*. (Revised Edition) Chicago, Illinois: Reilly and Lee, 1958.

Correspondance de Napoléon Ier. Paris: Plon and Dumaine. Published in 32 volumes from 1858 to 1870.

Crosscup, R. (Ed.) *A treasury of the world's greatest speeches*. New York: Barnes and Noble, 1993.

Daly, L. *Aesop without morals: The famous fables and life of Aesop*. (Translated by Lloyd Daly) New York: Thomas Yoseloff, 1961.

De Bruhl, M. *Sword of San Jacinto: A life of Sam Houston*. New York: Random House, 1993.

Dickson, H. *The Arab of the desert: A glimpse into Badawin life in Kuwait and Saudi Arabia*. London: Allen and Unwin, 1949.

Dodge, T. *Great captains: Showing the influence of the art of war on the campaigns of Alexander, Hannibal, Caesar, Gustavus Adolphus, Frederick and Napoleon*. Port Washington, New York: Kennikat Press, 1968. (Originally published in 1898)

Durant, W. & Durant, A. *The lessons of history*. New York: Simon and Schuster, 1968.

320

Du Picq, A. *Battle studies: Ancient and modern battles*. (Translated by John N. Greely and Robert C. Cotton) In *Roots of strategy: Book 2*. Harrisburg, Pennsylvania: Stackpole Books, 1987. (Originally published in 1880 by Hachette and Dumaine.)

DuVal, Jr., M. *And the mountains will move: The story of the building of the Panama Canal*. New York: Greenwood Press, 1968.

Eade, C. (Ed.) *The war speeches of Winston S. Churchill*. (Volume I) London: Cassell, 1952.

Eggenberger, D. *An encyclopedia of battles: Accounts of over 1,560 battles from 1479 B.C. to the present*. New York: Dover, 1985.

Emerson, R. *The collected works of Ralph Waldo Emerson. Volume II. Essays: First series*. Cambridge, Massachusetts: Belknap Press of Harvard University Press, 1979.

Erickson, J., Hansen, L. & Schneider, W. *Soviet ground forces: An operational assessment*. Boulder, Colorado: Westview Press, 1986.

Fenn, C. *Ho Chi Minh: A biographical introduction*. London: Studio Vista, 1973.

Foch, F. *The principles of war*. (Translated by Hilaire Belloc) New York: Henry Holt, 1920. (Originally published in 1903 as a summary of lectures given to the French Staff College)

Forisha-Kovak, B. *The flexible organization: A unique new system for organizational effectiveness and success*. Englewood Cliffs, New Jersey: Prentice-Hall, 1984.

Frankl, V. *Man's search for meaning: An introduction to logotherapy*. Boston, Massachusetts: Beacon Press, 1992. (First published in 1946)

Fuller, J. *A military history of the Western World*. (3 Volumes) New York: Funk and Wagnalls, 1954.

Goldberg, P. *The intuitive edge: Understanding and developing intuition*. Boston: Houghton-Mifflin, 1983.

Govinda, A. *Foundations of Tibetan mysticism, according to the esoteric teachings of the Great Mantra, Om Mani Padme H Um*. New York: Dutton, 1960.

Graves, J. "Leaders of corporate change." *Fortune*, 1992, 126 (13), 104-116.

321

Hall, E. *The dance of life: The other dimension of time.* New York: Doubleday, 1983.

Herodotus. *The histories.* (Translated by Aubrey de Selincourt) New York: Viking Penguin, 1972.

Herold, J. *Bonaparte in Egypt.* New York: Harper and Row Publishers, 1962.

Hersey, P. & Blanchard, K. *Management of organizational behavior: Utilizing human resources.* (Fifth Edition) Englewood Cliffs, New Jersey: Simon and Schuster, 1988.

Hickman, C. *Mind of a manager, Soul of a leader.* New York: Wiley, 1990.

Hitler, A. *Mein kampf.* (Translated by Ralph Manheim) Boston, Massachusetts: Houghton-Mifflin, 1971. (Originally published in 1925)

Hittle, J. *Jomini and his summary of The Art Of War: A condensed version.* Harrisburg, Pennsylvania: Military Service Publishing, 1985.

Hodgkinson, C. *The philosophy of leadership.* London: Blackwell, 1983.

Hoffer, E. *The passionate state of mind.* New York: Harper and Row, 1954.

Howard, J. (Ed.) *Letters and documents of Napoleon: Volume One, The rise to power.* New York: Oxford University Press, 1961.

Huey, J. "The new post-heroic leadership." *Fortune*, 1994, 129 (40), 42-50.

International Religious Foundation. *World scripture: A comparative anthology of sacred texts.* New York: Paragon House, 1991.

James, T. *An introduction to ancient Egypt.* London: British Museum, 1979.

James, W. *On some of life's ideals.* Norwood, Pennsylvania: Norwood Editions, 1976. (Reprint of a 1910 publication by Henry Holt of New York City)

Jouvenal, B. *The art of conjecture.* (Translated by Nikita Lary) New York: Basic Books, 1967.

Jung, C. *Memories, dreams, reflections.* (Revised Edition) New York: Pantheon Books, 1973.

Kahn, H. & Wiener, A. *The year 2000: A framework for speculation on the next thirty-three years*. New York: Macmilliam, 1967.

Kotter, J. *A force for change: How leadership differs from management*. New York: Free Press, 1990.

Kuhn, R. *To flourish among giants: Creative management for mid-sized firms*. New York: Wiley, 1985.

Kumar, K. *Utopia and anti-utopia in modern times*. New York: Blackwell, 1987.

La Fontaine, J. *The fables of La Fontaine*. (Translated by Marianne Moore) New York: Viking Press, 1954. (Originally published in 1668)

Lacey, R. *Ford: The man and the machine*. New York: Ballentine Books, 1986.

Lanier, H. (Ed.) *The photographic history of the Civil War*. (Volume 1) *The opening battles*. Secaucus, New Jersey: Blue and Grey Press, 1987.

Lanning, M. & Cragg, D. *Inside the VC and the NVA: The real story of North Vietnam's armed forces*. New York: Ivy Books, 1992.

Lecestre, L. *Lettres inédites de Napoléon Ier*. (Two Volumes) Paris, France: Plon and Nourrit, 1897.

Lewis, P. *Martial arts*. New York: Gallery Books, 1987.

Liddell-Hart, B. *Thoughts on war*. London: Faber and Faber, 1944.

Liddell-Hart, B. *Strategy*. (Second Edition) New York: Praeger, 1967.

Long, J. *Duel of eagles: The Mexican and U.S. fight for the Alamo*. New York: Morrow, 1990.

Madigan, C. & Elwood, A. *Brainstorms & thunderbolts: How creative genius works*. New York: Macmillan, 1983.

Masson, F. & Biagi, G. (Eds.) *Napoléon inconnu: Papiers inédites (1786-1793)*. (Two Volumes) Paris: Ollendorff, 1895.

McAlister, G. *Alamo: The price of freedom*. (Second Edition) San Antonio, Texas: Docutex, 1990.

Mill, J. *On liberty and Considerations on representative government*. (Edited by R.B. McCallum) Oxford, England: Blackwell, 1946.

Mill, J. *The autobiography of John Stuart Mill*. New York: Columbia University Press, 1960.

323

Morgan, K. (Ed.) *The path of the Buddha: Buddhism interpreted by Buddhists*. New York: Ronald Press, 1956.

Nanus, B. *Visionary leadership: Creating a compelling sense of direction for your organization*. San Francisco, California: Jossey-Bass, 1992.

Nanus, B. *The leader's edge: The seven keys to leadership in a turbulent world*. Chicago, Illinois: Contemporary Books, 1989.

Neave, H. *The Deming dimension*. Knoxville, Tennessee: SPC Press, 1990.

Nguyen Du. *The tale of Kieu*. (Translated by Huynh Sanh Thong) New Haven, Connecticut: Yale University Press, 1983.

Noss, J. *Man's religions*. (Fourth Edition) London: Collier MacMillan, 1971.

Nutt, P. *Managing planned change*. New York: Macmillan, 1992.

Parke, H. & Wormell, D. *The Delphic oracle*. (Volume I) *The history*. Oxford, England: Blackwell, 1956.

Paul, C. *The thoughts of Blaise Pascal*. (Translated from the text of M. Auguste Molinier) London: Kegan Paul and Trench, 1885.

Perla, P. "Wargaming's widening world." In *Military History*, 1994, 11 (5), 38-44.

Peters, T. *Thriving on chaos: Handbook for a management revolution*. New York: Knopf, 1987.

Petrie, W. *The pyramids and temples at Gizeh*. (Revised Edition) London: Leadenhall Press, 1885.

Phillips, T. (Ed.) *Roots of strategy: The 5 greatest military classics of all time*. Harrisburg, Pennsylvania: Stackpole Books, 1985.

Pickthall, M. *The meaning of the glorious Koran: An explanatory translation*. New York: Dorset Press. No date given.

Platt, S. (Ed.) *Respectfully quoted: A dictionary of quotations requested from the Congressional Research Service*. Washington, D.C.: Library of Congress, 1989.

Priesmeyer, H. *Organizations and chaos: Defining the methods of non-linear management*. Westport, Connecticut: Quorum Books, 1992.

Pritchard, J. (Ed.) *The ancient Near East: An anthology of texts and pictures.* Princeton, New Jersey: Princeton University Press, 1958.

Puccino, J. & Shoemaker, D. *The path to vision and beyond: Achieve business success through the power of the human spirit.* Irvine, California: The INTEC Corporation, 1992.

Pümpin, C. *The essence of corporate strategy.* London: Gower, 1987.

Quigley, J. *Vision: How leaders develop it, share it and sustain it.* New York: McGraw-Hill, 1993.

Richards, D. *Zamyatin: A Soviet heretic.* New York: Hillary House, 1962.

Schwartz, P. *The art of the long view.* New York: Doubleday, 1991.

Seltzer, T. *Savva, The Life Of Man: Two plays by Leonid Andreyev.* (Translated by Thomas Seltzer) Boston, Massachusetts: Little, 1917.

Senge, P. *The fifth discipline: The art and practice of the learning organization.* New York: Doubleday, 1990.

Shah, I. *Thinkers of the East: Teachings of the dervishes.* Baltimore, Maryland: Penguin Books, 1972.

Shaw, B. *Prefaces by Bernard Shaw.* London: Constable, 1934.

Shaw, B. *Sixteen self sketches.* New York: Dodd and Mead, 1949.

Shaw, B. *Back to Methuselah: A metabiological pentateuch.* (Revised Edition) New York: Oxford University Press, 1947.

Sherman, H. *The new TNT: Miraculous power within you.* Englewood Cliffs, New Jersey: Prentice-Hall, 1966.

Simmons, E. *Leo Tolstoy.* Boston, Massachusetts: Little and Brown, 1946.

Singer, I. *The meaning in life: The creation of value.* New York: Free Press, 1992.

Sokolovskiy, V. *Military strategy.* (Voyennaya Strategiya) Moscow: Military Publishing House, 1968.

Sokolovskiy, V. & Scott, H. *Soviet military strategy.* (Third Edition) New York: Crane Russak, 1975.

Spinoza, B. *The ethics and selected letters.* (Translated by Samuel Shirley) Indianapolis, Indiana: Hackett, 1982. (*The ethics* was first published in 1677.)

Stacey, R. *Managing the unknowable: Strategic boundaries between order and chaos in organizations*. San Francisco, California: Jossey-Bass, 1992.

Steiner, G. *After Babel: Aspects of language and translation*. New York: Oxford University Press, 1975.

Stern, A. *The search for meaning: Philosophical vistas*. Memphis, Tennessee: Memphis State University Press, 1971.

Tatum, L. *Confidence: A child's first weapon*. Los Angeles, California: Delsby, 1984.

Taylor, A. "How to murder the competition." *Fortune*, 1993, 127 (4), 87-90.

Thomas, B. *Walt Disney: An American original*. New York: Simon and Schuster, 1976.

Thoreau, H. *Walden: A story of life in the woods*. New York: Burt, 1902.

Tichy, N. & Sherman, S. *Control your destiny or someone else will: How Jack Welch is making General Electric the world's most competitive corporation*. New York: Doubleday, 1993.

Titus Livius. *The history of Rome: The first eight books*. (Translated by D. Spillan) London: Bell and Daldy, 1872.

Tolstoy, L. *Confession*. (Translated by David Patterson) New York: Norton, 1983. (Originally published in 1882)

von Franz, M. & Hillman, J. *Jung's typology*. New York: Spring, 1971.

Washington, J. (Ed.) *A testament of hope: The essential writings of Martin Luther King, Jr.* San Francisco, California: Harper and Row, 1986.

Waterman, Jr., R. *The renewal factor: How the best get and keep the competitive edge*. New York: Bantam Books, 1987.

Wick, C. & Leon, L. *The learning edge: How smart managers and smart companies stay ahead*. New York: McGraw-Hill, 1993.

Wilkins, E. *"Know Thyself" in Greek and Latin literature*. Chicago, Illinois: University of Chicago Libraries, 1917.

Woodward, J. *Leonid Andreyev: A study*. Oxford, England: Claredon Press, 1969.

Index

329

About The Authors

James Puccino ventures beyond our educational and cultural boundaries in pursuit of a deeper understanding of the human spirit and the future. Academically trained as an applied behavioral scientist and engineer, his insights influence the leadership of a variety of organizations. As an author and personal development consultant, Jim provides conceptual tools to help individuals boldly respond to change and gain greater meaning from the true challenges of work and life. He holds the M.S. degree in Management and Organizational Behavior and has completed advanced studies in Physics and Health Sciences. A student of ancient cultures, Jim occasionally wanders abroad to immerse himself in the timeless lessons of the past.

David Shoemaker holds the Ph.D. degree in Psychology. Dave has worked for several large organizations including the U.S. Department of Education in Washington, D.C. and a federally-funded educational research laboratory in Los Angeles, California. Over the years he has taught graduate and undergraduate courses at several universities. Dave enjoys traveling and meeting people who see the world differently than he sees it. Like many others over the centuries, he finds the pyramids and people of Egypt to be fascinating. Whatever he may have learned here and there, he continues to think of himself as a student, and a student he will always be.